Martin Wells Knapp

Revival Tornadoes

Or, life and labors of Rev. Joseph H. Weber, evangelist, the converted Roman Catholic. Third Edition

Martin Wells Knapp

Revival Tornadoes
Or, life and labors of Rev. Joseph H. Weber, evangelist, the converted Roman Catholic. Third Edition

ISBN/EAN: 9783744774956

Printed in Europe, USA, Canada, Australia, Japan

Cover: Foto ©Lupo / pixelio.de

More available books at **www.hansebooks.com**

Revival Tornadoes;

OR,

LIFE AND LABORS

OF

Rev. JOSEPH H. WEBER, Evangelist,

The Converted Roman Catholic.

BY

REV. MARTIN WELLS KNAPP,

Author of "Christ Crowned Within," and "Out of Egypt into Canaan."

"Like Harrison, he just delights in excitement, and seems never so happy as when in a religious hurricane." — *From a report of Mr. Weber's Lakeside Meetings.*

"Do the work of an Evangelist." — Paul.

THIRD EDITION — SIXTH THOUSAND.

McDONALD, GILL & CO.,
BOSTON, MASS.

THE REVIVALIST PUBLISHING CO.,

DEDICATION.

UNTO THE

Blessed Holy Spirit,

whose mission it is to convict, renew, witness, sanctify, fill, lead, and illuminate, and who with the Father and Son is able to overrule any mistakes that may be herein, and with divine energy apply its truths;

and to all of

The Great Family of God's Children,

who by this same Spirit have been baptized into one body, this book is

Humbly Dedicated

By ITS AUTHOR.

PRESTON, O., July 4, 1889.

"REVIVAL TORNADOES; OR, THE LIFE OF REV. J. H. WEBER," by Rev. Martin Wells Knapp, has my endorsement as being the only book in which my life and labors have been written in full. May Heaven's smiles illuminate the readers, and when the Light of lights we stand before, may each one be ushered into His presence, where there is fulness of joy. Amen.

Yours under the blood,

J. H. WEBER.

AUTHOR'S PREFACE.

The writing of this book is a surprise to myself. I had planned for a year of aggressive revival work, and had also another book on my mind to write as soon as circumstances would permit.

Unexpectedly my health, for a season, failed, and I was compelled to give up public work altogether. Then the question of writing this book was presented so forcibly, clearly, and repeatedly, that I was made to feel sure that it was of God, and have undertaken it, in Jesus' name, with that assurance.

The opposition of the enemies of the cross to Brother Weber's work, and the misconceptions of it by others, even of God's children, the extraordinary features of his labors, his marvelous success even in the most forbidding fields, and the fact that in the few years of his ministry thousands have professed conversion, make the publication of what God has wrought in him and through him of intense interest both to friend and foe.

The Scripture promise that the righteous "shall do exploits," has in him been so abundantly verified that he has been called "a wonder of the nineteenth century."

After reading of his miraculous deliverance from the manacles of sin and the clutches of Catholicism, and his confirmation by God Himself, as one of the most successful soul-winners of any age, one is led anew to magnify the mysterious grace of God which thus exalts one who humbles himself under His mighty hand.

It is humbly hoped and prayed that this book may be used of God in confounding the enemies of gospel truth, leading its readers to accept of forgiving grace; in detecting spurious revivals; in pointing to the secrets of success in revivals that are true; in inspiring evangelists, pastors and all other workers with new and more zealous efforts for the salvation of the people; and that it may prove a "tornado," destructive only to that which Christ came to destroy, but a blessing to all that is precious in His kingdom.

Many thanks are due to Brother Weber and his many ministerial and other friends for the furnishing of material without which the book could not have been written. Its circulation, like that of those which the author hitherto has written, is committed to the Great Head of the Church. If a like blessing, or greater, shall attend this, to Him shall be the praise.

It is hoped that the reader, remembering that the

writing of this book was not of the author's own seeking, but of divine direction, and that he "did what he could," will look leniently on any defects that may be found, and pray that God, who is able, will over rule them to His own glory. May His grace abide with each forever. In Jesus' perfect love,

M. W. KNAPP.

ALBION, MICH.,

PREFATORY NOTE TO THIRD EDITION.

THE writer wishes to express his gratitude to God for the wonderful blessing which has attended the preceding editions of this work. Also his thanks to the many editors, ministers, and others, who, by their helpful words, have aided in its circulation. As was expected, it has called forth from some unfriendly criticism, but even this seems overruled to its good.

Brother Weber is at this writing at Portland, Ore., where new "Revival Tornadoes" continue to attend his ministry.

May this book continue to inspire them wherever it is read. The praise, as hitherto, shall be given to Him who prompted the writing of it.

M. W. KNAPP.

INTRODUCTION.

REVIVALS are essential to the spiritual prosperity of the Church. What spring is to the year, what showers are to the thirsty earth, the seasons of spiritual refreshing are to the life of God's people. Men may talk about the desirability of continuous revivals, as compared with revival seasons, but save in rare instances such does not seem to be the experience of the Church. The religious life has its variations. There are periods of growth and development, of steady progress and ordinary activity, but these are generally interspaced with occasions of rarer displays of power and blessing, quickening the spiritual vitalities, arousing the dormant religious energies, and enlisting all the powers of the soul in an effort for conquest and an experience of victory. Such occasions are called revivals. The Church feels their power and profits by their fruits. Without them the life of many professed Christians would wane and die. Revivals keep them alive, feed them, strengthen and encourage them, bring others to their support, brighten their surroundings, clarify the atmosphere, tone up the lives of fellow Christians, and help things generally. All live Christians desire revivals, and all dead Christians need them. Therefore, whatever helps to the promotion of revivals should be encouraged and welcomed. We believe the present volume will prove to be such a help. The life and labors herein chronicled have been blessed of God in the salvation of many souls. The writer of the book, like its honored subject, is an efficient toiler in his Master's vineyard. He understands revival methods and conditions, and can distinguish a genuine "revival tornado" from a sound of wind and fury signifying nothing. Let his work be read. Let the facts become known. Let the world understand that there is power in our holy religion not only to convert sinners from the error of their ways, but to rescue deluded souls from the ignorance and superstition of popery, and make them burning and shining lights in the free and joyous service of God.

JAMES H. POTTS.

CONTENTS.

CHAPTER I.

BIRTH, Ancestry and Early Formative Influences — An Ohioan — Poverty — Influence of Catholicism — Saloonism — Dancing and Theatricals — Love for Liquor — Sabbath-breaking — At the Gates of Death — Good Traits 15

CHAPTER II.

CONVICTION, Conversion and Call to the Ministry — His Mother's Warning — Conviction — Reformation — Fearful Struggle with Appetites and Passion — Catholicism No Comfort — Seeks Rest in a Variety Theatre — Converted under a Baptist Missionary in an Out-door Meeting — Joins the M. E. Church — Called to Preach — The Call Confirmed — The Tornado Forming . . 28

CHAPTER III.

SCHOOL-LIFE and Pastorate — Salvation First in School — Made a Sabbath-school Superintendent — His Independence — Narrow Escape from a Catholic Mob — Prison and Missionary Work — Liberality — A Tempting Offer Rejected — Successful Pastorate — A Sketch from His Experience as Pastor 44

CHAPTER IV.

HIS Call to Evangelistic Work — Evangelists — Scriptural Authority and Status of — Increasing Demand for Evangelists — Relation to the Church — Their Peculiar Experiences — Bro. Weber Enters the Evangelistic Field 63

CHAPTER V.

REVIVAL Tornadoes — No New Name for Revivals — Tornadoes are from God — Governed by Certain Fixed Laws — Purifiers — Terror to the Wicked — Attended by Lightning — Compel Attention — Source of Alarm — Often Preceded by a Dead Calm . . 78

CHAPTER VI.

REVIVAL Tornadoes — No Respecter of Persons — "Undignified" — Provoke Unfriendly Criticism — Come Contrary to Preconceived Ideas — Move On, Notwithstanding Opposition — Out of the Regular Order — Are a Great Blessing 92

CHAPTER VII.

TORNADOES, 1882-1884 — Republic, Wauseon, Marseilles, — One Hundred and Twenty-five Saved in a Day — A Church Killed and Made Alive — First Mad, then Converted — Findlay — Five Hundred and Thirty Conversions — Prays for Hours — A Moralist Converted — Marion and Ridgeway — Some Sanctified — Marysville — A Midsummer Revival — Fasting and Prayer — Camp-meetings — Confirming the Converted — Everybody Prostrated 109

CHAPTER VIII.

JACKSON, Mich., Tornado — Severe Struggle — Great Excitement — Newspaper War — "Weber's Frolics" — A Wandering Star — The Whole City Shaken — "Zaccheus, Come Down" — Killed by the Tornado — "A Starless Crown" — Eight Hundred Profess Conversion — "Running Over" — A Touching Farewell Service — Millersburgh, O. — Fort Wayne, Ind. 131

CHAPTER IX.

TORNADOES, 1884-1885 — "Knee Work" — "Catholics Converted" — An "Elder" Converted — Berea, O., Five Hundred — An "Incurable" Healed Through Prayer — Niles — A Fearful Warning — Camp-meetings Again — Muskegon, Buchanan, St. Joseph, Mich. — Geneva, O. — Rock Rapids, Sioux Falls,

Ia. — Wilton, Ia. — Strongville, Cleveland, Royalton, O. — St. Johns, Mich. — Lost Fifteen Pounds of Flesh — A Well-dressed Vixen 146

CHAPTER X.

OVER the Ocean — Sea Voyage — London — Wesley's Pulpit — Paris — Egypt — The Great Pyramids — Nearly Shipwrecked — Palestine — Mt. Carmel — Gethsemane — The Birthplace of Jesus — The Jews' Wailing Place — Jericho — Jordan — The Early Home of Jesus — Damascus — Athens — Rome — "Home Again." 163

CHAPTER XI.

1886-7 — Algona — Eagle Grove — Correctionville — Fort Dodge — Clarion — Spencer — Sioux City — Piero — A Country Tent-meeting 178

CHAPTER XII.

MICHIGAN Tornadoes — Marcellus — White Pigeon — Bronson — Coldwater 187

CHAPTER XIII.

MICHIGAN Tornadoes, Continued — Leslie — Quincy — Coldwater Camp-meeting — East Rochester, N. H. — Haverhill — Union City — Hillsdale — Adrian 199

CHAPTER XIV.

A LOVE FEAST — Sunshine after the Storm — A Banker's Testimony — "Is My Name Written There?" — Where and When Converted — Victory — Convicted by a Card — A Teacher Rescued from Infidelity — A Problem in Loss and Gain — A Kiss the Key to His Heart — Where Will You Spend Eternity? — Saved from the Rink and Dance — Sometime Is Never — Bro. Weber as a Musical Director and Composer — His Song Book, The Evangelist 223

CHAPTER XV.

SERMON — Entire Sanctification. 244

CHAPTER XVI.

SERMON — Prayer 257

CHAPTER XVII.

BRO. WEBER'S Experience as Related in His Meetings . . 273

CHAPTER XVIII.

SECRETS of His Success — "Luck" not in the Bible, nor Christian's Vocabulary — A Positive Experience — Prayer — Faith — Earnestness — Humility — Plainness of Speech — Perseverance — Tact — Hits Sin — Preaches Terrors of the Law — Of Hell — He Loves Sinners — Liberality — Punctuality — A Student of the Bible and Holy Books — A Leader, not a Driver — Utilizes Song — Thoroughness — Fasting — Adaptability — Physical Exercise — Neatness — Persecuted — Eccentricity — Consecrated — "Filled" and "Led" by the Spirit — Preaches "Full Salvation" — Gives God the Glory 286

CHAPTER XIX.

To Whom Shall We Liken Him? — Noah — Joshua — Daniel — John the Baptist — Whitefield — Summerfield — Finney — Thomas Harrison — Jacob Knapp — Peter Cartwright — Sam Jones — Closing Remarks 313

Revival Tornadoes.

CHAPTER I.

BIRTH, ANCESTRY AND EARLY FORMATIVE INFLUENCES.

Soon will come the close of time, the dissolution of worlds, the final judgment, and after that the unfoldings of eternity.

As our eyes shall then behold the countless constellations of the redeemed, and view the different degrees of glory with which they shine, an index of their deeds below, not faintest among the many that glow with surpassing splendor we, doubtless, shall behold a spirit, who, when here below, was known by the name of Joseph H. Weber.

When the question shall be asked by saints of other ages and beings from other worlds, "Whence came he?" thousands saved through his agency will make ready answer, "From old Earth, where he found us lost souls and led us to the Saviour."

While it is true that the revelations of the judgment will reveal all the details of his marvelous life, yet there are many who do not wish to wait until then to learn them. Many to whom his life has been a benediction, and many others who have heard of his great and continuous success as a soul winner, are anxious to know all about him, his methods, his works, and the secret of his power with God and man. Nor is it idle curiosity that prompts them to seek this knowledge, but a desire to thus be better fitted for their especial work. It is also humbly hoped that many who have never met the evangelist may be, in this way, blessed.

BIRTH AND ANCESTRY.

Of the eleven children given to his parents, Louis and Elizabeth Weber, Joseph Hulse Weber was the second. He was born Oct. 12, 1855, in Cincinnati, Ohio. The state so prolific of Presidents, and others famed in the annals of political renown, has the honor of being his birth-place.

If souls won for Christ is in a great degree to determine man's glory at the judgment and through eternity, then, doubtless, of Ohio's sons this consecrated worker will be among the most illustrious of them all.

His father was born in Alsace, and was a German. His grandfather was a brave soldier under the first Napoleon, and an educated man. His mother, whose maiden name was Elizabeth Oatman, was born on Blennerhaset Island, situated in the Ohio river. Her father was born in New York State and her mother in Virginia.

With the Wesleys, Moody, Bishop Taylor, and the Booths of Salvation Army fame, he had the honor to spring from a large family, having five brothers and five sisters with whom to share his sorrows and his joys.

He loves homes in which the happy voices of many children mingle, and sometimes gives sharp thrusts at those false standards of society that have led her votaries to resort to criminality to keep their families small.

With the worthies mentioned above, Lincoln, Grant, Garfield, John Bunyan, Bishop Simpson, Spurgeon and hosts of others who have reached the topmost round of earthly fame, he also was privileged with being born in the vale of poverty and in a humble home.

His father was a cooper in the earlier part of his life, and is now a farmer. He, himself, in his boyhood and youth, was first a bar-tender in a saloon and then a laborer in a paper factory.

Hence Mr. Weber adds another to the long list of worthies that have sprung not only from homes of poverty but from the haunts of vice and have by God's help risen to be a boon to their fellow-men and thus a blessing to His kingdom.

The names of such will shine on the pages of history, and many of them in the annals of eternity, when the memory of myriads of the children of luxury and ease shall have dissolved like the morning mist. Such examples ought to nerve every child of poverty and toil, yea, of ignorance and vice, with an impulse to follow in their footsteps.

They ought to rebuke every proud and haughty Pharisee, who, with averted face and tighter grasp of robe, passes such persons "on the farther side," and also stimulate the Christian worker to everywhere be looking for these "diamonds in the rough," that, polished by saving grace, shall shine in the new Jerusalem when the names of the proud and haughty of earth, however exalted here, shall have rotted in oblivion.

CHILDHOOD AND YOUTH — EARLY FORMATIVE INFLUENCES.

"Heredity and early environments determine the currents of the after-life," "As the twig is bent the tree is inclined," are in a sense very wise and truthful sayings, but the hero of this book is a marked exception to the sentiments therein expressed. Herein is one of the many mysteries that shroud his eventful life.

Among his ancestry, as nearly as we can learn, prior to his own conversion, there had not been one really spiritual person. Therefore, whatever may be found in him as a Christian must be traced not to his first birth but to his second. On the advent of a soul into this world two forces seek to mould its character, right and wrong. Two beings, Christ and Satan, seek to place around it influences that will so impress it in its earliest years as to determine its destiny. In Mr. Weber's life wrong and Satan seemed from his earliest moments to possess great vantage ground, and early deprived the boy of safeguards such as Christ seeks to throw around the young, and swept him, well-nigh defenceless, into a current of subtle and mighty influences which, if not counteracted, would secure his certain ruin for time and for eternity. These were:

1. *The example of unconverted parents.* His father was a slave to strong drink. His mother religious in her way, but that way was the way of Catholicism.

2. *Roman Catholicism.* His ancestry on his father's side for centuries had been stanch Roman Catholics.

His mother on her marriage espoused her husband's faith and became one of the most ultra of the adherents of the Roman Church. Hence the children were reared at the feet of priest and pope and baptized into that faith. Thus by the minions of popery in the susceptible days of childhood he was bound with influences which proved chains such as only the "Lion of the tribe of Judah" would be able to break, not to Jesus, but to the icy altars of Ritualism and Formality. Lest he should early see his sad condition his eyes were blinded by a bandage rightly named "Popish Error," and thus from his earliest impressions he was in darkness, error, and superstition. Satan laughed and felt his victim sure. Rome said triumphantly, "I've got the first ten years of the child's life, I now defy Protestantism to win him back." The challenge was afterwards taken up, and with what results the coming pages will declare.

3. *Indulgence.* The parents, through false views of training children, perhaps thinking that indulgence was an index of parental love, allowed the boy to usually do as he pleased, and so the poisonous plants of disobedience and kindred vices grew almost unchecked in his young life. Oh, when will parents learn that such indulgence is keenest cruelty to the child, and that prompt obedience to the father and mother is to be the foundation, in after-life, of obedience to the Government and to God, and of a life of purity, happiness and usefulness, both in this world and the world to come!

4. *Strong drink.* In his very early boyhood it was regularly given him by the hands of his own parents, and a love for it, doubtless in part inherited, soon took

possession of him. What a marvel it will be if any power in the universe shall rescue and save from this demon, who has ruined millions in his murderous career.

5. *Dancing.* Under this deceptive syren he soon learned to love society and the indulgences connected with such gatherings, and all the baser elements of his nature being thus appealed to through circumstances entirely beyond his control, what wonder if, as one has written of him, "he naturally became very wild and hard; he was, like Bunyan, a 'ring leader' in all kinds of wickedness and sin," and knowing as he does all of the seductive wiles that this enchantress uses, first to charm and then to ruin the young, no wonder that at times he exposes them in tones that startle her defenders, and cause hundreds of the young to flee from her murderous thraldom. He was a great lover of music and became owner of a violin. He then was invited to play for the dances. He took great delight in this and went from bad to worse. Thoughts of these scenes of revelry, and the dissipations connected with them as he grew older, have never ceased to cause him pain. No wonder that he shudders, for thousands at the dance-house have left virtue behind, and arm in arm with lust have followed swiftly in the steps of her whose "house is the way to hell." Some one whispers, "But I know church members who uphold dances." The church member who upholds them in all the light of the way they have led and are leading thousands, is either a fool or a farce, or both, and is preparing an awful reckoning for the judgment.

6. *Saloonism.* Twin brother to the ball-room is the

saloon. Each have blighted thousands and sent them reeling under the cruel lashes of black despair to the grave and an agonizing eternity. Both are paid servants of Satan, and well do they work for him. Both are greedy whirlpools, whose outer currents at first amuse, then excite, then startle, then, as they near the gurgling centre, affright and then engulf. On their fatal currents is borne modesty, virtue, honor, industry, innocence, hope, love and life itself. Both are fiends who seek to lure with cunning wiles their victims, until they have slain their guardian, Self-control, and then they bind them with huge chains in the dungeons of despair, from which none but Christ can deliver. This agent of the enemy sought the boy who, as we have seen, though but a lad, was already terribly tangled in the meshes of sin. It is said that, "One day, while selling brooms, he went into a saloon to 'drive a bargain,' when he was accosted by the proprietor with, 'I don't want a broom but I want to buy you,' at first the boy was somewhat startled, but upon explanation, and further conversation, a bargain was made that he should attend bar. He was done with brooms, matches, shoe-strings, and fans, for he would actually be a salesman, which struck him as being something rather elevating. He returned home in high glee, and informed his parents of his project. They were both unfavorable to the move, but he prevailed on his father to go down to the saloon and see the man. The father's better nature and judgment prevailed, and Joe was informed that he must attend school rather than tend bar. He was not to be so easily frustrated in his coveted honors. When the following Monday came, his mother said, 'You must go to school,' but he desired to become a rich man, and so went to the saloon and began work as a bar tender. He was so small that the proprietor had to erect a rack behind the bar so that he could stand to deal out 'hell and destruction,' as he now terms it. He was with this saloon-keeper for five months." Here his love for liquor was further strengthened, and as if all of these influences were not sufficient to secure both the present and future ruin of the boy, another agency was brought to aid those already doing all too well their work in insuring the permanent downfall of the youth.

7. *Theatricals.* It would seem as if enough agencies were already devoted to his ruin without the last mentioned. Well did Satan understand, however, that, unless captured and kept, that his kingdom would be a tremendous loser, and so he plied all of his most cunning arts. Theatricals appeared to him as to many others in the stolen robes of innocence, and so like many others he thus was easily led astray. At her suggestion an amateur minstrel troupe was organized, of which he soon became the leading spirit, and with him, as with many others, this was a stepping stone to that which was even worse.

The dance-house, the rink, the saloon, the circus, and the theatre are Satan's churches, in which he seeks to ripen spirits in their alienation from God and in their fitness for the penalty beyond the grave. Their associations chime with the chords of an unregenerate heart, whether it beat in the breast of the openly profligate or of the false professor. As men in poisoning rats hide the poison in much meal, so Satan mingles the poison with which he seeks to ruin, through these agencies, with the meal of music and much else that is pleasing and in other relations would be unobjectionable.

"The Sabbath to him was a day of evil and high carnivals. His associates were all evil, as bad as he, and together they broke all of the commands of the Decalogue." Such was Joseph H. Weber in his early life. Young in years, but old in vice. Quaffing iniquity as if it were some delicious nectar, and loving the deadly draught. Manacled by evil habits, yet caressing the very irons that bound him! Chained to evil companions, which, as Satan's sheriffs, stand ready to bear his spirit to the cells of hopeless doom, yet revelling in such associations. Like Bunyan, he was a master-piece of what sin could do. Evidently Satan has done his work so well that it never can be undone, unless a miracle shall interpose. By these seductive influences "Joe," as he was then called, was pushed out into the Niagara of sin and dissipation, and yet there were many traits in the boy that, if redeemed from sin's service, would be of more value than gold or precious gems.

He was born to be a leader. At home, at school, in sports, at his work, and wherever he moved among the youth of his acquaintances, he was the center. This trait, consecrated to God in after life, has done much to help him lead on to spiritual victories.

He easily made friends. One has said of him, "He was not without friends, for he always won them wherever he went. His warm heart could only invite; he was himself friendly."

He had mental grip. He could apply himself to his studies, quickly master them, and then have plenty of leisure time in which to play the rogue.

He was possessed of an iron will. Whatever he undertook he persisted in. Doubtless this element was one thing that led his parents to oppose him as little as possible. His will was like an engine under high pressure upon a down grade with no brakes, every thing had to get out of his way or suffer. Referring to this, a former biographer writes, "We notice here an element of firmness cropping out, which is a requisite of success in his present work; this is seen prominently in all his meetings. He has a will, and that must govern."

He was benevolent. By nature, he knew not what it was to be stingy. He loved to make money, and had, even when a child, unusual faculties to succeed in business, but it was not that "gold fever," which loves to hoard, but a desire to get for the pleasure he might have in its using. It is said of him, that he would share the last farthing, and always delighted in giving to the needy. It may be that we shall finally find that the Master's teaching, "Give, and it shall be given unto you," found verification in his life.

These, and other traits, characterized his early life and, like gold dust on the surface, speak of what may yet prove a rich mine underneath. If it be there, it is bedded so deeply beneath the adamant of sin, that no one with less than Almighty power will ever be able to reach it. Perhaps he yet may come in contact with such an One. Be patient.

EARLY PERILS.

Not only was the soul of the youth, by such agencies as have been described in constant jeopardy, but sickness and accident both conspired to deliver his body into the hands of greedy Death, and thus shut him forever from the great life-work that God was finally to fit him for.

Jesus in Childhood had his Herod; Moses his Pharaoh; Wesley, the fire fiend. Some way it seems as if all the destructive forces of both the moral and material world are permitted to spend their fury upon many whom God is fitting for great usefulness.

Weber was to be no exception. This part of his experience is thus related by another: When between two and three years of age, he was taken very sick; no one expected him to recover. Before he was six, he had fallen into the canal twice, and once came very near drowning, but was rescued by a gentleman who happened to be passing by at the time. These warnings were not accepted, but his parents allowed him to go on in the way of sin, either without questioning the propriety of their course, or else feeling, with many foolish parents, that they were unable to control their son, and hence not responsible. When eight years old, he was again taken sick, and for long days his parents and friends despaired of his life. It was the dreaded scarlet fever, but careful nursing and proper medical attention enabled him so completley to recover that his parents were again hopeful. But immediately the dropsy set in, and for five long months he was at death's door, gyrating between life and death; most of the time the symptoms were decidedly unfavorable. One day the anxious mother went to market to purchase the necessaries for the table. She was naturally in a great hurry, as her boy was " sick nigh unto death." The old lady who was selling vegetables asked her why she was in such a big hurry. Her reply was, "I have a very sick boy at home." The market woman's sympathy was at once elicited, and upon inquiry found the disease to be dropsy. Like most "old ladies," she had her remedy, and said, "Oh, I can give you a cure for that." The mother, all the more credulous by her vigils and anxiety, was eager to learn the remedy in which the market woman had so much confidence. The remedy was "carrot seed and juniper berries," from which a tea was made of equal parts. These were immediately tried, and to the astonishment of all, proved to be *the* remedy, for he commenced at once to improve, and in two weeks' time the dropsy had all disappeared. For a few weeks, Joe improved, he became more like himself, and all were rejoicing that the boy was out of danger. But the way of the transgressor is hard. Before convalescence was complete, he was taken with intermittent fever, and again the death angel seemed to demand his prey. He grew worse rapidly, and at one time so near gone that the family and friends gathered around the bedside, weeping and expecting that each moment would be his last. While thus watching, their hearts beating wildly and their faces suffused with scalding tears, the dying child began to sing a song of rare sweetness. To the sad listeners it seemed as if the gates of heaven were ajar, and the angelic choirs were chanting his requiem. It seemed more the music of heaven than of earth. Amid the sobbing the grand-father said, "Now he is gone." They thought of the dying swan, "who chants a doleful hymn to his own death," and the song became the portent of his dissolution.

But his time had not yet come, for the God who rules in all the affairs of men had a work for him yet to do. He rallied, he gradually grew better, but his convalescence was slow and tedious. For nearly a year he was sick, confined for the most part of the time to his bed or the house. Though slowly, yet surely, he recovered, and in time was able to start again to school; but as is the case with many who are older, the impressions thus made, wore away or were drowned in the whirl of sinful pleasures, and so the young life sped on, a perfect "tornado" of frivolity and sinfulness. What a transformation, if, by some unseen power, it should yet become a tornado of righteousness and vehement zeal to save a lost world!

CHAPTER II.

CONVICTION, CONVERSION AND CALL TO THE MINISTRY.

A MEMBER of the Romish Church, but not converted. Such was the experience of Mr. Weber during all the days of his childhood and youth. When conscience would speak to alarm him, Satan would give the cradle of Catholicism, in which he had been placed, a nudge, and soon he would be fast asleep again.

Were such scenes confined only to the Roman Church, it would be a sad enough picture; but it is a startling fact that the churches of Protestantism are likewise replete with such members. As Mr. Moody says, "Many are as ignorant of spirituality as Nicodemus was of the new birth." The writer a few months since asked Mr. Weber, in the light of all of his experience as an evangelist, the proportion of people in the churches of Protestantism that in his judgment are really converted. He answered, "If I should say but one in four, I would not be putting it strongly."

In the spiritual tornadoes that are sweeping over the land, thank God thousands of these are being convicted, and we trust converted. Otherwise they remain drones in the gospel hive, that hinder, instead of help,—worms in the gospel tree that sap its very life.

Reader, are you, as he was then, a church member but

still unsaved? If so, may you, too, be led to see your error and danger and seek the grace that giveth life.

The chief agent — as in all other cases — that led to Joseph's conviction, was the Holy Ghost. He used, among other things, especially *his mother's warning.* When he was about nineteen years of age his relish for wickedness was such that "his mother became alarmed and threatened to send him to the Reform School" if he joined a show company. This was the first thing that seemed in any way to have checked him as he was plunging madly down the abyss of dissipation and of doom. This evidently "set him to thinking" about his real condition and prospects of the future.

The Roman Catholic Church holds clearly the atonement through Jesus, and the reality of future reward and punishment; also a hell just as awful as Christ has pictured it.

These truths had been vividly put before him by the teachings of the priest and as illustrated by the many impressive paintings that adorned the walls of the Roman cathedral.

Protestantism, while she shuns her errors, might learn much from Rome in her perseverence and success in impressing the minds of the young. The spirit of God now uses the truths which the boy's mind has "been like wax to receive and like marble to retain," though loth to practice, and he begins to feel that he is "guilty, helpless, lost, undone," and that he has a hell to shun and an offended God with whom he must make his peace at once. The life boat of Salvation was awaiting him, but Satan drew his eyes from that to another craft called Reformation, and he said, "I'll enter that, I'll reform and live a better life."

He vowed not to drink any more beer, and told his companions that he would give them five dollars if they caught him drinking it any more. He kept this vow, but continued to drink whiskey until the following March, when he became a total abstainer.

His associates plied all their arts to prevail upon him to give up these "new notions," but they might as well have pleaded with a whirlwind.

For four years he had been working with an ice company at Hamilton, Ohio, but May 6, 1874, he was apprenticed to Peter Hecks to learn the trade of carriage trimming. After working here for about half a year, while visiting the Cincinnati exposition, he saw an advertisement in the paper for one who had experience in carriage trimming, responded and secured the place. When his mother was first informed of this change she said, "You will surely be lost." Up to this time he had made his home with his parents, and his affectionate nature had twined around the parental household like the ivy around the oak.

No one knows the worth of a home, be it ever so humble, until he is called upon to leave it. Then some tendrils will break and bleed. The Holy Spirit used this occasion to touch the young man's heart for good as it had never been touched before. Under this strange, sweet, and to him melting influence, "as he was passing from the parental roof, his heart was touched with the parting. His better nature gained the supremacy. When almost out of view of his home and loved ones, he lifted his eyes toward heaven, and asked God to make him a better boy. That simple prayer was answered. From this time we find him different. God moves in a mysterious way. What seemed to his mother the ruin of her boy was his making. His old associates, especially those of the later day who had so much influence over him for evil, were now separated from him. It is true, the distance was not great, but the dire influence of constant evil companionship was broken, and an opportunity for better influences to operate was given."

If it be true that

> "Satan trembles when he sees
> The weakest saint upon his knees,"

then he doubtless began to tremble now lest this captive should escape.

Has he not used all that Satanic power can suggest to bind him fast? Can it be possible that his blindfolded prisoner is to pierce the thick pall of ignorance, vice and superstition, and even now behold that light that will turn the darkest night of sin into a day that knows no ending? So Satan soliloquizes. In the blackness, from the lips of the youth there wings a simple prayer to the ears of Him who ever listens to the faintest sigh of penitence, and has said, "Ask and ye shall receive." An answer comes, though not the one he expected, nor in the way he looked for. He is not pardoned yet, but he will be, cost what it may.

> "Oh, where can rest be found,
> Rest for the weary soul?"

He will seek it through the ordinances of the church of his fathers. Is not that the true church? So by the ladder of good deeds and devotions he will climb up into the peace and divine favor that is beginning to seem worth more to him than all else besides. So "he attended the Catholic Church faithfully in all kinds of weather. He would kneel upon the stone floor of the church and try to pray, but it seemed that he could not pray. The more he tried the worse he felt. No relief came to him, yet he would be faithful. He fought his appetites and passions the best he could with the light he possessed and the aid he could command. Thus he spent weary months seeking light, but there was no one to guide him aright. He had turned his face from the evil. He must win or die in the effort." How many like him must learn, as preached by Paul and learned by Luther as God fitted him for his life's great work, that "by the works of the law shall no flesh be justified," and that the "just shall live by faith."

Painfully was the lesson learned that

> "Nor bleeding bird, nor bleeding beast,
> Nor hyssop branch, nor sprinkling priest,
> Nor running brook, nor flood, nor sea,
> Can wash the dismal stain away."

His condition becomes desperate. Like Pharaoh, when Israel determined to fly for freedom, Satan marched down upon him with charging hosts of doubts and fears and strong temptations.

He worked early and late, and was soon rewarded by being made foreman, and being industrious he began to work in another shop at night. It was difficult to break from old companions, but now he saw that they were hindering him, and they must go.

God loved him too well to let him alone until he was saved and safe.

The Spirit continued to enlighten him and to strive with him. One morning he arose more restless and uneasy than usual. All of his old amusements had lost their charms. His soul was hungry for something that would satisfy. He had sought in Rome's way — in his own way, but still had found it not.

Unprepared for life, for death, for judgment and for eternity! what could he do? "His old associations crowded upon his mind, but were repelled. In this anxiety and temptation he wandered from place to place, but nowhere could he dissipate his heart's forebodings. He wandered across the 'Rhine,' into a variety theatre, seeking rest, but finding none. In these places he did not yield to temptation. He had not the least idea that they were unfit for a seeker of religious peace. He was educated to believe that these places were no worse than those of legitimate amusements, and that the Christian could enjoy the musical treat without any danger of sinning, or of injury to himself. He was uneasy, but had no idea of its cause or nature. He did not attribute it to the Spirit of God, but that Spirit was leading him in a way he knew not. After hours spent in this fruitless effort to find peace, he was attracted by a crowd of people listening to a Baptist missionary preaching on the site of the Exposition building under the archway crossing to the Art Gallery in Washington Park. The name of this minister was Rev. Joseph Emery. It was mere curiosity that led him to hear this man talk, for he was not aware that he was preaching the Gospel, or he probably would not have gone to hear the heretic. His preaching had no apparent effect upon him, but when the crowd began to sing lustily,—

'Almost persuaded now to believe ;
Almost persuaded Christ to receive,'

he became more attentive. His soul responded to the song, and when the last lines of the last stanza were being sung, —

"'Almost' cannot avail ;
'Almost' is but to fail !
Sad, sad, that bitter wail—
'Almost'—*but lost!*'

his soul was peculiarly touched, and looking toward heaven he said vehemently within himself, 'I WILL NOT BE LOST; I WILL BE SAVED.' In the quickness of thought the burden was rolled away in this decision for heaven. His heart was made light and happy. He felt that he could fly. What a change! and how suddenly it came upon him! He had never been taught in the way of life, and did not realize what the change was, but he knew he was happy."

Thus was Satan defeated, his chains broken, and the soul of Joseph set at liberty.

Christ did more for him "in the quickness of thought," than Roman rites in a life-time. From this day, Aug. 14, 1874, he dates his conversion. Henceforth, he will be known as the " Converted Catholic."

Among all of his wicked associates he is the only one that to-day is saved. Let that be remembered, lest some reader say, " Like Weber, I 'll quaff the pleasures of sin's cup, and after that will make my peace with God."

Unlike many who resist the truth, " as soon as the way of salvation was made plain to him, he walked in it." His conversion was as marvellous as Daniel's deliverance from the den of lions, or the Hebrew children's from the fiery furnace.

His deliverance was from the jaws of the lions of habits and passions, which already were crushing his soul; from the fires of sins that nothing in the universe, except the blood of Jesus, could ever quench. For this deliverance let every reader give "glory to God in the highest!" What this new experience was, in his spiritual darkness he hardly understood, but was conscious of the long-sought, great and blessed change.

Having enlisted under his new Commander, with all the energy he had shown in the service of sin, he now begins to work with Him.

Not like some foolish persons who wait for "some great thing" did he tarry, but seized the first opportunities to do good. The Young Men's Christian Association, the Sunday-school, and, above all, the Methodist class-meeting, were places that he loved.

No man need be anxious about something to do for the Master after he has settled the question that he will cheerfully do ANYTHING that He may bid. Of all such "it is written," "I have set before thee an open door, and no man can shut it."

Mr. Weber proved the truth of this. The work first given him was such as was fitted to his undeveloped capacities.

God did not send Moses upon his great life-work until he had been disciplined by years of preparatory training. The same was true of the apostles, of Luther, Wesley, Moody, and all of those who have been greatly honored in God's work. Mr. Weber was glad to belong to this class, and ready for any discipline.

Now we come to his first public religious work. What was it? *Teaching a set of rude, wild, street Arabs from the slums of Cincinnati.* He did not feel "qualified," but was too loyal to a Kingly voice,—whose whispers now he loved to heed — to say "no," and so with Bible and Journal he began his work. At first, of course, he made blunders. Who does not? Is not failure the first letter in the alphabet of success?

There was one thing he could do, one thing of greatest moment, one thing of more value than the recital of the most elaborate, Scriptural disquisitions, or systematic, analytical explanations of the lesson; and that was the giving of his own, *living*, personal experience of the practical truths in it.

He was now in possession of something that for soul-saving work was of more value than archangel eloquence, "all knowledge," and all "gifts," as valuable as these may be, and this talent of a genuine Christian experience, he would use as God might lead. God set His seal early upon the labors of the young worker, and many who belonged to his class were converted.

Brother Weber and his early co-workers were evidently and fortunately free from that false refinement and spurious idea of religious dignity which would confine gospel-meetings between church walls, and abandon God's great temple with "curtains of azure and dome of blue" to the circus, medicine vender, political pedagogue, and the Salvation Army. Therefore, at their Master's command, after the Sunday-school is over, they hasten to the "highways" and in the market places, and at their singing a crowd collects, and they unfold to them that gospel, which, like the sunshine and the free air of heaven, is at home in all places, and is for rich and poor alike. Though, like Jesus and the Wesleys in their out-door work, they sometimes met with hisses and opposition, yet they continued it, and much good was done.

The influence and counsels of Mr. Thompson, the superintendent of the Elm Street Sunday-school, were heaven-sent inspirations to him in this stage of his experience. Best of all, Jesus was his companion, the Word his instructor, and the Holy Spirit his guide.

The next great question that he had to settle was, "Where shall I make my church home?"

His quick perceptive powers saw clearly, to remain out on the "devil's commons," with church membership nowhere, would be a perilous course. And then he had too much honor to try and "tramp it" without taking a regular church train.

As cattle turned loose in the road browse through the fences a wisp of clover here and some wheat there and some timothy from another owner, so some people try to eke out a spiritual existence by what they in a like manner can browse from different churches, and sometimes they justify themselves in such a course by saying, "We don't want to be tied up to any one church; we want to be free."

The embryo evangelist with a divine instinct preferred the freedom of the "pasture" to that of the "roadside," and united with the St. Paul's Methodist Episcopal Church, Cincinnati, Ohio, November 1, 1875, on probation, and came into full membership April 9, 1876.

Now Satan was more enraged than ever, and he so influenced Mr. Weber's employer, that he discharged him because he had turned Protestant. Trusting, praying, often severely tried, yet learning new lessons, nearly a year passed away, and now we come to the next great event in his life,—

HIS CALL TO PREACH THE GOSPEL.

"He had been feeling ever since his conversion that he was called to preach the Gospel of Jesus, but he pleaded ignorance and the want of means to acquire an education as the excuse for his refusal. Amid all these discouragements, in debt for his board, with no work available, he knelt down in his room, alone with God. This was February 2, 1877. He had been raised as a Catholic, to believe in signs and wonders. While thus alone with his heavenly Father he poured out his soul unto God in this plaintive strain, 'Now, dear Father, I am not satisfied with thy Spirit saying, "You must preach;" I want something I can see and feel with my hands.' It seemed to him that the Lord replied, ' Well, my child, what shall I place before you?' He answered, ' A piece of money, Lord, in the space of one week." This hour of secret pleading and covenant was not forgotten. It was always before his mind. Ofttimes he would see a shining object before him, when he would approach it expectantly, only to find it a piece of tin or glass shining in the sunlight. His heart would then be sad, and misgivings would come to him. He felt that if God wanted him to preach he would give him the sign in the form of a piece of money. At times he would take the lamp at night to look around the room, or feel on the bed, searching every nook and corner, expecting the sign and evidence of his call to the ministry.

"The week was rapidly passing away. He went to his aunt's, who was living in Corryville, a suburb of Cincinnati, on Monday, February 5th. This aunt had become highly incensed on learning that he was out on the street preaching and had turned Protestant. She had sent for him on a previous occasion, and told him that he was crazy, and would go where all the crazy Methodists go, to the lunatic asylum, and that she did not want anything more to do with him, nor to see him afterward. After this interview he prayed for her, as he always did for all who persecuted him. She became reconciled to him, especially when she saw the power of the new religion over his life, so that she was prepared to welcome and encourage him in this trying hour. He opened his heart to his reconciled aunt, told her of all his trials, misgivings, his financial difficulties, etc. Her heart was touched. She invited him to remain with her until he could find a job. He accepted the invitation. On the following Wednesday, Feb. 7, 1887, he attended service at the Mt. Auburn Methodist Episcopal Church, where they had been holding a revival, and were now receiving the converts into probationary membership. This seems to have been a very excellent meeting. His soul was aglow with peace and joy.

"At the conclusion of the meeting he was talking with a young man who had been converted, telling him of his own experience and abiding hope in the Lord Jesus. While he was thus administering comfort and consolation to this new convert, he saw something sparkling on the floor, about twenty feet away. Then the vision dawned upon him: Here is the piece of money, the sign of his call to the ministry of the blessed Saviour. Ecstasy filled his soul; joy thrilled every chord of his heart; gladness reigned supreme. Turning his face toward heaven, his soul in its fulness exclaimed, 'Lord, I will go.' He picked up the shining objects, which proved to be two pennies, new from the mint. He gave them to the pastor, William W. Case. He had asked for a piece of money. God gave him two, — the emblem of a double call, to the ministry and to evangelism. They were but pennies, the smallest pieces of money, in token that the kingdom of Christ does not consist of the riches of this world. They were new, bright pennies, displaying the glory of the mission of an ambassador of the Lord Jesus."

On his way home the stars seemed to dance in participating joy; all nature was gorgeously arrayed in gladness to his happy soul. When he arrived at his aunt's, he told her about his prayer, the sign, and the answer. She said, "You ought to accept it." He replied, "I will." Then and there the question of his life work was settled. Thus step by step he was led by God into the great harvest field of soul-saving work. More and more he felt,—

> "The love of Christ doth me constrain,
> To seek the wandering souls of men;
> With cries, entreaties, tears, to save,—
> To snatch them from the gaping grave."

In his call to the ministry we are struck with the young man's caution and his honesty. In view of the great responsibility, like all whom God calls to this great work, he at first recoils from the call. He must *know* it to be of God before he can accept and act on it. How can he know? He had not been instructed, as we are clearly taught, that if such an impression is of God it will be followed,—

1. By gifts for the work.
2. By the call of the church.
3. By open doors for work, or preparation for it.

As he was ignorant of these tests, and must have one that would put doubt to flight, God met him in the way described and gave the craved assurance.

Like Mr. Moody, he received little or no encouragement from his pastor; but assured now that his call was of God, instead of sinking in the Slough of Despond, he mounts to the summit of fixed Purpose, and plans for the needed preparation. He is wise enough to know that, if he would teach others, he must himself first be taught; that if he would preach to others, he must possess the Gospel to be proclaimed; that if the Apostles must be with Jesus himself as pupils for three years, and then graduate with a special Pentecostal finishing course in the upper chamber, that he must, like them, seek the needed preparation of both head and heart in order to win success. Providence pointed him to the Ohio Wesleyan University at Delaware, Ohio, and here he determined to go.

He was now without employment and without money. Persons with less pluck would have folded their hands and said "Impossible." Not so with him. He prayed and planned and sought the means, and his efforts were blessed of God.

At this point young men who are called to the ministry are usually met by several ememies sent by Satan, clad in robes of light, to prevent their thorough preparation for the work of life. The name of the first is Gain. He says, "Follow me, and I will make you a millionaire." Many look at the luxuries that Gain will give, and allured, turn aside. The next is Political Renown. He says, "Follow me, and I will give you political position and the applause of men." Many have listened to him, and too late have seen their folly and lamented it. The next is Matrimony. She whispers, "Lay your books aside and heed my counsels, and I will give you a beautiful home, redolent with the perfumes that are wafted from fadeless flowers, thrilled by entrancing music and adorned by paintings, such as only Love can paint." Thus with honeyed words she often charms her victim and he often yields, only in later life to become the victim of deep regret.

If a youth remains unswayed under all of the seductive wiles of these subtle tempters, then a fourth, more dangerous than them all, appears to make a final effort. His name is "Zeal-without-knowledge." He looks pious, talks pious, and sometimes is pious, but in infancy his brain was impaired and he never recovered; hence he is a perilous advisor. He says "See, thousands of souls are being lost while you are tarrying at this preparatory work; if you love them, leave it and hasten to their rescue." He ignores the fact that while persons are engaged in preparatory work they can be winning souls, and that to go out unduly prepared is to be like a farmer who is in such a hurry to save his ripened grain that he has not time to grind his blunted sickle knives. This enemy, strange as it may seem, deceives some whom all the others are unable to ensnare.

To the sophistries of all of these deceptive voices, Mr. Weber turned a deaf ear. When Poverty arose and said, "I positively prohibit you from putting your plans for needed preparation into practice," he laughed Poverty in the face, and fell upon his knees, pleading the interposition of Divine help.

The next morning he said to his aunt, "I am going to get a job to-day." She asked where he would get it. He replied, "I don't know; but God has given me the evidence, and he will give me a job." Her only reply was, "You are a peculiar fellow." His prayer was answered. Work and good wages were given, and Oct. 3d, 1877, he started for the university with a thankful heart, glad hopes, and $225 in cash.

If such a young man as this lives, and proves as persistent and wise in seeking and retaining the education that is found in the "Pentecostal upper chamber" as the head culture that is also essential, the time will come when his prayers will make thrones tremble and kingdoms crumble. Some with clear spiritual perceptions will begin to see that a cyclone centre is forming, which, nursed in the tropic zone of spiritual and mental light and fire, will ere long sweep through the regions of drought and death with a fury that is born from above.

CHAPTER III.

SCHOOL LIFE AND PASTORATE.

"Gaining knowledge is a good thing, but saving souls is better. We ought to throw by all the libraries of the world rather than be guilty of the loss of one soul" (M. E. Discipline, ¶. 142). Such is the spirit of true Methodism, and of the Gospel.

Strong as was his desire for knowledge, pure as was his motive in gaining it, and strong as are the incentives in our institutions of learning that tend to impel a young man to put his studies before everything else, young Weber resisted them all, and, like a true son of Wesley, kept salvation first. He did this to such an extent that his evangelistic work might almost be said to have begun with his school life.

Students often become just as absorbed and secular in delving for knowledge as men do in delving for gold. Sometimes they enter college to study for the ministry, and postponing soul-saving work until school life is done, are graduated walking encyclopedias, as spiritually lifeless as Egyptian mummies. This comes from an abuse of golden privileges.

Within three weeks from the time our knowledge seeker entered school, he was elected superintendent of a Sunday-school. Soon the school burst its shell, and a larger room was sought and found. Then followed a gracious revival in St. Paul's Church, of which he was now a member, and many of the Sunday-school pupils were happily converted.

If young converts want to know how to keep from backsliding, and students how to stay in school and at the same time grow in grace, let them study and profit by this experience. Several characteristics are worthy of especial mention.

1. *His independence of surroundings.* Whether in his study or in Sunday-school, or in the mill or elsewhere earning money to meet his school expenses, his mind was staid on God. Whether his companions were good or godless, whether his superiors smiled or frowned upon him, he looked to Jesus, and was kept. Opposition seemed to intensify his determinations.

The following incident illustrating this, occurred at Minster, a Catholic town where he went to sell some buggies. They do most of their trading there on Sunday, and insisted that he should sell them buggies on that day. He explained that he was a Christian, made clear to them what a Christian is, and spoke of the sacredness of God's holy day.

The people, by this enraged, forbade his doing business there. He continued with success, which, with what he had said, turned his enemies into a mad mob. As he was leaving the place, a saloon-keeper sought a quarrel with him; but he would not come down to such unchristian conduct, and went his way, trusting Him who is able "to give power over all the power of the enemy" for protection. The saloon-keeper appealed to the already incensed mob, and they determined to kill the Christian. This with our hero was a time of most earnest prayer, for he heard their words, and perceived their intention. Then came the chase; the flying Protestant, and the pursuing Catholics. They chased him through the streets, throwing stones and bricks after him, and crying angrily, "Kill him! Kill him! Kill him!" The whole town was in an uproar. Excitement prevailed. He ran into the mayor's house for protection. The mayor proved to be a friend, and as one burly fellow rushed into the house, cursing the heretic, he was informed that he could not take the fugitive from there. After some parleying, the leader said he would protect Mr. Weber if he would go out to the crowd and make acknowledgements. This Weber refused to do, saying he had done nothing requiring an acknowledgement. As the leader promised protection, he went down to the mob, and talked to them, and finally succeeded in pacifying them. He claimed the victory through the blessing of God, to whom he poured out his soul in this trying hour. He passed through many trying scenes of a similar nature, but he came out of the active warfare whole through the mercy of God.

2. *His persistence in personal work.* He not only resisted the temptations offered by the unsaved, but, like Billy Bray and John Bunyan, wherever he went sought their salvation, so that his fellow-laborers learned to respect him as a Christian, and several of his fellow-students with whom he had labored, including his own room-mate, were converted.

3. *He loved to labor among the outcasts and the lowly.* "He took charge of the jail meetings, visiting

the prison, very often distributing books there which were chiefly donated by Dr. Payne and wife. As a result several of the prisoners were converted.

"He took time from his studies to visit the poor people in the vicinity of the mission, and supplied them with clothes and fuel when necessity demanded.

"He was always ready to visit the sick and dying. When laboring there he often preached upon the streets in Cincinnati. While in school at Delaware he became a missionary to the heathen Chinese, by going to the laundry and offering to instruct them in English. His offer was accepted. He taught them English, and at the same time taught them the Gospel. His work was successful.

"He preached for the colored people in a revival, in which many were converted. While on business in Buffalo he labored at the Canal Street Mission, where, it is said, the worst people in the world congregated."

Thus he faithfully did the humble work that he found always at hand. He that does this shall some day be "made ruler over many things."

Where others stood looking for great opportunities, he saw and gathered soul jewels that shall shine eternally in the diadem of Jesus. Ever busy, he had no time to parley with the devil.

This kind of work, both when in school and toiling for means to meet his school expenses, was his "recreation and pastime," and physically, spiritually, and intellectually, his strength increased. If students everywhere would systematically engage in such gymnastics, what blessings to themselves and others might flow thereby.

He was very liberal. "Papa," said a little girl who overheard her father say he soon should need more money, "if you want more money, you will have to begin to give more." She had learned the lesson that Jesus meant what He said when He declared, "Give, and it shall be given unto you." The truth of this Mr. Weber proved in early life. Most young men in school, particularly if devoting their lives to the ministry, would have felt that it was theirs to receive, not to give. Not so with Mr. Weber. No good cause could appeal to him in vain, and he was continually aiding the needy. In one instance he hired a man to stop drinking; in others supplied fuel and raiment to the destitute. While in Cincinnati earning money for school expenses, he organized a young people's Missionary Society, and raised quite a sum of money for that. When in canvassing he found a poor family, he frequently supplied their needs. Some one asks, "How could he give so much when he needed all to educate himself?" It was with him as with a liberal Detroit layman. When asked how he could give so much, he answered, "God shovels in, I shovel out, and He is so much stronger than I am that He continually keeps ahead of me." Whether working in the mill, canvassing on the road, or whatever he did, God prospered it, and though at times he must needs leave school to labor, those periods were short, and crowned with both spiritual and financial prosperity. Many young converts are led astray by giant Stinginess. His very breath is withering, and if his presence is cherished, like mown grass in June, so his victim will shrivel up and die. Another of the keys to his growth as a convert, and his success in whatever he undertook, was persistent and prevailing prayer. Early he realized that "prayer moves the Arm that moves the world," and wisely he availed himself of the benefits of such a mighty leverage.

He was much of the time on his knees, so much of it that "it was there that his pantaloons first wore out." He took the promises of Jesus just as they read, and meeting the conditions upon which they were offered, pleaded and expected their fulfillment, and thus prevailed with God. If he needed employment, he prayed for an opening until he felt sure of it, and soon he would find it.

On one occasion he left school to earn more money, but as for some time he had been out of practice, could earn but about twelve dollars a week, and that with the greatest effort. His constant prayer was that God would bless his labor and enable him to earn enough to carry him through college. When he was weary from excessive work he would pray for strength. He soon was able, with a slight increase of wages, to earn from twenty to twenty-eight dollars a week, nearly as much as two men would usually earn.

Satan utterly failed, where he has succeeded with so many, in persuading them that little things must be ruled out of the realm of prayer. "In everything" he made known his requests unto God. His great success in canvassing he attributed to this. When others in the same work with him were less successful, and inclined to listen to discouragement, he would tell them the secret of his success. Thus he carried his religion into his business and his business into his religion. Had he have met with a loss, which he seldom did, he would have felt as an honored Grand Rapids layman, J. C More, president of the Grand Rapids Furniture Co., when his property was destroyed by fire. The next day was Sunday, and he was in his place at church as usual. After service his friends commenced to condole him on the loss of his property. They were surprised at his cheerfulness, and still more by his reply. He answered, "I have not lost anything; it's my partner that meets the loss." "But who is he?" "Jesus Christ. I had consecrated all to Him, and the loss is His."

We give the following incident, written by another, as an illustration of the way Brother Weber trusted God in little things as well as great. "During the examination a student exchanged hats with him. His hat was a new one, while the student's was an old one. As he had to be economical, and at the same time did not like to wear an old hat when he had expended money for a new one, he was anxious to get his own hat. He prayed over the matter. He asked God to overrule in the return of his hat. When he prayed, he expected that his prayer would be answered. In a word, he took the Lord at His promise. When he was riding on horseback to preach for a friend, he saw a boy on the road; the Spirit seemed to say, 'That boy has your hat.' He at once looked up and thanked God for the answer to his prayer. He was positive the boy had his hat. A day or two after he met the boy again, when he accosted him, demanding his hat, believing in confidence that the Spirit had directed him to this boy. The boy denied having the hat, but finally acknowledged it, and Weber received his new hat, for which he had paid his money."

"To pray well," taught Luther, is the better part of an education. In the light of this statement, our coming evangelist, even in this stage of his training, was more highly advanced than many upon whom colleges have showered their highest honors. We may yet expect to see him "tarry in some upper chamber," pleading the "promise of the Father," until he comes out with power such as "all his adversaries shall not be able to resist." Such were some of the characteristics of Weber, the college youth.

For the following additional light on his life in school we are indebted to one of his personal friends, Rev. C. A. Galimore.

In the fall of 1877, Joseph H. Weber entered the Preparatory Department of the Ohio Wesleyan University, at Delaware, as a student.

He immediately identified himself with the religious work of the college, and, by showing his colors at the beginning of his student life, avoided the temptations which beset those who do not thus take an early and decisive stand for God. He was, however, far from content with mere identification with the Christian element of the college, and soon became quite prominent on account of the aggressive character of his religious life. He seemed to realize that the college presented a fertile field for Christian work; and, as one who must give an account of his stewardship, he gave himself, with all the earnestness of his ardent nature, to the work of securing the salvation of his class-mates. For this work he was eminently qualified, being possessed of a high type of moral courage, which feared not to seek out and rebuke all forms of immorality and vice; and, such was his love for souls, that he would subject himself to any inconvenience in order that he might lead them to Christ.

He was possessed of a remarkably magnetic manner, which drew the students, and especially the younger portion of them, to him, as the iron is drawn to the lodestone; while his love for and interest in them seemed as intense as that of a maiden for her lover. These characteristics, together with a bright, cheerful spirit and great earnestness of manner, rendered him peculiarly adapted to the work of influencing the students for good ; and, it is safe to say, that, during his stay in college, no man had a greater hold upon so large a body of students, nor drew so many to Christ as he. There are many students, who are now out in the world and some who have passed into the unseen world, who will thank God through all eternity for the influence exerted by J. H. Weber on their lives.

But, as though having a reserve of power unutilized, and needing a larger field for the exercise of it, he sought other fields wherein he might labor for the Master he so well loved. These he found in Sabbath-school and Mission work. Interesting himself in what was then known as the South Delaware Mission, he was soon elected as its superintendent, and the work immediately felt the impetus of his power. The dark, contracted and dilapidated room, occupied by the Mission, was speedily exchanged for a commodious, cheery, comfortably seated apartment ; while the meagre attendance of twenty-five to forty soon grew to two hundred and over. This change was not consummated without great labor. Homes were visited and solicited for scholars ; students and others were interested in the work, and secured as teachers and officers in the school; and means for the purchasing of supplies, and the procuring of necessities were raised.

In this work he manifested great organizing ability, bringing order out of confusion, and laying plans for active and effective service. Very rarely was he mistaken in his judgment of any one whom he selected for any position, as to his fitness for it. Having decided what was needed, he usually secured it. Obstacles seemed to make him but the more determined, while his faith was of that kind which "laughs at impossibilities," and cries, " It shall be done."

He asked, and received; sought, and found; knocked, and the doors of opposition, as well as those of desire, were opened to him. There were few indeed who could resist his fervent appeals in behalf of the work that lay near his heart.

Personal visitation was a prominent factor in the securing of his success. His Saturday afternoons were given, almost entirely, to visitation among the poor ; and many a sad heart has been gladdened by the sight of his joyous face, and the sound of his heart-felt words.

The South Delaware Mission has advanced, until it is now an

independent organization, having its settled pastor. Many earnest workers have labored to contribute to this result; but among them all there has been none more earnest, none more beloved by the people, nor any whose impress on the work is more indelible than that of him who is now known as Weber, the evangelist.

Looking out still for other avenues of usefulness, his attention was directed to the County Jail, and he entered this new path in the name of Him who came to " Proclaim liberty to the captives, and the opening of prison to them that are bound." Organizing a band of helpers, he instituted Sunday afternoon services, and with prayer, exhortation and sacred song, endeavored to lead the prisoners to a knowledge of the sinner's Friend. Realizing, also, that the body and mind are the handmaids of the soul, he sought to minister, in all possible and practical ways, to their physical and mental comfort and well-being. He enjoined personal cleanliness and neatness; and, by securing wholesome literature, furnished healthy food for the mind. The change in the appearance and manners of the prisoners was noticeable, in a very short time. The rough, unkempt heads, and unshaven faces, which first greeted the visitor, soon gave evidence of care; while the oath was unheard, and the gaming card was superseded by the wholesome periodical, book, or Word of God. Who can estimate the value of the work done in softening the hearts of men incarcerated for crime, and in bringing them to the realization that the pathway to virtue, integrity and manhood was still open to them, and that helping hands were not wanting to aid them in securing their lost inheritance.

As far as the writer's knowledge serves, there was no systematic visitation at the jail until Mr. Weber inaugurated it.

The impress left upon the college and town during his brief stay in them—for feeling the call to a wider field—was phenomenal, and is only exceeded by the larger, wider and more potent influence which he is exerting for God and the Church in the world at large.

His college days extended from October, 1877, until the spring of 1881. During this period he was alternately in school, or by working at his trade in Cincinnati, canvassing for a sifter, or other labor, earning money to pay his school expenses. The discipline of mind that he received in business, and in soul-saving work, and the knowledge of dealing with human nature, then garnered, more than counterbalanced what he thus lost by absence from his books; so at the close of these four years we find that he has made much progress, and is ready to remain in school or hasten now to life's great harvest-field, as God shall will. He had been licensed to preach March 3, 1879, by the quarterly conference of the St. Paul's Methodist Episcopal Church, Delaware, Ohio. He made good use of this privilege, and the results were favorable and encouraging. This year, as during the year before, there was a gracious revival of religion, in which he had no little part.

May 28, 1881, he went to Buffalo, and engaged in an agency to earn money to enable him again to return to his studies, if God should will.

PASTORATE.

"'Tis not a cause of small import,
The pastor's care demands ;
But what might thrill an angel's heart,
And fill an angel's hands."

Scene, a young man on his knees earnestly pleading with God for needed guidance. Place, Buffalo. Time, September, 1881. The person was Joseph H. Weber. The time had come when he must know whether to continue school or enter at once the pastorate. In a short time he had accumulated between eight hundred and nine hundred dollars, and was, financially, able now to return and resume his studies without interruption at Delaware. There are two extreme and mistaken views in regard to preparation for the pastorate. One is that no man is fitted for it without a complete college course; the other is that if one is called to it he needs no special drill, but at once by the Holy Ghost is prepared for the service. Both of these views are unscriptural, and the truth lies between them.

Some, for the special work to which they are called, need all the preparatory discipline that they can command; others are called to a different field of work, and the discipline they will get in that work will be worth more to them than college drill. God, who is marking out the life-work of the man, knows just the discipline he needs, and will reveal it if that revelation be faithfully sought.

He is wise, who, like Weber, appeals at such a time to Him who will not misdirect. With his wonted earnestness and expectancy he held this matter before the throne: Shall he again return to college, or enter the itinerancy? This was the all-absorbing question to him. His heart's desire was to do God's will; to obey in all respects. He believed in the special providence of God, and would be governed by the indications of His will, taking that as final.

Worldly prosperity at one time tried to bribe him to give up the ministry. He had been "offered a situation to travel with a gentleman, who said he was making from five to six thousand dollars a year, and that, if he would travel with him, he could increase the business to ten thousand dollars." Whether the man told the truth or not, we see the principle which actuated Mr. Weber at this time, as he refused the offer, feeling that the gain of this world would be nothing if in that gain he should lose his own soul. He felt it to be a duty to preach, and preach he would at any sacrifice.

He had learned to study, and college honors and the positions following them doubtless awaited him should he return to school, and he would be glad to heed the counsels of his advisors if he could and at the same time retain the smile of Jesus.

He had committed his way to God, and he confidently awaited the answer. It came. "In a few days, after praying over the matter, a letter came from the presiding elder of Lima district, Central Ohio Conference, Rev. L. M. Albright, asking him to join the conference, about to convene at Marion, Ohio. This was taken as the will of the Lord, and he replied that he would accept the invitation if he could get a place that he could properly fill. The answer came that there would be no trouble about the place. He replied that he would come, and that the elder might expect at least two hundred conversions the first year of his ministry. He purchased the necessary books at Buffalo, and began at once to prepare himself for the conference examination."

Conference convened Sept. 24, 1881, and having passed a satisfactory examination in the course of studies prescribed, he became a probationary member of the Central Ohio Conference, Bishop Merrill presiding.

The reception of the new pastor is a great event in the church which gave Mr. Weber his appointment. By many of its members time is measured by the pastorates of the past. This event and that event "occurred when Bro. ——— was pastor, and he was here — years, and then Bro. ——— came, and was pastor so long," etc., is the common way of recalling the time of events in many Methodist families.

As to who the incoming pastor should be, the local church in other days was as ignorant as of the character of the people of the North Star, or as the coming minister himself. While that still is true in some of the smaller appointments, yet official boards now often exert a strong influence in securing a desired appointment. In either case the people are on tip-toe of curiosity and expectation to greet "our new minister." "Is he strong in the pulpit?" "Is he a pastor as well as a preacher?" "Will he draw?" "Is he married, or is he single?" "If single, won't ——— be just the helpmeet for him?" "Has he a large family?" "Hope his wife is a 'tidy housekeeper,'" "and governs the children," and "always goes with him when he calls," "and is economical," "and don't dress so plainly as to condemn us," "and will keep up with the fashions," and has "literary ability," and can "attend all the prayer meetings," and "take a class in the Sunday-school," and "be president of the Ladies Aid Society," and the "Woman's Foreign Missionary Society," and "resurrect the W. C. T. U.," and "visit the poor and sick," etc. "Is he a revivalist?" "Can he remove debts," and "preach the plain truth," and "please the people," and "keep sweet," etc.

Amid such kindly hopes and questions, the new minister comes and receives a cordial welcome, and at once begins his work. If he be a true man of God and has the good of his people at heart, they soon learn to love him just as deeply as they did Pastor Patience who preceded him, and whose place they honestly thought "no living preacher would ever be able to fill." They expect only "that the new man will do the best he can under the circumstances." Happy people! Happy pastor!

Pastor Weber was appointed to South Lima Circuit, and reached his new field Oct. 6, 1881. He entered this work in full view of all the weighty responsibilities, which he, as a pastor, would be heir to, and "trembled like a leaf."

He realized that, though a "conference might send a man to Egypt, yet the Lord could put him on the throne," and that it is an honor to have even the least place in God's great harvest field, and so, with a faith firmly grounded on fail-less promises, with confidence he began the work that God had given him. The second day after reaching his charge, he began the work that every true pastor will not neglect, of "visiting from house to house." The people, at once convinced that their pastor was a "shepherd to feed and lead," seeking "not theirs but them," opened their hearts and gave him a cordial welcome.

Such a field as here invited his best efforts, was enough to tempt a Paul or Wesley back to earth again. Precious souls, like priceless diamonds, met his gaze on every side. Some of them saved and shining, but the great majority awaiting the hand of this consecrated jewel-gatherer for Jesus' crown. The societies met in school-houses, which soon became too small to accommodate his growing congregations.

He was privileged with leading in the building of a church edifice at an out-appointment, and at South Lima, which stand as memorials of his labors there. But infinitely more precious than houses made by hands, stand the

> "Temples divine of living stones,
> Inscribed with Jesus' name,"

which "immovably founded in grace" will reflect the glory of God in the new Jerusalem, world without end.

Early in the year, in answer to his prayers, and in response to his faithful labors, revival breezes began to blow, and ere the year closed a tornado of converting grace swept over the entire charge, and through St. John's, Kalida and Cherry Valley, where he was called to aid the respective pastors. A part of these revivals was a great quickening of the churches, between three and four hundred conversions, and the building of two churches and repairing of another.

This was the visible result. The homes made happy, the debauched reformed, the liberations from doubt and fear, passion and prejudice, lust and liquor, infidelity and formality, and the increasing joy and influence that shall be the outcome of this year's work in the world to come, only eternity can tell.

The following mention of events occurring in this stage of Mr. Weber's experience is from his own pen:

I was stationed at Lima, Ohio, and at this time we had no church, but were worshipping in a private house, but before winter we dedicated our church free of debt; then we began revival meetings, and God gave us very many souls. Having two other places to preach, and then I still took another, so as to be sure and have plenty to do (as I knew, if God's work did not keep me busy, the devil's would). After having a sweeping revival at Lima, I began meetings at Allentown. From the first the crowds came, and for eleven nights I preached to the church. But something seemed the matter, so one night a brother from another church invited me home with him, and there told me the reason things did not move was, that the members did not like the way I preached and jumped about; so, loving my people, I went with the intention of being like other ministers, as the outsiders were calling it "a monkey show," and every other name, and saying, "what fun they were having." I stood as straight as a straight edge and looked as solemn as a Presbyterian deacon, but God was not to be thwarted that way. When I began to preach He paralyzed my tongue and I dropped to the floor, weeping. The brethren gathered around me and asked the cause. So I told them, "I came to please you instead of God, and now I must close the meeting; I cannot offend God and go on."

So, many of the brethren got up and said, "We want this meeting to go on," and "Let Bro. Weber work in his own way," and then a proposition was made, "those that wanted the meetings to go on, and were sorry they criticized Bro. Weber, to stand up. The whole house rose. But being so broken up, I could not go on, and said, "Come to-morrow night." The next night twenty-five said, "I want to be saved." The meeting went on, and such a meeting as they had not seen for years was the result.

After closing there, I went to this school-house for ten days. They said, "There are only two in the community that can be induced to be saved." I said, "That is a lie of the devil." The people wanted a church there, but I said, "Pray for a revival, and then the church will come."

The little class that was formed was true as the needle. The first night every member promised to do anything I would ask them.

The second day, at a prayer-meeting, a young lady was very anxious to be saved, but was afraid her ma would not like it. So that night, after preaching, I went to her ma and began to talk to her about letting her daughter come, and she became enraged and struck me with her fist, so I called the church and we began to pray with her, and in the midst of my prayer she slapped me on the right cheek, so I said, "The Bible says, 'If they smite you on the right side, turn the left also,'" so I turned the left and she gave me another slap harder than the other. Every one in the community began to pray, "Lord, bless the woman that slapped our little preacher." The next night after the sermon, I said, "Let us see the salvation of God, just you pray." I went to sixteen consecutively, and reached out my hand and they came to the altar. The next day, I made one of the brethren build an altar clear across the school-house. He said, "What for?" But I said, "Build it and do as I tell you. They are coming."

Having prayed all that day, at night I came in shouting and said,

"God is coming to-night." So I called first one and then another of the members and stationed them among the seats and said, "Every one of you begin to pray;" and then I exhorted sinners in the aisle, and then I said, "Now, sinners, come to the altar," and they almost fell over each other in coming. They came until nearly forty came. Praise God!

The tide rose higher and higher. The woman who slapped me could not stay away but one night at a time; and one night I went to her and asked her to come. She said, "Let me alone and I will come." Soon she came and was gloriously converted, with two of her children. We raised enough money to build a church, and now they have a flourishing society.

Began another revival at Shawnee, and here God did manifest his power and very many were saved. God gave us over two hundred souls on my charge. This was the greatest revival in the conference. At Allentown we put on a new roof, belfry, and painted the church. Here were two new churches, remodeled another, and my audiences grew so large in Lima, that, if you wanted a seat, you must needs go from a half to an hour ahead of time to get one. They wanted me to build another church the same year. The next year they built a large church.

I visited every family but one, and took a meal with nearly every one. I used to spend many hours in prayer. We had a revival all the year around, and one time, in an ordinary prayer meeting, we had seven saved. At times men would want to thrash me and threatened to egg me, and every threat was made, but I gave them red-hot shot all the same. My people were alive for God and souls. Went away and held three other meetings, at which over one hundred were saved.

One time I invited the elder to preach for me. He came, and prayed such a cold prayer! Then I prayed and said to him, "No preaching for you this evening," and immediately invited them to the altar, and several were saved. He said, "If you had let me preach, there might have been more saved, but I said, "I don't believe one would have moved."

All this time I felt my work was that of an evangelist. My elder said I would fail. He wanted me to remain.

While at Sidney, at conference, I began to look for souls. Found a preacher's son, and other boys that were not saved, and began to pray for them. Visited one at his home. He was indifferent to my appeals at first, when all at once he broke down, and some of the ministers who heard me praying for him, came up, and he was saved. Went down stairs and found the Holy Ghost at work there. Found a backslider and she was saved, and while we were rejoicing, a rap was heard at the front door, and a young man, who had just graduated at the high shcool, stood weeping and saying, "I want to be saved." He was saved, and is now studying for the ministry, at the O. W. U. at Delaware, Ohio. Went and stayed with a doctor's boy, and he was saved, and also another boy at conference. Began then at Republic, Ohio.

My presiding elder said I would not succeed and would starve. I told him the other day I had not starved but had the fat of the land, and had given away about $10,000, and that I believed 100,000 people had been blessed in one way or another in my meetings. Dr. Paine tried to get me to stay at school, and talked to me hours to get me to graduate, and said, "If you don't listen to me you will regret it, and at some conference you will come and say, 'I am sorry I did not listen to you." I would do the same thing over, if I knew what I do now.

Thus "always abounding in the work of the Lord," he rises rapidly on the ladder of success in soul-saving work. To rescue the lost has become the passion of his life, and no wonder that he now feels that all of his energies must be bent to this one great work.

CHAPTER IV.

EVANGELISTS — MR. WEBER ENTERS THE EVANGELISTIC FIELD.

Do the work of an evangelist.— Paul.

HAVING noticed his call to the ministry and successful pastorate, we now come to one of the most eventful periods in Mr. Weber's life.

Soon after his call to the ministry he became convinced that his life work was to be that of an evangelist. That God was calling him to fill

> "An office which a man could scarcely hold
> And live. A gift of burning coal
> To hands that must not tremble holding it for God.
> A robe of costly white on which one stain
> Meant shame and death."

The Scripture authority for this office is found in Eph. iv. 11, 12, where the distributing of gifts of "apostles," "prophets," "EVANGELISTS," "pastors," and "teachers" are all attributed to the Holy Ghost. Also in many other places.

It may not be amiss for us, at this point, to stop and study the status of this calling, and notice some of the duties pertaining to it. Rev. A. B. Hyde, who, in his sparkling "Story of Methodism," gives a charming chapter on "Evangelists," has, in said chapter, collated many of the facts connected with them and given what appears to be the substance of the results of the investigation of many of our best authorities, such as Barnes, Bengal, Olshausen, and others. He says,—

" The term 'evangelist' is used in the New Testament to indicate a class of laborers well known and valued in the constitution of the early church. They are shown to be a certain class of Christian teachers who were not fixed to any particular spot, who travelled either independently, or under the direction of one of the apostles, for the purpose of propagating the gospel. The absence of any detailed account of the organization and working of the early church, at least of the first century, leaves us a little uncertain as to their function and position. Their title, 'Publishers of the Glad Tidings,' might belong to all the Christian ministry, yet evangelists are named next after 'apostles and prophets' and before 'pastors and teachers.' If, then, apostles were those who immediately represented Christ, and prophets were those who spoke under the special impulse of the Holy Ghost words mighty to effect men's hearts and consciences, then it would follow that evangelists were in authority below the apostles and in power below the prophets. Yet their office was higher and more conspicuous than that of pastors who watched over a church that had been founded, or the teachers who carried on the work of systematic instruction. They were apparently set forth by the apostles as they had been set forth by their Master as missionary preachers of the gospel, preparing the way, calling congregations and founding churches to which pastors and teachers should afterwards minister.

The evangelist was then a preacher with no pastoral superintendence. In the Middle Ages these evangelists were called Gospelers, and they have remained in the church of Rome as Preaching Friars.

"Methodism itself is an evangelism, and the early Methodist preachers were evangelists more than anything else. One can easily see that the work of an evangelist was wholly that of Whitefield, and more than half that of Wesley. The former went from place to place, not to organize, but to cry aloud; and his career was wonderful. Wesley did the same, going free among the dead and dark of the English parishes, as the apostles and evangelists had gone to the utter heathen."

That God in His infinite wisdom has appointed these different orders of workers in His ministry is evident. It is also plain that all the duties devolving upon each calling is not as clear as might be wished. It is also a fact that, like the mingling of the tints of the rainbow, so the labors connected with each of these callings sometimes are blended in the life of one person, and he becomes evangelist, pastor, and teacher all combined. Wesley and Finney and others have belonged to this class. It is also a fact that there has been a tendency to exalt the pastorate and minify the distinct calling of the evangelist; also a tendency to think that the work of pastor and evangelist must always blend in all who are called to the pastorate.

"Every pastor his own evangelist," sounds nicely, but is as unscriptural as it often is impossible. Otherwise would the office of evangelist ever have been instituted? It is also unjust to a large number of true and faithful pastors whom God has called to that office, and in it abundantly blessed their labors, but who have not evangelistic gifts.

That there are many evangelists in the pastorate, and that an evangelist may, like Paul and John, labor three years, more or less, in one place, there can be no doubt. It is also true that every Christian should seek the salvation of souls; but to hold that a minister is not called to the pastorate because he has not evangelistic gifts, is to be wise above what is written.

As one star differs from another star in glory, so it is among these different yet divinely instituted constellations in the church of God; and in each constellation there is diversity of gifts, of graces and of usefulness. What the especial work of each is, it would be profitable for us to know, and particularly, at this time, the duties of an evangelist. There seems to be much darkness here, but some light — enough to keep them busy.

There is another class of workers mentioned in Scripture under the name of "helps," who at the present sometimes wrongly pass under the name of "evangelists." Many are called to be "helps" who are not called to be "pastors" or "evangelists." They have special gifts for prayer, or song, or personal persuasion, or exhortation, or house to house visitation, or for all of these combined, which make them a mighty power under wise leadership to help in revival work. They may not have evangelistic gifts to lead a service successfully, but in the place where God has set them they are a power.

Evangelistic pastors who are striving to do their

own preaching and conduct their own revival services, often feel the need of such workers to aid them in inspiring their membership to work, and in the exercise of their peculiar gifts as "helps." Such were often utilized in the Methodist Church under the name of "exhorters." As has been seen, no calling is more clearly defined in the New Testament, or has been more abundantly blessed of God, than that of "evangelists." Early Methodism was extensively organized through "helps" and itinerant "evangelists." As churches sprang up the work of "pastors" and "teachers" was more and more manifest, and God has "set them in the church," with special gifts and training for their special work.

The following are some of the providential openings that invite the labors of the evangelist.

1. Destitute places where there are no churches established. In our rural districts there are thousands of persons who "never read the Bible nor hear the Sabbath bell." Pastor's hands are so tied by other imperative duties that they are unable to reach them. Our towns and the country both are being filled with a foreign element that must be converted or they will ruin our nation. God has two ways of reaching unconverted foreigners.

First. He sends us to them.

Second. He sends them to us.

Thousands come to us to one of us going to them. God commands us with judgment-day solemnity to Christianize them.

If we turn from the call and do not all we can for their salvation, we will sink down to hell with their blood upon us.

Christ poured out His life's blood for their redemption and now bids us to tell them the "good tidings, and preach to them the gospel of repentance," and, if they will not come to our services, to "go out into the highway and hedges and compel them to come in." They are precious souls whom our Father loves, for whom our elder Brother died, and whom we must soon meet in judgment. Unconcerned they are sleeping the fatal sleep of sin at our very doors.

They must be awakened! THEY MUST BE SAVED!!

What is done must be done *speedily*. Jesus says of his workers, "As thou hast sent me into the world even so have I also sent them into the world."

Should there not be some system generally adopted that would more fully utilize the "helps" and "evangelists" whom God summons for their special work, to the taking of these strongholds of sin for the King?

The Canada Band movement, under Dr. Savage, and the Michigan State Revival Band under Rev. D. W. Parsons and his associates, both of which have been instrumental in the salvation of thousands of souls, seem to be wise steps in this direction.

If organized effort works good in the distribution of pastors, why not in that of "helps" and "evangelists?" Or, can they be better trusted to make their own appointments?

2. Where churches are already organized, but have become cold, formal and lifeless. Like a stumpy, stony, weedy "fallow ground," they need the application of extraordinary measures, and God provides for them through the advent of the evangelist.

3. Where a man is called to be "a pastor," yet has

not evangelistic gifts. Because the Methodist Church in its origin was a sort of an evangelistic association, and nearly all of her preachers were evangelists, some of her children have become blinded to the fact that a man may be called of God to be a "pastor" without being an "evangelist," just as truly as he may be a pastor and not "have gifts of healing" and other powers which are granted to those to whom Christ sees fit to give them in his church.

4. Where the pastor is not physically strong enough to bear the burdens of his charge and at the same time conduct a revival.

5. Where the powers of darkness are so strongly intrenched that the combined efforts of both "pastor" and "evangelist" are required to dislodge them.

Knowing that such fields as this would await them, no wonder that God "set them in the church" as a permanent part of it, and has kept them there and demonstrated their divine calling by the success with which he has crowned their efforts.

No wonder that progressive churches are framing their regulations so as to recognize and utilize this right arm of power with which Jehovah puts to flight his foes.

That some of their number prove unworthy is no argument against their calling, but should be an incentive to the providing of proper regulations, by which those unworthy may be relegated to their proper places. What a stupid simpleton the man would be considered who would sneer at the office of pastor, because some who fill it are recreant to their trusts. In God's sight, all who belittle the office or work of the evangelist for a similar reason, are guilty of a like folly.

The silences, sneers and opposition, with which evangelism has been met by some professed followers of Christ, argue either the grossest ignorance of Scripture teaching and Divine leadings along this line, or else a heart hatred of it which the profession of piety and the possession of official position is utterly unable to hide. That their work is "superficial" is doubtless sometimes true. Fallow ground gets so hard, and is so stony, that sometimes it is impossible for the best of plows to go in deeply.

Should all "superficial" workers among them be relegated to the rear, it is probable, however, that their ranks would suffer no greater depletion by such a process than those of other classes of workers. While it is true that in most of the churches at present, the evangelist has no "regularly fixed field" in which to labor, yet in this respect he is not unlike his Master, and with "the world" for his parish, "Victory" for his battle cry, "Salvation" for his watchword, "Holiness" for his motto, "Saints" for his companions, the "Church" for his mother, the "Word" for his instructor, "God" for his Father, "Jesus" for his bosom friend, the "Holy Ghost" for his guide, and hosts of angels always on hand to report his meetings to the heavenly host, he is, even on earth, as happy as an archangel, and would not, unless God should will, exchange places with any created being. For such a delightsome post of duty he will praise God through all eternity.

The following excellent extract on "Evangelistic Work," taken from the *London Primitive Methodist*, is expressive of much in this relation which is true:

There is evidently a very general feeling in the connection that more aggressive work should be done. We have one district advertising for ten evangelists, full of faith and the Holy Ghost; and in nearly all the districts we have some movement on foot for evangelistic purposes. No doubt the legislation of last Conference on mission work has given a stimulus to this movement, but the real cause lies beyond that.

The travelling preachers, as a rule, have not the time to devote to aggressive work which they desire, and which is needed. We may talk as we like in conference and convention about laymen attending to the business of the churches; but, after all, it has to be done by the preachers. They have to look after chapel affairs, and the demand made upon them in this respect, in many stations, is most exacting, consuming time and energy, and burdening the mind. And it must be done. We have the property, and the property is needful for the housing of our people, and in a few years it will be a great blessing; but at present it consumes many of the ministers. The men who are doing this work are doing heroic service for the connection and cause of God, and are worthy of all honor. But they cannot give the attention they would like to evangelistic work. In other places the ministers are engaged in educational work, training the people in the grace and knowledge of Jesus Christ. It ought not to be impossible to combine an educational and evangelistic ministry, but there cannot be the concentration as where only the one thing is sought. And we should never forget the pulpit demands upon our ministers are much more exacting now than ever, and that many of the ministers have received only partial furnishing, and require more time for preparation. Without assuming that there is any lack on the part of the ministers—indeed, assuming, which is correct, that they are anxious to see more aggressive work,—they have not the opportunity and means to engage in it as they would desire.

The evangelist's field of labor is the world; the pastor's his pastorate. Evangelists devote all their time and strength directly to the promotion of revivals; pastors, for manifest reasons, are unable to do this. The peculiar work of the evangelist is to ring the gospel-bell and gather pupils into the gospel-school; that of the pastor to shepherd them. Evangelists, like the prophets of the old dispensation, usually receive their appointments "irregularly," but pastors through agencies instituted for that purpose. Both are called of God and are essential factors in His church below.

Like different wheels in the same watch they are designed to work harmoniously and for the common good until "all come into the unity of the faith, and the knowledge of the Son of God, unto a perfect man, unto the measure of the stature of the fulness of Christ." As in our public schools, the parents, school-board, superintendent and teachers, all work harmoniously together for the banishment of ignorance and the enthronement of knowledge, so it is designed that all of the offices of the Church of God shall unitedly and harmoniously labor together for the dethronement of sin and the coronation of Holiness.

During Mr. Weber's pastorate he was called upon to aid in revivals on neighboring charges, and at these places, as we have seen, God abundantly owned his efforts. His success was such that he received many pressing invitations to evangelistic work from other places. These calls were so many and pressing that he began to feel that they were Providential voices telling him that the time had come when he should devote all his energies to the work of an evangelist, a work to which he now felt that God was calling him. Experience had shown him that he could not do justice to that work and remain in the pastorate.

(*a*) The people need the presence of a pastor and have a right to expect him to remain in their midst.

(*b*) It is difficult to keep special revival meetings running with profit constantly on any one charge.

(c) Constant revival work at one point compels neglecting care of converts in the places where the revival is not in progress.

(d) Much of a pastor's time is necessarily taken in church building and debt-raising projects, "sermonizing," attending weddings and funerals, and in doing many other things that those can do who have not evangelistic gifts.

(e) Constant revival work and the faithful discharge of the duties of the pastorate are too much for any ordinary minister. He will have to neglect one or the other. Hundreds of evangelists in the pastorate break under this double work. Other true pastors get discouraged and break down in trying to exercise gifts that they have not. God's plan of apportioning his work is best. With these facts before him, and both the Spirit's call and Providential voices ringing in his ears to begin a work for which a burning love is given, a man like Brother Weber wisely weighing the matter, will not be likely to make a mistake.

On his old battleground, his knees, the question is finally and fully settled, and he starts for Conference with a fixed resolve to be true to the voice divine. At this point such a pressure is brought to bear upon those who feel called from a successful pastorate to this work as only those who have been there know. I have a letter asking advice from a gifted evangelistic pastor in a Southern Conference that fairly makes one's heart bleed. He had come to the same point in his experience where we now find Mr. Weber. He had felt the call, and wisely and prayerfully weighed the matter for months. He had good appointments and apparently bright prospects as a pastor for the future, but was fully convinced that he should give all his time to evangelistic work. He went to his conference determined if possible to take a relation that would allow him thus to labor. Like Bishop Taylor, he had counted the cost and at his Master's call was willing to make the sacrifice of giving up good appointments, a good salary, a pleasant home, the tender ties that bind a pastor to his people, and the society of his precious wife and children. For a number of years he had been a member of his conference, and the strong and tender ties that attach men in these bodies of heroes of the cross were to him especially dear. He sought some way whereby he could be true to his convictions and at the same time retain his conference relation. Through some oversight, this branch of God's great church has neglected to make disciplinary provision for the recognition of this class of her ministry that the Scripture, her own best interests, and their rights demand. This neglect is doubtless due, in part, to circumstances that have so changed since her origin; in part to the fact of the new questions to which such a step will give birth; in part to a fear of new measures; in part to a conservatism that wants to be sure it is right before it acts; in part to a jealousy of any new order, and in part to an ecclesiasticism which is always slow to see and adopt the leadings of the Holy Ghost. One of the many signs of spiritual awakening and advance of our beloved Zion is that her sons are agitating this question, seeking to know just the right thing to do, and determining that early in her councils this matter shall be made right.

As matters now are, our brother found that for "poor health" men could take a supernumerary relation and still remain with their brethren in the conference. He found that a very broad meaning is often attached to that relation, and that men are sometimes allowed to take it, engaging in secular business. He found that for "sickness in the family," a man might resign the pastorate and still be a member of his conference. He found that by regular conference appointment, a man could pass from the pastorate to become a college president, a college agent, a temperance, tract or book agent, or an editor. Express provision is also made whereby a minister may retain his conference relation and "attend any of our schools."

But for a man to labor DIRECTLY AND EXCLUSIVELY FOR THE SALVATION OF SOULS, GIVING ALL OF HIS TIME, AS AN EVANGELIST, TO THE PROMOTION OF REVIVALS OF RELIGION, he found no provision whatever to be made. It is needless to say that this defect in the disciplinary provision of the church of his choice, his mother, the church whose founder said, "Gaining knowledge is a good thing, but saving souls is a better," and that "We ought to throw by all the libraries in the world, rather than be guilty of the loss of one soul," caused him deep pain. He also saw that this defect in her machinery would compel him, if true to God's call, to take a location and thus be where he would no longer be amenable to his peers. He also saw that he would be misunderstood by many of his ministerial brethren, and that doubtless some whose counsels he thus would disregard, might whisper, "Disloyalty to the church," forgetful that loyalty to the

Spirit and the Word is always loyalty to the church, no matter how much opposition to the views of those whom the church may have clothed with dignity and power, and that loyalty to ecclesiasticism may be disloyalty both to God and to His church.

The pressure at the conference was so great that he resisted convictions, took another pastoral appointment and went to it, like Sampson, shorn of his strength, to lament his mistake and rectify it as early as possible. When Mr. Weber reached this critical and testing point in his career, convinced of the divinity of his evangelistic call, he remained true to his church, true to his convictions, and true to God. He attended his conference held at Sydney, Ohio, Sept. 13, 1882, and giving his report for the year, asked for and obtained a certificate of location as the following extract from the minutes of that body attests:

"Joseph H. Weber was before the committee of examination, and his character was passed, and he was discontinued from trial in the travelling connection or ministry on his own request, with a view to entering upon evangelistic work."

Though his church does not officially appoint evangelists, yet unofficially she employs them, and gives them her support and all that they can do. So we soon find Mr. Weber thronged with invitations and busy in the work to which the Lord had called him. Thus he passed from the vestibule of his ministry into its great auditorium, henceforth to be, if God should will, like Whitefield,—

"A homeless pilgrim, with dubious name,
 Blown about on the winds of fame,
 Now as an angel of blessing classed
 And now as a mad enthusiast;
 Called in his youth to sound and gauge
 The moral lapse of his race and age,
 And sharp as truth the contrast draw
 Of human frailty and perfect law;
 Possessed by the one dread thought that lent
 Its goad to his fiery temperament,
 Up and down the world he went
 A John the Baptist, crying, 'Repent!'"

CHAPTER V.

REVIVAL TORNADOES.

"A TORNADO is a tempest distinguished by a progressive whirling motion, usually accompanied by severe thunder, lightning and torrents of rain."

A genuine revival is like a tornado, in that it is a mighty progressive movement in the spiritual world, accompanied by the lightning strokes of divine truth, the thunder of the disturbed elements and torrents of saving power.

"Revival tornadoes" is no new name for great religious awakenings. Ezekiel, with inspired vision, looking down the ages from Babylonian Chebar's banks, saw, beyond the Babe in the manger, His miraculous life, His death and His resurrection, to this revival dispensation, when the Spirit's power should be manifest as a "whirlwind which came out of the north a great cloud and a fire, unfolding itself, and a brightness was about it."

The same prophet, pleading over the "dead bones" of Israel backslidden, "Come, from the four winds, O Breath, and breathe upon these slain, that they may live," simply uttered a prayer for a mighty soul-saving REVIVAL TORNADO.

Jesus Himself compared the Spirit's work to the wind, and His coming at the great initiatory revival of this pentecostal period is compared to "a sound from heaven as of a mighty rushing wind."

All who are acquainted with Bro. Weber and his extraordinary religious awakenings, will see at once the especial appropriateness of this figure to his work. Rescued by saving grace from vice and Catholicism, he has been marvelously led of God, until thousands of souls have been converted through his agency, and the facts that he has never given an invitation but that souls have responded, and that his work is thorough, and that for years he has engaged in no revival meeting that has not been a blessing and that hundreds of souls are often saved in his meetings in a very short time, make him and his revivals startling wonders, such as have their counterpart, in part, at least, in the tornado, and furnish, in many respects, as inviting a source of revival inspiration as can be found anywhere in the history of the Christian Church.

It may not be amiss in these pages, introductory to his revival work, to stop and see in what particulars real revivals are like the cyclones of the atmospheric world.

They are from God. He declares that the mission of the wind is to "fulfil His will." "Revival tornadoes" are sent by Him upon a like errand. Men cannot "get them up," but must pray them down from above. Men may get up "protracted meetings," coax the unconverted to come out, to rise for prayers, express a desire to "go to heaven when they die," say that they "believe on the Lord Jesus Christ," be baptized, and to unite with the church, and yet there be no more of revival power in it all, than there is in the purring of a cat, the cooing of a dove, or the twitching of a corpse under the currents of an electric battery. Such efforts are "clouds without water," and are evidently from some other source than above.

Tornadoes are governed by fixed laws. These laws determine their existence, their movements, and their cessation. Like laws govern the revival movements of the spiritual world with the exception that, in the material world the storm is not conditioned on human action, while in the spiritual it is. God declares, "If my people . . . shall humble themselves, and pray, and seek my face and turn from their wicked ways; then WILL I hear from heaven, and forgive their sin and will heal their land." And again, "Bring ye all the tithes into the storehouse, . . . *and prove me now herewith*, saith the Lord of hosts, if I will not open the windows of heaven and pour you out a blessing that there shall not be room enough to receive it." God cannot lie. The conditions of the revival are plain, and the promises of it are great, precious and changeless.

From John the Baptist and beyond, God has seen fit to employ, and bless with great success, "evangelists" in special revival work. Ignorance and ecclesiasticism have sometimes been arrayed against them, but "God is not mocked," and very often one of the conditions of revival victory is the engagement of their aid. The true evangelist, like the true pastor, labors, not where some wild impression might suggest, but where the Spirit leads, and providential openings point the way.

Mr. Weber's engagements are conditioned upon the call of God, corroborated and confirmed by invitation of pastor and official board, and their pledged agreement to sustain him in the work.

Then let the conditions of prayer, of fasting, of humiliation, of confession, of turning from all sin, of seeking the Father's face, of personal work, in a word, of bringing "ALL the tithes into the storehouse," be faithfully met, and just as certainly as the thunder's peal follows the lightning bolt, just so surely will the spiritual temperature rise, the air become heavy with spiritual moisture and charged with electricity from above, and soon the Church become the center of a cyclone that shall be awfully destructive to all spiritual buildings that are not founded on the Rock of Ages, and to all trees that are not rooted and grounded in love; and whose lightnings shall leap with gleeful and destructive fury upon all who are not insulated from the power of sin.

Tornadoes purify the atmosphere. The air that was heavy and hot and malarious, breeding all kinds of deadly diseases, is left sweet and pure and healthful. So with their counterpart in the spiritual world. Moral miasma disappears, and many that were wild with delirium, caused by fevers contracted in the swamps of sin, or in the hot, foggy atmosphere of unbelief, or on the burning sands of atheism or infidelity, are completely cured in an instant by the atmospheric change, and will praise God forever for the tornado.

The following reference to the results of the great revival which attended Bro. Weber's labors at Union City, Mich., is forcibly illustrative of this point. In scores of places where he has labored the same is true.

Readers of this paper (*Michigan Christian Advocate*) have read accounts of the work of grace here. I give a demonstration of its reality. Some three months since I had occasion to travel through the southern part of the township, where at one time were but two Christian families. Desolation marked many a familiar spot. Ruin seemed to be written on the face of many homes, while their owners were at town spending their time and money in the various vice-dealing dens that infest our beautiful city. A few days ago I paid another visit to this same neighborhood, and such a change as had taken place. Buildings were repaired; men were industriously working at the different kinds of business pertaining to a farmer's life. Everything bore an indication of thrift. What had caused this change? It was because the power of God had been at work, and by his love, his kindness and his gentle persuasion, had turned the hearts of these men from the low depths of degradation and lifted them to the best, the grandest and highest attainment within the reach of man. In other words, they had been converted to the religion of the Lord Jesus Christ. Thus are the benefits of Christianity practically demonstrated.

Tornadoes are a terror to the wicked. So are revivals. "Behold," shouts Jeremiah, "the whirlwind of the Lord goeth forth with fury, a continuing whirlwind; it shall fall with pain upon the head of the wicked." The wicked have heard that they "shall be like the chaff which the wind driveth away," and when revival gales begin to blow, they are reminded of the near approach of their long-dreaded doom. The hypocrite has been warned that "his hope shall perish," and the formalist that his trust is foundationless, and the disobedient that they are "building upon the sand," and all who are determined to resist the truth feel that the revival tornado is but the outer circle of the mighty cyclone that shall sweep away all their props and hopes, and continually gather new force until finally it will sweep them up to the left hand of the judgment seat and from thence, with mighty momentum, bear them forever along, the sport of hissing fiends, upon the broad expanses of eternal doom, where it must be said of them,—

> "O sin-cursed souls, wind-driven and tossed,
> Henceforth to find no resting place,
> But ever along the shores of the lost
> To be beat by the living storms of God."

Tornadoes are usually attended by chain-lightning, and it often hits someone. A revival in which the lightning of divine truth hits no one and kills no one, is a stupendous sham. God save us from sheet-lightning revivals, that bring no rain and destroy no malaria. On every form of modern and antiquated evil, on saloon and ball-room, and brothel, on pen and press inspired by Satan, on gambling hells running under the names of agricultural fairs, and otherwise, on political trickery and private dishonesty and public roguery, on hypocrisy under the cloak of religion and without it, on worldliness and formality, on secret vice and open sin, a black thunder-cloud is gathering, and upon one and all death-bringing lightning of divine truth shall leap, attended with such tornado power as shall destroy them all forevermore. Then will come the sweet and peaceful reign of Christ, and the holy atmosphere of His heavenly kingdom will prevail.

. There is a tendency in every age to forget that the Lamb of God is also the "Lion of the tribe of Judah," and that Jesus' character, less the lion-like in it, would be just as imperfect as if shorn of the lamb-like. That His mission is to "break every chain" just as really as to atone for the sins of His people, and that He "came to send, not peace, but a sword," to all who will persist in impenitence. A tendency to forget that Jesus, in all ages, has hurled red-hot thunderbolts upon pharisaism, pride, hypocrisy, and formality, just as really as He has sent the sunshine of pardon and the dew of His sanctifying grace upon the humble believer. Every revival that Jesus has honored by His abiding presence has heard not only the tender bleating of the "Lamb of God," who taketh away the sins of the world, but also the thunderous roaring of the "Lion of the tribe of Judah" against sin and those who will defend it. Both of these elements of true Christian character are prominent in Bro. Weber, and here lies much of his strength.

Like Savanarola,—

> "To him the smiles of earth
>   Are little worth,
> His eyes have seen the lifted sword
>   Gleam wild in the north,
> And he speaks as one to whom is given
> To know the wrath of outraged Heaven
>   And to pour it forth.
>
> Yet are there softer hours
>   When his voice sinks low,
> And they see as it were an angel's face ;
>   So sweet the glow
> With which he prays them all to come
> To the arms of Christ, who is our home,
>   And loveth so."

While towards the weeping penitent and the honest inquirer he is overflowing with tenderness, at the same time towards hypocrisy and his hydra-headed children, who seek deceptively to hinder God's work, he is as furious as a lion robbed of her whelps.

Tornadoes are a test to the righteous. When the sky

is black, and storm clouds, like runaway steeds, are plunging swiftly by, men are brought to think of death, judgment, and eternity. If really right, they may be able, like the saved Moravians, who, when with Wesley were crossing the Atlantic, sang joyful songs of praise, when all the angry elements of air and ocean conspired to sink their ship. Within a few rods from where I now am sitting, some time since, there passed a cyclone. A few days before it came, a Christian woman dreamed that she was going to heaven in a whirlwind. She did not fear it, but sure enough it came, shattered her house, and upon its currents, like Elijah, she was borne to her Father's many-mansioned house. She was tested, but found true. Just so truly will a revival try God's people. The testings of experience, the vivid unfoldings of the truth and the pressure to do personal work, all combine to compel people to examine themselves, whether they be in the faith or not. The true saint challenges such inspection, and, rejoicing in the storm, comes out of it, as gold from the crucible, purer for the process.

In the opinion of some tornadoes do more harm than good. The man whom God chastises by it often hardens his heart and curses both the storm and the God who sent it. Such, beholding an unroofed house or a few uprooted trees, forget that but for the tornado to purify the earth and air thousands would have died by fever and by pestilence. "Don't go to the revival, Aaron; it's a place of wildfire and excitement," said a minister to Aaron Burr, when a young man under conviction he was inclined to seek revival influences. He staid away, and his convictions were quenched. Who would want to stand in the place of that false minister at the judgment? Ministers whose pet theories are spoiled by its success, worldlings and formalists whose hypocrisies are exposed by its plain preaching, weak professors who fear that its plain proclamations will offend, Jezebels and Jehus who are determined to rule or ruin, Ananias and Sapphiras persistent in their perfidy, and other slaves to sin, who had rather be lost than to give up their wickedness, usually will unite in proclaiming that a revival does more harm than good, and especially a revival tornado attended by the power of the Holy Ghost. Such raise this cry on the same principle that saloonists shout, "Prohibition won't prohibit." The daughter of one of this fraternity once said to Evangelist Sam Jones, "My father don't believe in revivals." "That's where your father and the devil are alike," was the prompt and truthful reply. Many of this class, like pirates who have stolen their country's colors, maintain a profession of religion, and are thus enabled to do double harm, and in the great day of reckoning will receive double damnation.

Brother Weber's meetings are no exception to this rule, as the following extract from a pastor's report of one of them indicates. "Some of the members of the church were so badly disaffected as never to be reconciled. For instance, one of the class-leaders met me one day, and when I asked him how he liked the meeting, he said, 'Not at all,' that the preaching was hypocritical and doing more harm than good, and that if the meetings continued on in that way, that he should not attend them. He came once more, but left the house in great rage and became an open enemy to the meeting from that time. Yet this was one of the most thorough and sweeping revivals ever known in Michigan."

This class-leader doubtless was spiritually blind, had backslidden in heart, had wrongs that he would not make right, or something similar. Of all such Jesus says, "For every one that doeth evil hateth the light, neither cometh to the light lest his deeds should be reproved."

Woe unto the man that by either open opposition or silence stands in the way of the salvation of the people. The prophecies of this class of revival opposers, like those of Baal's prophets on Mt. Carmel, prove false, for, in answer to the prayers of this modern Elijah, the fire falls, multitudes are saved, and the people shout, "The Lord He is God, and this is His servant." All glory to the Lamb!

Tornadoes compel the attention of men to an unseen power. No matter what their minds are centered on, the cyclone will compel them to see and feel the power of God as manifested in the aerial elements.

A revival tornado makes men see and feel this power in the spiritual world. Unless Attention can be captured Soul Town never will surrender. Men's minds are fixed and their affections centered on things below, and in many instances the question of their salvation is a question of getting their attention from things ordinary to the things of eternity. The sunshine, the dew, the zephyrs and the gentle showers of ordinary religious effort, fail to move them. Then God sends forth a John the Baptist, a Luther, a Wesley, a Whitefield, a Finney, a Harrison, or a Weber, as the storm centre of a mighty revival tornado, and the attention of the people is arrested and they are won for God. In the revivals with which God honors Mr. Weber, a whole city will stand awe-struck at the displays of Divine power.

Tornadoes are a source of alarm. The following illustrative incident is related by Evangelist Caughey, who was present when the incident occurred, and declares it to have been a "solemn and awful hour." He says, "We had preached every night, but could make no impression on hardened sinners. One night just as the congregation was retiring, and before we knew of a single case of *awakening*, and I should think before fifty of the audience got out, a most tremendous storm of thunder, lightning and rain burst over the town. The windows of the church were unusually large, and they seemed all ablaze from the effect of the lightning. The mass of people were arrested in a moment . . . the storm raged in fury, and one of the preachers, a plain young man, began to exhort, and wielded with power that passage in the eleventh Psalm, 'Upon the wicked He shall rain snares, fire and brimstone and an horrible tempest; this shall be the portion of their cup.'

"Thus while God thundered and lightened outside, the minister did the same within. It was a scene of terror and awful grandeur. Some began to tremble and weep and pray. At length there was a movement toward the ministers, where they were standing at the altar; not to take vengeance upon the fiery exhorter, but to cry for mercy from that God who was thundering through the heavens, and to seek an interest in the prayers of His people. Still the storm continued, with peals of loudest thunder, which were re-echoed by successive bursts of most impassioned appeals to the consciences of terrified sinners. Nothing was heard but,—

> "'See the storm of vengeance gathering
> O'er the path you dare to tread;
> Hear the awful thunder rolling
> Loud and louder o'er your head.'

And all of this attended by the deep, subdued groans of sinners slain by the sword of the Spirit. Victory was on our side from that hour; and the victories achieved through a preached gospel during the three or four weeks following amazed the whole town. A large majority are still living in the enjoyment of that grace which 'the terror of the storm' drove them to seek. . . I visited some of them on their death-beds, and the scenes of holy triumph I witnessed there were sufficient to convince the most abandoned infidel of the truth of religion."

True revivals, like this tornado, often prove a source of alarm to the unconverted. Under the influence of the piercing preaching, the persistent prayer, and the persevering and ardent personal appeal, all mighty through the Spirit's power, the sinner sees himself as he really is, suspended by but a brittle thread over a yawning, bottomless abyss. His past sins, like lead, seem bound to his back, and about to sink his soul forever. On every side he sees the darting of the lightnings of the "wrath" of an offended God. Judgment scenes startle him with all the great realities about to be, and he sees himself standing condemned before the Judge and an assembled universe, Heaven's gate closed to him forever. He hears the hoarse grating of the hinges of the gates of doom as they close behind his lost soul, and the click of the key that makes his exit hopeless forever pierces his soul like a javelin. As he seeks a place of safety, an evil nature, acquired habits, inherited propensities and wicked associations, like so many huge cobras, seem to paralyze him in their murderous folds. "Oh," he moans, "why did I not see this sooner! How could I have sported as I have with destiny!" Moved with fear that takes his appetite, his mind from his business, his sleep and absorbs all his powers, he seeks safety, and finds it in a look at the Saviour of the world.

During the revival tornado at Quincy, Michigan, when Mr. Weber was laboring there, a man found himself in just this condition. His sense of his awful danger grew deeper and deeper, until he could not wait for help another hour, and in the night he sent for the pastor and was brightly converted to God, and to-day is one of the most earnest members of the church in that place.

Tornadoes are often preceded by a dead calm. So are revivals. "What was the condition of the church here when the revival began?" asked the writer of the presiding elder in the midst of a great revival in a prominent appointment. "It was spiritually hopeless; they were a dancing, card-playing, theatre-going people," was the sad answer. Many memberships before the revival begins, if united at all, are frozen together. Often all other means have been used to no avail before the evangelist is sent for, and he is invited as a last resort.

"Many of the churches in southern Michigan are dying of the dry rot, and, unless something is done, will have to be put on the missionary list," said a prominent church official, as he referred to the deadly calm that had settled down upon them. Such was the sad condition, that the question of consolidating Districts was being agitated. Thank God, this deathly calm was simply the forerunner of an on-coming spiritual cloudburst and the revival tornadoes which shortly followed left life, strength and beauty where there was but present or threatened desolation.

CHAPTER VI.

REVIVAL TORNADOES.

TORNADOES *are no respecters of persons.* God "directs their way." They do His bidding. They treat pauper and patrician alike. So does revival truth. It condemns sin alike in all, and smiles on real righteousness, whether in kings or common people. Money, learning, or position cannot bribe it nor turn its edge. The man who is the centre of the revival must, fearless of man, present God's truth, realizing that an emperor or president, a king or a doctor of divinity, will, if unconverted, be lost eternally as surely as the most degraded. This point is illustrated in the story which, oft told, will bear repeating, of Peter Cartwright and General Jackson.

A fastidious preacher had invited Cartwright to preach for him. As he was about to begin, the preacher whispered loudly to him, "General Jackson has come in. General Jackson has come in."

"I felt," writes Cartwright, "a flash of indignation run all over me like an electric shock, and facing about to my congregation, and purposely speaking out audibly, I said, 'Who is General Jackson? If he don't get his soul converted, God will damn him as quick as he would a Guinea negro.'"

The next day General Jackson said, "Mr. Cartwright,

you are a man after my own heart. A minister of Jesus Christ ought to love everybody and fear no mortal man. . . . If I had a few thousand such independent, fearless officers as you are, and a well drilled army, I could take old England."

The next day after Bro. Weber had preached at Hillsdale, Mich., on "Hell," he was met on the street by a Universalist preacher, who accused him of personally attacking himself and his church. "I know nothing of you personally," replied Mr. Weber; "but if the shoe fits you, wear it." Such was the lightning bolt that thus leaped upon this nettled prophet of infidelity.

Tornadoes pay no attention to men's ideas of dignity. Their business is to arrest and bear away every germ of malaria they can find in earth or air, and with search warrants for such from the great God of the tempest, they accomplish their work without consulting men's notions of dignity or how it should be done.

Revival tornadoes act in a similar way. Their mission is to seek the destruction of "sin germs," from which men are dying eternally by the million. They find men bearing in their breasts the fire of rebellion against God, which, unless quenched, will burn their souls forever. They find them wrecked upon the shores of Time and sinking beneath the angry billows of eternal despair. Their work is to seek them out and save them. So in plain language that all the people can understand, they vehemently warn and point to the one place of safety. Souls which are moved by such mighty currents of faith and quenchless love are not like the weak one who, when asked to help inquirers in an after-service, said, "*I cannot; I'm not acquainted with them,*" but like sailors rescuing sinking seamen, will first get them to a place of safety and then get acquainted with them afterwards. Lost souls to them are more precious than rubies, and wherever these can be found, there they go.

Whatever ways or words they can devise to get their attention and rivet their minds to things eternal, they do not hesitate to use. If they will not come to the meetings, then they will go to them ; and if at their homes they cannot be found, then away to their places of business ; and if needs be from hence, at the Master's command, into the "highways and the hedges" to "compel them" to come in. Their Saviour gladly flew on such errands of love and mercy, and is the servant better than his Lord?

If those unversed in the Master's arts of reaching souls shall feel annoyed by their earnest, practical efforts, and shall complain as some have of their "lowering the dignity of the Gospel," in the unanswerable language of another they can say, "What constitutes the dignity of the Gospel? Is it human dignity, or Divine? It was a very undignified thing, looked at humanly, to die on the cross between two thieves. That was the most undignified thing ever done in this world, and yet, looked at on moral and spiritual grounds, it was the grandest spectacle that ever heaven or earth gazed upon, and methinks the inhabitants of heaven stood still and looked over the battlements at that glorious, illustrious Sufferer as He hung there between heaven and earth. . . . That was the dignity of almighty strength allying itself with human weakness in order to raise it. It was the dignity of eternal wisdom shrouding itself in human ignorance in order to enlighten it. It was the dignity of everlasting, unquenchable love, baring its bosom to suffer in the stead of its rebellious creature — man. Ah, it was incarnate God standing in the place of condemned, apostate man — the dignity of love! *love!!* LOVE!!!

"Oh, precious Saviour, save us from maligning Thy Gospel by clothing it with our paltry notions of earthly dignity and forgetting the dignity that crowned Thy sacred brow as Thou didst hang upon the cross!

"That is the dignity for us, and it will never suffer any gentleman here carrying the gospel into the back by-slums or alleys of any town or city where he lives. That dignity will never suffer by any employer talking lovingly to his errand boy, and looking into his eyes with tears of sympathy and love, and trying to bring his soul to Jesus. That dignity will never suffer, even though you should have to be dragged through the streets with a howling mob at your heels, like Jesus Christ, if you have gone into those streets for the souls of your fellow-men, and the glory of God. Though you should be tied to the stake, as were the martyrs of old, and surrounded by laughing and taunting fiends and their howling followers,— that will be a dignity which shall be crowned in heaven, crowned with everlasting glory. If I understand it, *that* is the dignity of love. I do not envy, I do not covet any other — God is my witness — than the dignity of love."

The success of the man and his methods show that, though Mr. Weber is a stranger to the sham dignity which attends the spiritual idleness or iceberg efforts of many of his critics, the dignity of the corpse and the shroud, yet that with the true gospel dignity that seeks to save men at any cost he is clothed as with a garment.

Tornadoes provoke unfriendly criticism. Instead of looking at the blessings which attend them, people are wont to magnify the discomforts which they cause, forgetful that even in these is some concealed blessing. Revival tornadoes have ever provoked kindred criticism, and of course such mighty cyclones of divine power as attend Mr. Weber's work will be no exception to this rule. In many places, as in Defiance, Ohio, as he has recorded in his journal, "The people criticised very much and some got mad because the truths were told so plainly. One complained and said, 'I would split the seats.' I heard about it and said, the next night, I hoped God would split some of their hearts and let light in so they could see their sins." The work swept on with mighty power. During his work at Jackson, Mich., where over 800 gave their names as being saved, two of the city papers criticised the work with a venom born from below. Referring to this in his journal, Mr. Weber wrote, "But this only drew out the crowds, and in fact stimulated the Christian people." Thus God makes the wrath of man to praise Him. The evangelist treats these criticisms as a planet would a pebble.

One of the most cunning devices of the devil is that in which he deceives people to persist in worldliness, formality and opposition to holiness and aggressive revival work, and then blame spiritual people for the "friction" thus caused. It is as if a bad man should censure faithful fellow-citizens, who stand firmly by the laws of their land, because of the "friction" which his own badness brings.

Wherever there is carnality, pure Christianity, when its claims are all pushed with Apostolic energy, is the occasion of "friction."

Noah, Elijah, Isaiah, Jeremiah, Daniel, John, Paul and Jesus were the prolific occasions of "friction" among the self-seeking formalists of their own day, and the truths they taught and the errors they fought are in essence the same as then.

> "Never on custom's oiled grooves
> The world to a higher level moves,
> But grates and grinds with 'friction' hard
> On granite, boulder and flinty shard."

The critics mentioned are usually of "the dog in the manger" class, who do not eat themselves, but snap at those who would. They are brethren to the Pharisees of old who would not go into Christ's kingdom themselves, but hindered those who sought to enter. What would have been thought of men, in the great Pennsylvania flood, who would not only refuse to aid in rescuing the dying, but would throw stones at those who were doing all they could to save them? Such persons are like men who would sit and find fault with the tone of the fire bell, the motions of the firemen and the noise of the busy rescuers, when the city is on fire, and fellow-mortals are perishing in the flames. O shame! *Shame!!* SHAME!!! Sad to say there are those who have been thus guilty. Only it was the evangelist, or pastor or other helpers that were criticized, and the souls of men instead of their bodies that were being rescued from ruin. They were seeking to save, not from a burning building, but from the quenchless fire of an eternal hell. Yet some, wearing the outer garb of a Christian profession, instead of encouraging them, keep criminally silent, and sometimes try, after the victory is won, to cover their treachery by saying, "Well, I said nothing against them." Jesus, by and by, will say to such, "Inasmuch as ye did it not unto one of the least of these my brethren, ye did it not unto me — Depart." Others, instead of praying for them, shrug the shoulder and curl the contemptuous lip, and instead of defending them, stab them again and again with the keen dagger of unfriendly criticism, and, saddest of all, sometimes this cruel, murderous work is done, as in the days of Jesus, by church officials, and even ministers!

Would that they would yet repent! The probabilities are, however, that they will not. Already they have been seen to point with a triumph poorly masked to one of the young converts who, in an unguarded moment, had yielded to the tempter's power and say, "We told you so." Already have they been heard to seek to justify self in the murderous course taken, and thus with the mantle of self-justification seek to cover the blood of souls with which their garments are spattered. May such be warned before it is too late! Otherwise, HOW WILL THEY STAND AT THE JUDGMENT?

Every true deep revival from Pentecost to the present day has awakened from opposers this same unkind hostile criticism. The unfriendly world has taken up the cry, "These men are drunk on new wine," and ringing ten thousand changes on it, hurled it into the face of every great revival that has ever blest the land. As in the beginning, it has been treated as an elephant would treat a gnat, or as the moon, moving onward in majesty, treats the cur that barks at her. Jesus did thus, and his Church can be no wiser than her Head.

Tornadoes come contrary to men's preconceived ideas of how showers should come. Men in a general way often in the time of a drought pray for rain and look for it. When the tornado comes they prefer it to continued drought, but it is not " just as they would have ordered." "The class that we expected to see converted have very few of them yielded yet," said a prominent member of the church at Adrian, during the great revival there. Over four hundred had professed conversion, but they were chiefly persons whose salvation had not been looked for. The unlooked-for way in which God's power often is displayed in revival time, often surprises those who are not close observers of his dealings. Such is the case when some rich pew-holder is hit by the truth and threatens to join some church where it never thunders nor lightens, where gospel gales never sweep, and revival tornadoes never come ; where from one year's end to another there is one parched desert of Formality and Worldliness, and a deadly spiritual calm in which most of its dwellers perish. Some, too, are frightened when the power of God rests mightily with official members that are not right with Him, as at Findlay, Ohio, where, under Brother Weber's labors, in about four weeks five hundred and thirty professed conversion. In the beginning of the meeting, some of the leading men of the church said, " I cannot and will not stand it," and some said, " I will take my letter and go elsewhere." Some of the daily papers echoed their opposition, but the pastor remained firm and said, " They get no letters from me," and the work moved mightily onward.

The spiritual tornado often acts in an unlooked-for way upon an unconverted husband. He declares himself "disgusted" at the "plain preaching" of the evangelist, or at the idea of an endless "hell," and declares that he will "never go to church as long as that revival continues." Sister Faintheart had prayed for the revival and felt almost sure her husband would be converted, but now all hope must go, "he means just what he says," and the tornado has struck him in such a way he never will go back to the meetings. She never thought it would bring about such a state of things. O dear! O dear! The next night he goes. The third night he asks his wife's forgiveness. The fourth, O glory! He is converted! Such events are not likely to occur in spiritual ice-houses, where spiritual mummies fumble their musty manuscripts, but in the tornado belt they are of frequent occurrence.

A tornado, notwithstanding all opposition, moves on. Contrary winds may cross its track, and forests, cities and even mountains rise up before it in its onward march, but they do not stop it. To fight against it would be a foolish if not a suicidal act. Revival tornadoes are centers of a similar might. As was written of the gracious revival conducted by Mr. Weber at Rock Rapids, Iowa, "The work has not been without opposition. Christians have been reviled to their faces, but since then some of these very men have been converted."

Jerusalem rose up to crush revivals in the beginning of this great revival dispensation, and like lightning God's judgment fell upon her and she was quickly pillaged and annihilated by a foreign foe. Herod threateningly shook his sword at them, and quickly he was "eaten of the worms." One of Mr. Finney's revivals was opposed by an influential clergyman, who made a public and violent speech against it. "There was great crying unto God that night that He would counteract any evil influence that might result from that speech. The next morning this man was found dead in his bed," but the revival swept on with power.

He who opposes the organized efforts through which God is saving the people touches the "apple of his eye." Such people are like a man who would stop and knock his head against the corner-stone of a cathedral every time he passed it. The structure could stand it all right, but it would be hard on the poor man's head. Some, by opposing holiness and resisting revivals, have acted thus foolishly. The holiness temple still stands in all its stately grandeur, and revivals sweep on like a resistless Niagara, but the "heads" of opposers are in a sad condition.

The revival tornadoes which are about to be noticed are all of them monuments to the power of God, which thus crushes mighty combinations that unite to impede the progress of His work and moves on like the "sun when he goeth forth in his might."

Some persist in their foolish opposition, and while the revival moves on, their children are prejudiced against it by their parents' influence, and remain unconverted. Or, if the person who thus exposes his folly and sin chances to be a pastor, his people, too frequently drinking in of his spirit, likewise remain aloof from the revival or oppose it, and thus grieve the Spirit and purchase to themselves and theirs an awful penalty. Such people are like men who would oppose others who are seeking to rescue drowning persons from a billowy grave, because, forsooth, they "talk too plainly to suit them," or are "too excited," or because they "don't believe that people who are excited or frightened when they get into the life-boat will stay there." Or, they don't believe in having a whole ship's crew "saved at once," but "think they would be more likely to live if they were picked up singly, here one and there one." Or, because so many that are rescued belong to the "riff-raff of society." Men who would sit still and make such excuses for not aiding in saving their drowning fellow-men, or, worse still, oppose those who were doing their best to rescue them, would be considered MURDERERS. Yet this is precisely the way that some act towards revivals. Are not such opposers in God's sight guilty of soul-murder? And if they repent not, must they not answer for it at the Judgment seat of Christ?

Tornadoes are out of the regular order of things. So are revivals, and yet, as Mr. Moody says, "that does not prove that they are wrong. Eldad and Medad were out of the regular succession. Joshua wanted Moses to rebuke them. Instead of that he said, 'Would God that all the Lord's people were prophets.' Elijah and Elisha did not belong to the regular school of prophets, yet they exercised a mighty influence for good in their day. John the Baptist was not in the regular line; he got his theological training out in the desert. Jesus Christ Himself was out of the recognized order. When Philip told Nathaniel that he had found the Messiah, he said to him, 'Can there any good thing come out of Nazareth?'

"As we read the history of the past few centuries, we find that God has frequently taken up those who were, so to speak, out of the regular line. Martin Luther had to break through the regular order of things in his day before he brought about the mighty Reformation. There are now some sixty millions of people who adhere to the Lutheran Church. Wesley and Whitefield were not exactly in the regular line, but see what a mighty work they accomplished!"

More rain frequently falls in one tornado than in a number of ordinary showers. More souls are frequently converted in one revival tornado than during years of the dews of ordinary means of grace or months of protracted drizzles. Listen to Talmage, the eminent Brooklyn evangelistic pastor, —

The church is the boat; the gospel is the net; society is the sea; and a great revival is a whole school brought in at one sweep of the net. I have admiration for that man who goes out with a hook and line to fish. I admire the way he unwinds the reel, and adjusts the bait, and drops the hook in a quiet place on a still afternoon, and here catches one and there one; but I like also a big boat, and a large crew, and a net a mile long, and swift oars, and stout sails, and a stiff breeze, and a great multitude of souls brought—so great a multitude that you would have to get help to draw it ashore, straining the net to the utmost, until it breaks here and there, letting a few escape, but bringing the great multitude into eternal safety.

In other words, *I believe in revivals.* The great work of saving men began with three thousand people joining the church in one day, and it will close with forty or a hundred million people saved in twenty-four hours, when nations shall be born in a day.

Tornadoes are a heaven-sent benediction. They find Nature gasping for a pure breath of air and choking for a drop of water to cool her parched tongue. Her birds, heat-smitten and thirsty, have ceased to sing. Many of her cattle that once rejoiced upon her thousand hills, and her sheep that gamboled in her pastures, are dead or dying, and the stench of their decaying bodies polluting the air, scatters deadly contagion far and near. Her fountains are dried, and also her lakes and rivers, which once were as mirrors in which she beheld her own beauty.

Her flowers long since have faded, and her forests now are no longer pictures of life but death. Her fields, baked by the burning sun that glares blood red from the brassy heavens, are barren wastes. Her granaries are empty. Food is worth more than gold, and water than rubies. Her people many of them are dead, others are dying. Pestilences, arm in arm with deadly plagues, stalk defiantly through the streets of her cities at noonday, claiming thousands of victims who are helpless to escape their power. At night they break into her homes, and snatch children from their parents and wives from their husbands, and with their breath poison whole households, and then with a fiendish laugh, which they have caught from long companionship with demons, they toss them all into the lap of greedy Death, who gloats over them for a moment and then consigns them to the grave. Through all her rural districts, where a happy, prosperous people had rejoiced in the rich profusion of her gifts, now Diseases hold high carnival. In secret counsel assembled, they decide that one of their number shall enter this home and another that, nor stay their deadly work, until all the people are prostrate through their power. Health is banished from her borders. Joy is smothered in her chamber. Plenty and Prosperity have been stabbed by Penury and Poverty, who have usurped their thrones, and now reign in their stead. Wolfish Want makes both day and night hideous with his cries.

But see, quickly the scene changes. The wind rises. Hope about to die lifts again her head and faintly sings. A cloud hovers in sight. It fills the western sky. Now the sun is darkened. The heavens now look black. Lightnings flash in the distance and the welcome rolling of the thunder once more is heard again. The clouds, like coursers on the track each bent on outstripping the other, move swiftly. Now the thunder peals, now crashes, then for a moment an awful deadly calm, then the elements all seem let loose and the tornado has come. Some fly to the cellars for safety, others, thankful that the reign of ghastly drought is over, sing songs of thanksgiving amid the tempest, and with contentment trust Him who holds the whirlwind in His hand.

'Tis ended now. How changed the scene! 'Tis true, some fences are blown down, occasionally a house unroofed, a forest tree laid low,—but oh, how small a price to pay for such a blessing! Look, Nature again wears the same glad smile that of old so brightened all her subjects. Drought and Blight and Malaria and Plagues and Pestilences, all, in one short hour have been driven from her realms. These, with the murderous company of Diseases that were lurking in the land, were sought out and seized by the tornado's might, and, like so many prisoners to the scaffold, were borne roughly to their destined doom.

As it hasted on its mission, it touched each bird and tree and flower, and at that touch the one burst forth in song and the others into beauty. It carpeted the earth as in the days gone by, and following in its train were rosy-cheeked Health and brawny Strength and blushing Beauty, and Purity and Happiness, Plenty and Prosperity, with all of their attendants of minor blessings. Innumerable are the benefits following in the wake of the tornado. This picture has its counterpart in the spiritual world.

In many places spiritual drought abounds. The water of divine truth no longer springs up into everlasting life. The flowers of Peace and Joy and Love, and kindred graces of the Spirit, have withered away. The "wheat and corn and wine" of the kingdom rejoice the heart no more.

Spiritual diseases, plagues and pestilences, as in the counterpart, have formed a conspiracy against the souls of the people, and in the employ of Eternal Death are daily bringing consignments of their doomed prisoners to the gates of Eternal Despair.

Many, starving on the burning sands of Formality, stagger up and down the land, beating their breasts and crying, "O my leanness! O my leanness!" Others, to satisfy the demands of greedy hunger, devour like starving swine the husks of worldliness and many of the poisonous fruits of sin, which seem to allay the momentary craving but which leaves the system with additional poison in the blood.

Satan, through a band of strong temptations which ever wait to do his bidding, has honey-combed the land with pitfalls, cunningly covered so as to snare the victim by treachery and surprise, and into these many fall, to rise again no more.

But soon there comes the mighty transformation, more marvelous than that mentioned in the material world. A faithful few beseech heaven in Jesus' name for showers from above. They meet the conditions, and soon mercy-drops are falling, and now they are in the midst of a sweeping spiritual tornado, the figure of which was just described.

As bolt after bolt of the lightning of divine truth

falls on every side, and as the revival currents in their majestic sweep make everything that is movable to tremble, some are frightened, and seek to run away from its influence, and others curse it, while all who know the secret of the Lord, sing His praises that the "rain has come and the drought is at an end." It soon passes by, but its fruits abide. Men who were dying of thirst now abide continually at the fountain and without money and without price partake freely of the water of life. Others that were dead of spiritual starvation, have been brought to life, and now, alive forevermore, partake gratefully of the gospel feast and "go from strength to strength."

Many afflicted with tongue paralyzing palsy, the loathesome leprosy of inbred sin, spiritual blindness, which makes men make "crooked paths" to the glee of devils and the grief of saints, spiritual deafness that had for years deadened the soul to gospel sounds, spiritual debility and nervousness that had for a long time made revival meetings a dread, and spiritual fevers that had well-nigh reached the fatal crisis, now are made "every whit whole," and strong in the strength which God supplies through His eternal Son, are fast becoming effective workers in His vineyard. Weaklings are transformed into spiritual giants, and the desert waste now blossoms as the rose. The land now is full of the wheat and the corn and oil and the wine of the heavenly kingdom, and the people partake and are satisfied.

The strength of the Church in quantity and quality is increased manyfold, and her children now are glad to work, to give, to speak or to pray, as need requires and as privilege affords. No questionable or sinful expedients to "meet expenses," or the benevolences of the church, are needed now, for the people "have a mind and *love* to give," as Jesus taught. No more sepulchral silences in meetings for prayer and praise and Christian testimony, for they "cannot but speak" the blessed experiences of the soul. No more godless musicians going through with musical performances for worship, but a people whose hearts are full of song and whose voices join those of devout leaders as together "with the spirit and the understanding" they praise the triune God. No more dearth of workers in the Sunday-school and other departments of lawful church activities, for God's people, having become willing in this, the day of His power, many are ready to say, "Here am I; send me, send me." No more urging the Christians to labor with sinners, for now they cannot keep away from them.

May such revival tornadoes multiply, until Ethiopia shall no longer stretch out her hands in vain for some to bring to her the gospel, and until all the kingdoms of this world shall become those of our Lord and of His Christ. The great revivals, a record of which is given in the succeeding chapters of this book, are all corroborative of the fact that real revival tornadoes are a blessed benediction from above.

CHAPTER VII.

TORNADOES.

Republic, Wauseon and Marseilles had the honor of being among the first fields to which the Holy Spirit directed Bro. Weber, in his work as an evangelist. The saying of a prophet being without honor in his own country, evidently has no application to him, as many of his grandest victories have been in his own state.

At Republic many evangelists had preceded him, without much apparent success, and the disheartened church was electrified, as by a shock from a battery, when, the "second night of the meeting, sinners were crying for mercy." The pastor, C. E. Ruddick, "a man of faith, of the evangelistic type, gave his full sympathy to the work and it swept on for four weeks. The power of God was wonderfully displayed, great crowds attended, and people of all ages were reached, until one hundred and twenty professed conversion," and many came out in a higher life. "I started out," records the evangelist, "on the faith plan," and God, true to His promise, supplied his needs. Referring to the meeting, a secular paper said that nothing like it had occurred there for years and years; that it reminded of the days of smiting with the "flaming sword and thunderbolts of fire;" that the evangelist was a "host in himself, bringing many bathed in tears of contrition to the penitential altar." "He came to us," it was written, "like a comet, and like the comet was brilliant and attractive."

It was here that a mother asked prayers for her boy in Kansas, and the next letter from him brought the tidings, "I am converted."

It was here that the man lived, of whom Mr. Weber writes, "He had been a drunkard for years, and was a terror to the whole town. Under deep conviction, he was out in the woods getting wood, and so powerfully did the Spirit work that he came to the parsonage in despair, saying, 'I want to be prayed for.' We got down on our knees, and in a few moments he was converted and shouting happy. His whole theme after that was 'Praise the Lord.'"

Here, too, it was that he visited a blacksmith, who had not been to church for years, to see him about his soul. The pastor had cautioned him not to speak to him about religion, as he was very sensitive and it would frighten him. "But," says Mr. Weber, "the second word I said was, 'Are you saved?' The pastor left abruptly, but before he got across the street the man was on his knees, in the shop, crying for mercy. He went over to his house and the wife also was crying, and both joined the church, happily saved.

"One of the business men, a professed infidel, had opposed the meetings. His wife came to make fun at first, but the Spirit took hold of her heart. I called to see her, and had prayers. She said she 'wanted to be saved, but could not come to the altar.' After she became willing, her husband said she must not go. I gave her books and a little Testament to read, and she was converted. The husband became very much alarmed. He tried to buy her, by offering anything if she would give up this subject of religion. He came also to meeting, was gloriously converted, and himself, wife and little boy all united with the church." Thus God honored the efforts of his servant, in this, his first field as an evangelist.

From Republic, Bro. Weber went to Bellevue, O., where there was a large church, "packed to overflowing night after night, and hundreds unable to gain admission." The pastor, a man of power and faith, worked with might, and the third night sinners came to the altar. When Mr. Weber gave his experience here, the Catholics, which are many, were greatly enraged. Over one hundred persons professed conversion. Among many incidents occurring at this revival is the following, which is an excellent lesson for all: A little boy, about twelve years old, noted for his quick temper and quickness to resent an injury, was converted. While coming home from school, another boy tried to provoke him, by calling him all kinds of names, but failed to accomplish his purpose. The little persecutor was lame, and often would have to call on other boys to aid him home. This time they all refused him, when up stepped the noble little convert and kindly offered him his help. The wicked little fellow wept and asked his forgiveness.

November 30, he began at Wauseon, O. As usual the church soon became too small. At the second meeting there was a seeker. This church had no altar.

When the pastor on the first night of the meeting asked for money to build one, Mr. Weber said, if they did not give the money, he would, and it was quickly raised. The work here was chiefly among the young people, members of the Sunday-school. In a Saturday afternoon service one hundred and twenty-five cried for mercy and seventy professed conversion. The names of over one hundred and fifty were taken at this revival and most of them professed conversion. Many were the servants of Satan, who threw stones at this tornado, but it was to their own shame. Howbeit the son of one of them was converted.

During the early part of the meetings, some young folks had a social at a private house, after church, " at which they held a mock revival, one imitating Weber and the other Charles, his helper in song. Mourners were brought forward and a general mock revival prevailed, until the pastor appeared and put an end to it. The participators in this were converted, and at last account were doing well.

The following incident occurring here illustrates forcibly the fact that honest seekers, who are not afraid to use the means of salvation, will not long be left in the dark. "A number of young men from the high school came to the evangelist one night and said, " Mr. Weber, we are honest and want to know the truth." He asked, "Are you willing to let the people know that you want to know the truth?" "Yes." They came to the altar, and ere long were rejoicing in the consciousness of salvation. "Seek and ye shall find."

The next place which this tornado struck was Defiance, O., December 20. The pastor, Rev. S. L. Roberts, had engaged brother Weber at Conference, but kept it from the people until about the time he wished the meetings to begin. Some objected to beginning meetings then, as the holidays were at hand, and they were preparing for a Christmas tree. Brother Weber told them that his time was precious, and at the first service, with the air thick with doubt, he announced that he had come to stay until there were from two hundred to three hundred conversions. The people derided it; many criticised; and some got mad because the truth was preached so plain. Soon the first gales of the tornado had passed, and there was a cloud-burst of revival rain which poured steadily, until about three hundred had professed conversion. The church woke up, and a spirit of labor came upon them, so that even children, from ten to fourteen years of age, would go out in the congregation and plead with sinners to be saved. The other churches remained aloof from the meetings, and the result was that nearly all of the converts united with the people who had labored for their salvation, about two hundred and fifty being received on probation and by letter.

One evening, just before time to preach, the fire-bells began to ring; the people were alarmed and a panic was threatened. Mr. Weber mounted the chancel-rail and warned the people of the fire eternal with such earnestness that soon they had forgotten the flames of earth that threatened, and there was a wonderful meeting that night. Some days the air seemed charged with almost resistless convicting power, as the Holy Spirit, in answer to prayer, fell upon the people. In one single day eighty-two in the Sunday-school and other services professed conversion. "I never," wrote Mr. Weber, "saw such a day; men, women, and children bowing before the same God, and being saved." The last day of the meeting, a man about seventy years old, who had not attended a single service, but for whom prayers had been offered, was so arrested by the Spirit that he sent for the pastor to come and see him. He was preparing to go when who should come but the man himself, his face radiant with smiles, saying, "I am saved, I am saved!"

A minister's daughter, who was a teacher in the public schools, when spoken to by Mr. Weber about her soul, repelled him with a look of hatred, that seemed to say, "You cannot get me." The last night he succeeded in getting her to promise that she would pray every night for two weeks that God would show her her heart, and give her a new one. She was shortly after converted. A farewell service was held Monday morning, January 15, and was attended by hundreds who came to bid the evangelist good-bye. Brother Weber in his journal says, "One not knowing we were leaving, would have thought there was a funeral, as almost everybody cried. I never before met at one time so many that loved us." Such scenes in his life were to become frequent. He who leads souls to Christ forms friendships deeper, tenderer, and more lasting than any other.

Taking advantage of every event, and turning it to the glory of God and the salvation of souls, Mr. Weber has been quick to see the value of watch-night services, and appropriate them in his work.

1883, full of hope, and early crowned with victory,

broke upon him in one of these watch-night services, at Defiance, O., in the midst of his meeting there. Renewing the solemn vows of the past, and with humble dependence upon Him for future victory, he began what proved to be one of the most eventful years of his life. During this year he was the cyclone center of blessed spiritual reformations in many places, laboring at Defiance, Marseilles, Findlay, McComb, Marion, Bridgeman, Clyde and Marysville ; also at Bayshore, Lakeside, and Franklin, Penn., camp-meetings ; then at Jackson, Mich., Williamsburg, O., and Fort Wayne, Ind. At each of these places overflowing houses and success continued to attend him.

January 15th, beginning at Marseilles, O., he asked for one hundred and twenty-five souls. The second night "twenty-one came forward" and fifteen professed conversion, and the work swept on, until one hundred and forty professed conversion in ten days. As victory followed victory, no wonder that Bro. Weber wrote, "Oh, how blessed to see souls coming to Jesus! I would rather see souls converted than have all the riches of this world!" While here, he went out to McKendree chapel, talked a little while, "and seventeen came forward and eight were saved. Glory to God." The people, to get seats, would sometimes come four hours before time.

That salvation is a mightier moral lever than reformation alone, is evidenced by the fact that the temperance people had tried in vain to dislodge a saloon at this place, which the "revival drove out of town." A very rich moralist came out to the meetings, and was struck with conviction. Mr. Weber visited him at his home and prayed that he might "sell out his interest in the devil, and take an interest in heaven." At this he "got mad," but soon became reconciled and was converted. To God be the glory!

An old man of about seventy years came to the meeting, so feeble that he could not kneel. Mr. Weber led him to the altar and he was converted. It was here that, when the meeting began, many of the members would look at Mr. Weber, "and stare, and then look away, as they were not used to seeing a man red hot all over." The pastor and people went to work after Bro. Weber left, and the revival fire spread in every direction, until over one hundred were converted. A pastor received the Spirit's baptism and went home, began meetings, and at once was blessed with a gracious revival.

FINDLAY, O., FIVE HUNDRED AND THIRTY CONVERSIONS.

This work began February 1st. The second night the evangelist preached from "Prepare to meet thy God." He was so weak that he nearly fainted several times; but the Holy Ghost attended the Word with power, and thirty-five came forward and nine professed conversion. The following from a report of this meeting by Rev. J. R. Henderson was published in the *Western Christian Advocate*, —

The pastor and official board of Findlay secured the services of Rev. J. H. Weber to hold a series of meetings. He commenced just before the great floods. After two nights' work, he was compelled to suspend for nine days, on account of the gas being cut off. February 11 was really the beginning of his meetings. He closed Tuesday morning, March 13. The results are five hundred and thirty conversions in a little more than four weeks. A more genuine revival I have not seen in twenty-five years. It commenced with the class with which our revivals should commence, namely, the Sunday-school, and after the Sunday-school was largely converted, it reached out, and up, and took hold of hundreds of adults of all ages.

It was the general opinion of all interested in the meeting that if Bro. Weber could have remained three weeks longer the converts would have reached one thousand or more ; but he was so pressed by other engagements that he felt that duty called him to other expectant fields.

Bro. Weber insisted from beginning to end on Holy Ghost conversions. I never saw a larger proportion of clear conversions. I never heard so many shouts around a Methodist altar. The whole town was never so moved before. The auditorium was crowded with an audience of one thousand for a month. If the church had been twice its capacity it would have been filled for the last three weeks. All of the other evangelical churches have been largely benefited by the revival. Nearly one-half of the converts have united with the Methodist Episcopal Church, and the other half have united with the other churches. The good work still goes on under the leadership of pastor Yingler, assisted by Mr. Starkey of the United Brethren Church. The pastor has been growing in the estimation and affection of his church ever since he commenced his pastorate, last fall. His coolness, and firm, earnest co-operation with the evangelist, contributed largely to the great results. The evangelist has the good sense of allying the pastor as prominently as he can to the revival and the converts. Singing was made to contribute all its power to the revival. The first fifteen or twenty minutes of each evening's service was devoted exclusively to singing. It filled the whole house, and thrilled all hearts. The singing was followed by prayer. This was followed by an earnest appeal to sinners, averaging in length from twenty to thirty minutes. The evangelist makes every word tell directly on sinners' hearts and consciences. After this he gives the invitation to the altar. He leaves the pastor in charge, and spends from thirty to forty-five minutes in the congregation, persuading sinners to surrender to Christ at once. By his own personal efforts, he has led hundreds to the altar. He has a sweetness of spirit that wins; has wonderful faith and courage; has a passion for saving souls that seems all-absorbing. His dash and bodily demonstrations and eccentricities are, at first, matters of general criticism, but after awhile the people, sinners as well as saints, come to believe most profoundly that God is with him, and their criticisms give way to co-operation. Up to this time, this was the evangelist's greatest battle and greatest victory. The devil combined all his forces inside of the church and out to crush the work. Men were maddened as of old at the exposure of their sins, and in many ways gave expression to their spite.

Weaker men than Weber would have been discouraged and have given up; but opposition but whets his determination, and by "SPENDING HOURS DAILY IN PRAYER," appointing a day of prayer and fasting, and using all the means at his disposal, the victory was won. The following, from his own pen, gives some idea of the contest,—

"The devil is very mad, and many of the church members are on their dignity. If you ask them if they are saved, they get real mad. I mean to stick to the truth if they tear my head off. Some said they would strike me. All right, dear Jesus, I am ready to bear anything for you. Glory to God, we can glory in tribulation. The devil knew we were going to have a good time, and that is the reason he gets so mad. Prayed most all day for power, and God sent it, glory to His name. I never saw a church in such an awful condition. 'If God be for us, who can be against us?' was my fortress text."

A little later he wrote, "The ice is broken; the officiary say they will stand by and work."

After this the work swept on with mighty momentum, as high as ninety-two professing conversion in a single day. Once, during the meeting, Bro. Weber wrote, "The devil is trying to get out lies about me. I am innocent. How gratifying to look into the face of Jesus and say, 'Thou knowest my life.'" And again, when the "interest was rapidly increasing and fifty at the altar," "Our God does the work; not me. O God, keep me humble. Success often kills people."

It was here that an infidel, about seventy years old, was converted. Mr. Weber saw him, a man over six feet tall, in the congregation, visibly affected. He went to him and he began to tremble. Then he was asked to come; but he said, "No." Mr. Weber said, "You must," and commanded him in the name of Jesus to come. He came and was converted.

The people now loved the evangelist even more ardently than at first they had hated him. They, above compensation for labor, made him a present of a calagraph, valued at $75.00, and to Charlie Blakeslie, an assistant in song who was with him at this time, a valuable watch.

A number of young men who were converted felt they were called to the ministry. Oh, for a host of men who will thus defy the world, the flesh and the devil, and claim the kingdom which already to our Lord belongs!

> "From victory on to victory,
> His armies He shall lead,
> Till every foe is vanquished,
> And Christ is Lord indeed."

McComb, Ohio, a town said to be "half a mile from hell," where many were so tinctured with Campbelitism that they did not know they were saved, was the next place the tornado's flight scattered the host of sin. "The pastor, J. N. Smith, full of the Holy Ghost, worked with all his might to help on the work. Remaining here less than two weeks, eighty-five professed conversion, twenty the last night of the meeting, and five at the eight o'clock farewell meeting the morning he went away." The following *warning* incident occurred at this place. A young lady attended the meetings and was deeply wrought upon, but would not yield. Mr. Weber personally pleaded with her the last night, but she refused. She was taken sick that very night, on her way home, and died that week, unsaved.

Pressing invitations now poured in upon him from many places. He had fully committed his way to the Lord, and like Paul went where the Spirit led him. God said, Marion, and thither the evangelist hastened. The officiary having invited him, were in a state of expectancy, and looked for great things. Rev. L. R. Belt, a "man of good intellectual power," was pastor. As usual, the truth was pressed, the Spirit worked, and all of the tornado attendants were manifest. It was declared to be the most wonderful meeting ever held in those parts. As high as fifty were converted at a single service. Here Brother Weber wrote, "I never was much more burdened for souls than this day, I felt like dying sometimes. It was so great that I had to leave the house and take a walk." Here he received letters from other places assuring him that "the converts are doing well all over." The gospel gales continued to increase, until over three hundred had professed conversion. He labored here about four weeks, and when he felt that he must close, many, even of the unconverted, urged him to remain, as so many more seemed on "the point of yielding." It was here that a secular paper sputtered, "Bro. Weber for breakfast, Bro. Weber for dinner, Bro. Weber for supper, day after day, for four weeks, has been a rather tiresome dish." It doubtless was to those who would not obey the truth, but to multitudes who obeyed the Gospel messages he brought, his name was next to that of the Saviour, to whom he had led them.

The pastor, reporting this meeting to the *Advocate*, referring to the evangelist, said, —

He is a success. He has a level head, kind heart, social nature, a vigorous body and mind, all of which he works to the utmost ability for the promotion of his work. He has the gift of knowing people by name, on sight, and in a few weeks will know more of the personality of a people than many men will in as many years. He preaches a whole gospel, dwells largely on the doom of the damned, the trickery of the devil, and the deceitfulness of sin. He finds no houses large enough to hold his audiences, and he grows in favor with the people the longer he stays. Marion was loth to give him up.

One of the business men prided himself on his morality, and that he was as good as the church members, for when a poor widow needed aid it was he that would send the necessaries of life, which many professors neglected; but God smote him on his sick bed, and there he laid with the streaming light of God's truth on his soul; and, when Bro. Weber arrived, the pastor and he visited him, and he was converted, joined the church, and since has gone to heaven.

An infidel came to the meetings, was struck by revival lightning, came penitently to the altar, cried for mercy and was saved.

As the evangelist was preaching on the Judgment, the people became terrified, and some came very near rushing to the altar before the sermon was done. When the invitation was given, it seemed a race as to who should get there first. The altar and the four front seats were crowded with earnest seekers; the presence of God filled the place, and forty professed conversion.

During this meeting Brother Weber was exposed to the mumps. He writes, "I was getting the mumps. In the midst of the meeting I asked the people to pray that, if it was God's will, He would cure me immediately." They did, and he recovered at once.

Among the many marked answers to prayer occurring here was that of a young lady convert who had a lover in the West. She asked the prayers of God's people for him, and when the next letter came he was saved.

Closing with victory in Jesus' name at Marion, he next labored a few days at Ridgeway, where, though feeling an "unexplainable indifference" and "tempted sorely," God gave him precious souls as seals to his ministry, and seventeen were at the altar on the last night of the meeting.

The last saloon was closed before he left the place, and among others the following incidents occurred, which should encourage workers to labor with the most indifferent. Mr. Weber approached a young man and asked him if he was saved. "No." "Do you want to be?" "I do not care to be." "Do you want to go to hell?" "I don't care." Mr. Weber then kneeled and prayed that the Holy Spirit would show him his need of a Saviour. The young man asked his prayers, and before he left was converted. Clyde, Ohio, was "noted for its wickedness." Among the young men "shocking licentiousness" prevailed and among the old Spiritualism and Universalism had been rampant and, as elsewhere, were the parents of many vices, making this the "most difficult" town to which the evangelist had ever been called. "The fourth night sinners came to the altar, and every night after that they were saved, until there were one hundred and fifty converted, and many came out into a higher life." Rev. G. W. Ball, "a sanctified man, filled with the fulness of God," was pastor. He declared this to be "one of the most powerful spiritual awakenings that ever visited Clyde."

The following incident occurred, illustrating faith and its reward, and is from Bro. Weber's pen, "We had a desperate fight with the devil. I got up, by being led by the Holy Ghost, and said a certain woman would come. Many declared the same thing, and we had to hold on till a late hour before she yielded; but God did hear. Glory to God."

Here Mr. Weber's "sister Emma came from her home, near Cincinnati, and was gloriously converted." Mrs. F., the wife of a spiritualist lecturer, was saved, and joined the church.

A young lady was saved on Thursday evening, and commenced at once to pray for the young man to whom she was engaged, and Saturday night of the same week her prayer was answered and he was converted.

Here Mr. Weber had a jubilee of two thousand saved in his work since New Year's. He invited the people to come in the afternoon and join in a jubilee street parade. The ministers led the van, and several hundred fell in line, and they "went through the streets praising God and singing songs of Zion." "Oh, what consternation," wrote Bro. Weber, "it produced on the people! Saloon keepers trembled, business men feared; but God was in it. We went back to the church, and the whole altar was flooded with penitents, and many saved."

A principle is here involved that will bear the careful thought of all who would be wise to win souls. Moses, John the Baptist, Jesus, Wesley and Whitfield engaged in frequent open-air services, and it is a suicidal policy that surrenders them to the "world, the flesh and the devil." The meeting was attended by one of the most fashionable ladies in town. At first she made sport. One night he gave her a card, on which was printed, "Where will I spend my eternity?" She went home to her husband, an unconverted man, and said, sportively, "I have a ticket straight to heaven." "Let me see," said the husband. He answered, "Wife, it is too solemn a thing to make sport of; you have a straight ticket to hell." That night, "a straight ticket to hell" would "ring in her ears, until she became so fearful she could not rest." She tried to find Christ at home, but failed. She was proud; and when her pride was renounced and she came to the altar, she was saved, joined the church, and became a devoted Christian.

MARYSVILLE, OHIO — A MIDSUMMER REVIVAL — OVER FOUR HUNDRED PROFESS CONVERSION.

Many have become so accustomed to seeing the devil have his own way, so far as salvation is concerned, that a midsummer revival surprises them like a lightning-bolt from a clear sky. And yet God worked in such a wonderful way that Bro. Weber was able to write, "I have not been to a place where the work seemed so easy as here." There seemed to be less of the opposition than usually had been shown. Perhaps the devil was off on a summer vacation. Marysville is a town of about three thousand people, with three churches, Congregational, Presbyterian and Methodist. The Congregational pastor worked faithfully in the meetings, and many of the Presbyterian people united to help the work along. The Methodist pastor was Rev. A. Harmont, full of zeal and earnestness to see a genuine work of God. Often the church would be full, and hundreds congregated outside to listen. The people flocked in from neighboring towns, and many of them were converted. At times " the heat was so oppressive that the penitents had to be fanned to keep them from suffocating." Sometimes it "seemed as if heaven was on earth." Fifty-four were saved in one day, and forty in another. The following is from the pastor's report of this wonderful work to the *Western Christian Advocate*, —

Our meeting, under the direction of Rev. J. H. Weber, which commenced June 10, closed to-day, July 9. It has been full of blessing to the churches of this place. Many in the churches, but not saved, have become converted and wonderfully interested. The interest has exceeded all we most fondly hoped. For five weeks, by day and by night, our house has been full, and the meeting has been the subject of thought and conversation through the city and community.

God has wonderfully owned the labor of Bro. Weber, whose faith in God triumphs over all obstacles. During the meeting four hundred and two gave their names as converted. The altar has been crowded from night to night.

Was not that a summer vacation worth having?

June 27th was set apart as a day of fasting and prayer. Hundreds came, fasted, and were blessed. Twenty-two professed conversion on that day. In this meeting a young man, who said he had been a "drunkard from his birth," was gloriously saved. A business man, under oppressive conviction, started for Bro. Weber's room seven times, but "failed because of fear." On the night of the "fourth" he came to church, and as there were a number of business men present, Bro. Weber addressed his remarks to them, and three of them came to the altar. They had been there about twenty minutes when the "fearful" seeker forgot his timidity in the glad consciousness of salvation, and forgetful of everything else, he threw his hat toward the ceiling, and in tones that made the air ring, at the top of his voice shouted, "H — Y — P — I — E!"

A young man on his sick bed was visited, converted and went home to heaven. At one service, a space was reserved for the militia, who came in full uniform. When the altar invitation was given, one was "so anxious to be saved that he would not take time to go around, but jumped over the seat."

On July 5th a jubilee service was held. "Meeting began at 10.30. Met at 3 o'clock and formed a procession of several hundred, and marched through town, singing. Stopped in front of a saloon and prayed. Went to a grove and about one thousand persons came. Two were forward."

At the last night of the meeting a young man, under conviction, was sitting on the fence, with others, talking about the meeting. He finally said, "Let's go to church." Jumping down from the fence, he caught his pantaloons on a nail and tore a great rent in them. At this he burst forth with an awful volley of oaths, but went home, changed his clothes, and came back to church, too late, however, to get in. While he stood by the window, the power of God came upon him, and his need of a present Saviour became so intense that he climbed through the window, saying, "For God's sake, let me get in to be saved," and was converted.

What human eloquence, reasoning and might, were powerless to accomplish, Mr. Weber, through the power of the Holy Ghost, was enabled, as elsewhere, to do at this place, demonstrating that a man, full of the Holy Ghost and led in everything by the Spirit, can have revival victory as great in July as in January. May midsummer revivals multiply, until earth is retaken for her lawful King.

Bro. Weber at Camp-meetings. The time has now come when Mr. Weber is to have his first experience in conducting services at camp-meetings, where,—

> "In the temple that never was made by hands,
> Curtains of azure, crystal wall
> And dome of the sunshine over all,"

great multitudes were to gather.

After the Marysville meeting, he paid a short visit to his father's home, which to him was a season of great rejoicing, the source of which is seen from the following entry in his journal of July 11th: "Praise the Lord! This is a day of days at our home. My ma has decided to be a Christian; was saved with her head in my lap."

From home he paid a short visit to Defiance and Clyde, "confirming the converts," and passed from thence to the Bayshore, O., camp-ground, which he reached on the 21st. Here he had been engaged to aid in the services, and here, as usual, the blessing of God was upon his labors. "A straight gospel was preached, and many hardened sinners fell beneath the strokes of the Holy Ghost. Many were saved and sanctified."

The trustees of the Lakeside, O., camp-ground, Aug. 8–20, 1883, where he next led the hosts of God to revival victory, had early secured the services of evangelist Thomas Harrison, but finding that he could stay but a short time, Mr. Weber was secured in his stead for the entire meeting. "Oh, for a TORNADO AT LAKE SIDE," had been the burden of the evangelist's prayer. He came expecting it, and, glory to God, he was not disappointed. Here he was greeted by the "largest audiences he had ever had," and was enabled to claim "power from on high" to sway them as the wind sways the forest leaves.

At the first meeting many manifested a desire to be saved. Pastors, people and the evangelist united their labors, and many were converted, and many others were wholly sanctified. Interest grew more and more intense, culminating in a sweeping cyclone at the closing Sunday service, when "the people surged from all parts of the auditorium to be saved, and the interest was so great that many stayed after the lights were put out, and were converted."

"INSTANT IN SEASON, OUT OF SEASON."

Passing from Lakeside to his next appointment, an incident of interest occurred which should inspire others to look for God's leadings, even in disappointments. At Ashtabula, O., he met with an accident that caused him to lose the train which he felt that he should have taken. This compelled him to lay over in a little town by the name of Andover. He writes, "The thought would come, 'The Lord could have held that train, but He has a work for you to do here.' So I said, 'What is it, Lord?' I started out, hoping to see some one whom I might help, as the Spirit said, 'I have a work for you,' but the people seemed to treat me so indifferently. Went and bought some taffy. Found some boys playing ball and gave them some, hoping that my work was talking to them, but they likewise seemed indifferent. I then went to the hotel, when a man came up and stretched out his hand, and said, 'How are you, Mr. Weber? I am from Marysville, O. I was in your meetings there.' After supper, I said to him, 'Would you like to go out for a little walk?' He consented. After walking some distance, I said, 'Are you a Christian?' He said, 'No; but I would like to be.' Then it dawned on me why God had me miss the train. As we walked, I unfolded to him God's Word. We walked a mile or so, then we came to the hotel, and sat on the porch. I urged him to make a surrender to God there and then, so I said, 'Let us go out to some place and pray.' He did not seem inclined, so I said, 'God will save you right here, if you will confess your sins, and accept Him as your Saviour.' So he prayed in his chair, and so did I; then I got up and got a drink, and came back, and said, 'Well, did you ask Him to forgive you?' 'Well, then, according to His word and not according to your feelings, what does He do?' 'Why, He forgives!' 'Are you lost or saved?' 'Why, Weber, I am saved!' His eyes sparkled and his face lit up with heavenly smiles, and he left that evening a happy man. I met his wife, a short time after, who thanked me for saving her husband."

The next morning he reached Franklin, Pa., where with the Ohio Camp-meeting Holiness Association, he had been invited to aid in a camp-meeting. This meeting "was carried on almost exclusively for holiness." But as genuine holiness always sets people to work for sinners, the work naturally took hold of them, and they, too, were saved. While here, the following fell from Bro. Weber's pen : "Had one of the most peculiar experiences in a meeting that I ever had. At the close of my talk, I got down and wept over sinners, and so did many of the people. Many came to the altar and were saved. Glory be to Jesus." Truly "they that sow in tears shall reap in joy." Here the evangelist would lay in his tent and "pray by the hour," and a "wave of salvation came, prostrating everybody."

This meeting closed August 27, and the time between that and September 30, when the great revival began at Jackson, Mich., he improved by visiting a number of the churches, where he had hitherto labored, being received as an angel of mercy, and everywhere praying the Father, "in Jesus' name," to bless the people.

CHAPTER VIII.

THE GREAT JACKSON TORNADO — EIGHT HUNDRED PROFESS CONVERSION, — SEPTEMBER 30 TO NOVEMBER 22, 1883.

This was one of the most remarkable revivals in the history of Michigan. Dr. F. Reasner, an official member of the First M. E. Church, met the evangelist at the Lake Side Camp-meeting and obtained a promise from him, that, if the church called, he would come and labor at Jackson. In due time the official call came, and, true to his promise, September 31st found Mr. Weber at Jackson, at the head of what was to prove a mighty revival movement. The following concerning the opening there is from his own pen, —

"Jackson, Mich., is a city of twenty-two thousand population. It is called the hardest city in Michigan. Several noted evangelists had been there without stirring the entire city. It seemed as if Satan had become so entrenched as to defy the churches and all that was good.

"The church, the largest in that conference, had been burdened with a debt of $40,000, which seemed to crush out all the spirituality, in fact all they could attend to was to raise money to pay the interest. Bro. J. Graham, a man full of tact and push, being pastor, crowded the question day and night of paying off the debt. Some said, 'It cannot be done'; but he, true as the needle is to the north, when he undertakes anything, said, 'It must be done.' This 'It must' was pushed night and day, until the debt was entirely liquidated, and now the church was in a condition to enjoy a glorious revival. . . . The church was in a very low state of spirituality and the signs of life were few."

A prominent member of the official board says, "The spiritual condition of our church, as also the community, was at a low ebb. Our prayer and class meetings were thinly attended and the singing of the old hymn,

'Live at this poor dying rate,'

seemed to express the real condition of our church."

There was a large Catholic population, and the Protestant churches were cold and formal. As truly as of New England towns in Whitefield's times, it might have been said, —

"To the lust of office and greed of trade,
A stepping stone is the altar made;
Everywhere is the grasping hand,
And eager adding of land to land;
And earth, which seemed to the fathers meant
But as a pilgrim's wayside tent, —
A nightly shelter to fold away
When the Lord should call at break of day,
Solid and steadfast seemed to be,
And Time has forgotten Eternity!"

Reports of Mr. Weber's successes and eccentricities had preceded him, and Sunday evening the people, wide-awake with curiosity, gathered to his first meeting. After singing, and fitting preliminary remarks by the pastor, the evangelist took charge of the service. His remarks were reported by the daily papers as follows,—

Bro. Weber said he did praise God for what He had done and for what He was going to do, for the people were going to have an old-fashioned Methodist time. He did not want scientific singing, but singing from the heart. "Glory hallelujah" was then sung, after which there was prayer by the Revs. M. S. Sly and J. Graham. "Bringing in the sheaves" was then sung, Mr. Weber remarking that the sheaves would begin to be gathered before next Sunday. After, "Shall we gather at the river?" was sung with great fervor, by the choir and congregation, led by the revivalist, prayer was again offered.

"The people had come to hear a sermon," Rev. Weber said, "but he did not come to preach. He just came to help Revs. Graham, Sly, and perhaps other ministers, who were in the congregation. In the afternoon he had taken a retrospective view of the situation in Jackson, in prayer in his closet, and as he had thought of the condition of a large portion here, his heart had bled for them, but the God who had given him thousands and thousands of converts had not deserted him. Perhaps some of his hearers did not like his ways, and perhaps he would not like them if he knew all about them; on this score he and they were mutual. He had not come to stay a few days. He had told his folks in Ohio that he was going to be gone between one and four months, and if the ministers would stand by him, his bones would bleach before he had left, until he had made five hundred to one thousand converts here in Jackson. At Findlay, O., thirty-five came forward the second night. When he left the tally, that showed five hundred and thirty converts. The church was not large enough to hold those who came, and hundreds went away. He was reminded of a story of a man who saw but one devil on the roof of a house. He asked what he was doing there, and the devil replied, 'There is a church quarrel here, and I can keep them in order alone.' Passing on, he found a church lined with devils, for there a revival was going on, and it took all the power of Satan to hold a few back. This town was going to be mightily moved for God, and multitudes saved, who are now going 'pell-mell' to hell. He expected that many would go away mad, but some of them would come back glad. At Marysville, O., during the hot weather in June, he had made four hundred and three converts in four weeks; the church and yards were thronged, and one young man was so anxious for salvation that he jumped into the church through a window. The people must be careful how they acted in regard to this work. He had heard of a little dog barking at the moon. The moon went on shining, and when the little dog died, even then the moon did not stop. The people could bark at this work, but it would still go on. All he asked of this people was a ten days' probation, and then they could look for a moving of the Spirit. There was so much preciseness that Christ was almost driven out of the churches. At his church in Ohio, the people had said, 'monkey show,' and would not stand it. Then he tried to preach in the usual precise kind of a way, but he dropped into the pulpit paralyzed. The people begged him to go on, and the next night twenty-five or thirty souls said, 'I want to be saved.' Last year he had seen three thousand converts. He had come to be just like himself; he could not be anybody else if he tried. In reply to the slander that he worked for money, the speaker said he had refused a position worth between $5,000 and $6,000 a year, and had given up a place at $10 per day, when he was through college, to go into this work, a place where he would not have been libeled by newspapers, cursed and damned by a good many people, in whose way he stood. He wanted personal work in the congregation, and night after night with penitents. He wanted the people to *know* that they were saved. For himself, he did not wish to go to heaven on a guess. He did not believe there were people enough, with red-hot personal experiences, in the congregation, to lead the coming throng to the altar, and the church was going to be too small for the congregations of the coming nights.

He then closed with the benediction.

The speaker's independence of man, earnestness, and confident prophecies of coming crowds and great success, aroused a great deal of criticism. Especially his statement that, under such unfavorable circumstances, there would be from five hundred to one thousand conversions.

Satan, who had been defeated through him many times before, and understood well that the evangelist meant every word he said, sent as strong a detachment of devils to Jackson as he could spare, and the battle at once began.

At the next evening service he "gave an invitation

for those who knew they were saved to stand up. A good number arose. He then asked any who would like to know they were saved to arise, and as many more arose."

His pointed sermons and earnest efforts, both in public and private, soon stirred the entire city. Peal followed peal of denunciation of the popular sins of the church and the people. They would hardly recover from one surprise before another was ready.

> "Through the ceiled chambers of secret sin
> Sudden and strong the light shone in;
> A guilty sense of his neighbor's needs
> Startled the man of title deeds."

Purity, Innocence, and Virtue waved their hands and rejoiced. Truth and Uprightness defended the evangelist, and urged him on. Error, Vice, and Hypocrisy counselled together how they might paralyze his power. As elsewhere, unconverted professors were among the chief opposers.

The *Jackson Star*, a "wandering star" to whom we fear is "reserved the blackness of darkness, forever," from the beginning ridiculed the revival and the evangelist, as the following extracts from its columns indicate,—

AMUSEMENTS — REV. MR. WEBER.

The M. E. Church has contributed its share to the amusements this week. Rev. Mr. Weber is a star of a considerable magnitude. Though he was not extensively billed, he has played to large houses all the week. Matinees every afternoon.

WEBER'S FROLICS.

The Rev. Mr. Weber continues his nightly performances at the M. E. Church, and, no matter what the attraction at the other theatre, he fills the house nightly. He is really a good actor, and the large houses are greatly pleased.

Tadpoles often fall during a tornado, and this was simply one of them. Two of the *Star* reporters were converted before the meetings closed. Glory to God!

The *Jackson Citizen*, the official paper of the city, and one of the leading newspapers in Michigan, by able editorials and reports of the meetings seemed to feel it an honor to use its extensive influence in every way to support the evangelist and the revival. This led to a sort of newspaper "war" which helped the work, and did honor to the *Citizen*. The following extracts from it give us something of an idea of the effect of the revival, even in the secular circles of the city,—

The revival services at the First M. E. Church, under the management of the young revivalist, Weber, are the talk of the city. While some have faith that God will use him for much good, others are wishing that he may be successful, and yet reserve their judgments. While some others have their fine sensibilities very much ruffled by the unusual manners of the man, others flatly denounce the service as wanting in common respect to the house of God.

Those who have faith that good will come of this effort *are mostly those who are devoted, earnest Christians*, that realize the necessity of the hour, and remember that God uses various methods and instrumentalities to bring about his purposes. Those who are afflicted by the style of the man, *are those who know but little of religion outside the forms and ceremonies of the church, rarely at prayer-meetings, seldom at class, never enthusiastic except at socials and entertainments*. And, strange to say, those who flatly denounce *are those who seldom enter a church, have little regard for religion, and have faith in nobody but themselves.*

Please note the sentences which we have italicised. They contain the secret of opposition to all genuine revivals.

In another issue, the *Citizen* said, —

The controversy going on in the minds of hundreds who have listened to the sermons of Rev. J. H. Weber, the evangelist, seems likely to be left to the city press for final settlement. The Christian churches believe that his mission is to do good, and the two thousand people who throng the Methodist church building every night to hear him, is pretty conclusive evidence that he is not repudiated by the citizens of Jackson.

While the newspaper duelling was going on, the tide of convicting and converting power was continually rising, and the attendance kept increasing, until hundreds would come and be unable to gain admittance. Did all the ministers of the city stand by the evangelist? We presume not; some did not by Jesus, nor Wesley, nor Finney. Very many people, regardless of creed, are drawn, as by magnetism, to the clear, crystal draughts of gospel truth, that are dispersed so freely in genuine revivals, and though offered from the tin cups of informality, they much prefer this to vainly sipping from the silver chalices of emptiness. They therefore naturally go where they can get and do the most good. So it is not strange that sometimes, as of old,—

> "Grave pastors, fearing their flock to lose,
> Prophesied to empty pews that
> Gourds would wither, and mushrooms die,
> And noisiest fountains soonest run dry."

This was true of, at least, one minister at Jackson, and has frequently been known to occur in the history of revival movements. No proselyting is allowed by Mr. Weber. All Christians are invited to co-operate, and his converts sometimes join different churches. He does a great deal of personal work, and proselyting preachers sometimes get terribly stung. In one town, the Presbyterian minister stood aloof from the meeting, but, like a hawk, would swoop down on any of the converts that he was anxious to have in his church. In one instance, as he was about to seize his would-be prey, he was met by this stinging rebuke, "You paid no attention to us before we were converted and we shall go with those who did." He flew back to his retreat a disappointed and we trust a wiser man.

Though the meetings of the first week were declared to be glorious ones, yet each week would surpass the former, until, under the head of "WONDERFUL CROWDS, WONDERFUL INTERESTS, WONDERFUL RESULTS," it was reported, " In the language of the pastor, it beggars description. He doubted if any church in Michigan or Detroit Conferences had ever seen such a day, — so full of tangible results. He did not think that any pastor had ever been permitted to administer the rites of baptism to so many people, all the result of one revival, as he had, during the morning service."

A special to the *Commercial Gazette*, headed, "EXTRAORDINARY RELIGIOUS REVIVAL — PHENOMENAL SUCCESS OF A YOUNG CINCINNATI EVANGELIST," declared the meetings " surpassed anything of the kind ever known in this section. The church, in its audience room and galleries has a seating capacity of over two thousand, which have nightly been crowded, while hundreds were turned away for want of even standing room, and even now the interest still increases, so that it has become necessary to throw open the lecture room and parlors of the church in the basement, which have been crowded as well, and thus two meetings were in progress at the same time. The records show nearly eight hundred conversions, over three hundred of which have already united with the First M. E. Church, and perhaps as many more at the different churches in the city."

A correspondent of the *Michigan Christian Advocate* wrote, —

Nothing in this city is so much talked of as the revival now in progress in our church. The Holy Spirit is doing His office work, and all over the city men and women are under powerful conviction. Those who once hated and reviled now sing glad anthems of praise unto Him who hath redeemed them. On Sunday evening our church was "packed," no other word will convey the idea. The city press places the number at two thousand five hundred. Bro. Weber preached from the text, "The great day of His wrath is come, and who shall be able to stand?" and for more than forty minutes, he held his audience before the judgment-seat of God, and many of the stoutest hearts "quaked and trembled." At one point in his sermon he spoke of the trump of God sounding, and he reached down and took the cornet from the hands of the cornet-player, and held it aloft, and his effect upon his audience brought to mind the incident in the life of Lorenzo Dow. "God is in His holy temple, and not unto us, but unto Him, be all the glory."

It was estimated that as high as from five hundred to one thousand persons went away, on a single evening, unable to gain admittance.

REVIVAL WAVE.

We copy the following important report from the *Lamp of Life*, Rev. J. S. Smart, editor, where it was published under the above caption, —

The following letter from Rev. John Graham, pastor of the first M. E. Church, Jackson, Mich., will be read with profound interest, and with thanksgiving and praise to God, for the wonderful works of his grace,—

JACKSON, Nov. 20, 1883.

DEAR BRO. SMART,— In respect to the revival now going on in our church, anything I might say will fall short of the reality. It goes beyond everything I have ever seen. We have been carrying forward service now into the eighth week, and since the third week the work has taken on the most solid type, spreading largely among young men, the middle aged, and reaching to some away up in the sixties. The conversions are clear, and, one thing remarkable, most of them are converted on once coming to the altar. Up to the present, there are reported eight hundred conversions. There are converted, nightly, from twenty to thirty. We have so far gathered into the First Church three hundred and fifty, and will, at least, get four hundred. Seven have just united with the Haven-street M. E. Church. The gain to Jackson Methodism, at present, by probation and by letter, will be over five hundred and fifty. Many old letters have been hunted up. A few have united with other churches, and many have been converted belonging to adjacent villages. The crowds are simply overpowering. The church is packed night after night. Then, some nights, we have an overflow meeting in the lecture room, that will be filled, holding about five hundred. The whole city and surrounding country are moved with a deep religious influence, and everywhere men and women are talking about the revival. Last Sunday was the most wonderful day I have ever seen. During the week, a baptismal service was announced, for Sunday morning. Every available seat in the audience room was filled. We gave an invitation to the candidates to come to the altar. It was first filled with parents, presenting their children, then by probationers, and for one hour and one-half I administered the rite of baptism. One hundred and forty-four were thus dedicated to God, one hundred and ten of whom were adults.

Mr Weber is a combination of eccentricity and force, is deeply in earnest, and works along the old lines of Methodism. He practises our altar service, and believes in people knowing they are saved. I have given you the main facts, without any attempt at finish whatever. Yours, J. Graham.

The closing service was a fitting climax to all that had gone before.

On the final night, persons were admitted only by tickets. The spiritual atmosphere, as compared with the first night, was changed as from January to June. The rainbow of promises fulfilled arched the spiritual sky. The songs of victory and praise rose from multitudes of happy hearts, and fifteen hundred came to bid the evangelist farewell. "He could not pronounce the benediction without giving one more opportunity to those who had so long resisted. The altar was filled, and eleven souls came out into the light."

Thus closed the labors of Mr. Weber in one of the greatest revivals of this or any age.

At Pentecost, there was at least one hundred and twenty evangelists baptized with the Holy Ghost, to aid in the meeting. Here there was only one. The Pentecost congregation was composed largely of devout Jews, who were walking in the light they had, and looking for the Messiah. The Jackson congregation was largely made up of slaves to Worldliness, Prejudice, and Vice. God was glorified in both. To Him be the praise! Amen.

Revival Incidents.

A LITTLE CHILD SHALL LEAD THEM.

Two little children went home and there begun shouting, praising God. The parents became alarmed about them, and the mother came to the meetings and was converted.

BREAD CAST UPON THE WATERS.

Here Mr. Weber met a man whose salvation he had sought years before, when they were laborers together in a shop. This man was converted, and said to the evangelist, "Many times I thought of the words you said to me at the shop."

"ZACHEUS, COME DOWN."

At the close of one service all who wished prayers were asked to rise. Among the number who arose was a person in the gallery. The pastor suggested to test them by asking them to come and kneel at the altar. She came from the gallery to the altar, "*and no more than knelt than God saved her.*" The gallery was nearly filled with young men. "When she arose," writes Dr. Reasner, "they broke out into a laugh. With a mighty energy, Mr. Weber leaped from the pulpit platform, ran down the aisle, and commanded them with a voice of authority, such as I have seldom heard, 'Stop, stop, in the name of God stop;' and then in burning words he denounced their irreverence and ungentlemanly conduct, until, like whipped children, they hushed into silence, and then to shame. Then with persuasive words, Mr. Weber excused them, saying, 'You did not mean to do wrong, did you, boys? Promise me you won't do so again.' To this they were only too glad to assent."

A WEBER COCKTAIL.

A young bar-tender was converted, but had promised to give the man a chance to get some one to take his place, and, being there the next day, a man heard of it, and when he came in, said, "Give me a Weber cocktail." *He was handed a glass of cold water.*

A STARLESS CROWN.

A woman had a dream that she went to heaven, and there she saw all her friends, with stars in their crowns, but she had none. This awakened her, and she was saved.

REDEEMING THE TIME.

Mr. Weber became greatly interested in a young man at the hotel where he boarded. He talked with him at the table and elsewhere about his business and his soul. He came to the meeting and was saved.

LIGHTNING.

"Oh, that the scales might balance for every one! What does it mean? It means to you, business men, thirty-six inches to the yard, two thousand pounds to the ton, and sixteen ounces to the pound. It means to the clerk, no 'knocking down.' If there is an ounce or nickle goes down, you are 'found wanting.' It means that, when you go away from home, you can come back and look your wife square in the face, and say you have not been in bad company."

PERMANENT RESULTS.

Dr. Reasner further testifies, in regard to the permanency of the work at Jackson, "I am not able to give the whole number who came into full membership, but this I know, that, now after more than five years, the effect of the work is very manifest, and some of the best workers in our church are those who were brought to Christ in those meetings."

ANNOYED BY THE TORNADO.

Most of the pastors of the place gave the meeting their tacit approval. One, however, was greatly annoyed, and said to his congregation, one morning, that he wished them to come out in the evening, and that he did not "think it necessary to stand upon his head to attract a congregation." Some of his best members were pained by the course he took. His congregation became greatly reduced, and before the year closed, he resigned. Moral: Don't fight revivals.

MUSCULAR RELIGION.

A man came into Mr. Weber's room, at the hotel, and wanted to fight him, because he had called attention to his wife, who was "cutting up" in church. The evangelist "put him out of his room."

One evening a woman was converted just as Mr. Weber was about to take his text, and shouted aloud in her new found joy.

"YE MUST BE BORN AGAIN."

In his sermon on the new birth, the evangelist said, "Some say, 'I do not understand this being born again. Don't you think people are educated to it?' Now, whenever I hear this, it reminds me of the story I have heard told of the Chinese emperor with the pig, who thought that the pig was dirty because always kept in an unclean place. He thought that, if kept in a clean place, it would be clean and nice like a little lamb, and so he called his wise men together, and they concluded to take a young pig, put him in a clean place and educate him. This was done, and they taught him many tricks, until at last they thought him all right and concluded to fix him up and take him out for a walk, which they did. Everything went all right until they came to a mud-puddle, when in went the pig. At this the emperor was wroth, and declared those in charge of him had not given him the proper education, and compelled them to be placed in dungeons, and others selected to continue the education of Mr. Pig. After a while, they took the pig out again. Many said, 'Why, he was tempted that time;' but by and by they came to another mud-puddle, and the pig was soon in again all over."

RUNNING OVER.

One of the tests of conversion which the people meet in genuine revivals, is liberality. At the close of this meeting, after all its expenses were met, there still remained three hundred dollars in the treasury.

Mr. Weber went from Jackson to Millersburgh, O., where over one hundred and forty professed conversion, and closed the year with another sweeping tornado at Fort Wayne, Ind., in which over four hundred professed to have found the Saviour. During the last two days of 1883, seventy were saved in his services, and between three thousand and four thousand during the year. Referring to God's blessing, he writes, "It is a great deal better than I deserve."

> "Praise God, from whom all blessings flow,
> Praise Him, all creatures here below,
> Praise Him above, ye heavenly host,
> Praise Father, Son and Holy Ghost."

CHAPTER IX.

TORNADOES, 1884-1885.

"BEGAN this year," writes the Evangelist, "as the previous one, on my knees in the house of God. My prayer was that this year might eclipse all others in soul-saving."

The general features of the following revivals have already been described in those that have gone before. The opposition of the devil and his agents, the diverse criticisms, the overflowing houses, the general agitation, the reconciliations, the restitutions, the prayer, personal work and fasting, intense enthusiasm, the clear conversions, the plain preaching, the thrilling songs, the tearful "farewell meetings," and other general features with some variety, as already mentioned, attend the revivals about to be noticed. Let the reader bear this in mind, not thinking that because not mentioned they did not exist.

At Fort Wayne, Ind., where the new year finds him, the spiritual temperature was like the atmospheric many days that month, away down below zero. Brother Weber had, in God's name, defied July heat and conquered, and now January ice must meet a similar fate.

Catholics claim about two-thirds of the population of

this city, and many of them were among the number converted.

"Impossible to have a great revival here," was the encouragement the Evangelist got from many, "which proves to us," he says, "that nothing is too hard for God."

The meeting lasted five weeks, and was one of the most successful of Mr. Weber's works.

Fort Wayne College shared largely in the results.

A Presbyterian elder, who had been a member of the church for twenty-five years, but never converted, under the Spirit's power, was brought to see his need of salvation, kneeled penitently at the altar, and was saved.

Another church member believed it impossible for one to know his sins forgiven. She firmly refused to go to the altar. So intense was her resistance that she thus became sick "fighting against God." At last she yielded; and, after meeting at a store the "witness of the Spirit," came and she exclaimed of her own accord, "I know I am saved!"

A young lady who had determined to enter a convent came to the altar, was saved, and is now a teacher in a Methodist Sunday-school.

Mr. Weber received a postal from a person who sarcastically "wanted him to go on the stage." He wrote him "that his Father had hired him for life."

As victory followed victory, Satan tried his old trick of defeating the Evangelist by spiritual inflation. Referring to this, he wrote: "The devil tries to get me puffed up, but God keeps me down. I triumph, because I let Jesus have his way."

THE GREAT REVIVAL AT BEREA. — FIVE HUNDRED CONVERSIONS.

Concerning this wonderful tornado, Rev. A. J. Lyon, who then was pastor, writes as follows, —

In the winter of 1884, the church at Berea, including the faculty of Baldwin University, united in inviting Rev. J. H. Weber to assist in holding a series of revival meetings, and promised hearty support in the work. The attendance from the first was large. While some were disposed to question the methods of Brother Weber, God owned him, and we were soon in the midst of a great awakening, — a revival of marvellous power, such as seldom comes in the history of any church.

The audiences soon increased to such an extent, and so eager were the people to hear, that the church would often be filled hours before the time of service. Excellent singing, done by home talent, was of great service. The preaching by Brother Weber was most earnest and stirring, holding attention and arousing the deepest religious interest with both saint and sinner.

While there was very little of wild excitement in any of the meetings, there often came upon the audience a wave of divine power and glory of indescribable effect. Sometimes during the preaching, then in the prayer, and then in the singing, a rapture of glory filled the house, and it seemed as though the angels came down in our midst to hear the shouts of new-born souls, witness the cries of the penitent, and join in the triumphs of the church. The altars were crowded from night to night, for nearly four weeks. And often a score or more would be converted at a single meeting. All classes were reached, young and old, including the mayor of the place, and many other excellent citizens. Sceptics scoffed, and many hardened sinners were saved; and some from other places were converted and went home rejoicing. About five hundred professed conversion. Over three hundred united with churches in Berea, and others united with churches in the vicinity.

The strengthened faith of the church, the effect of the manifest power of God on the whole community, the advance of public sentiment on all moral questions, these are some of the secondary results which came.

Brother Weber labored hard, kept himself close to God, and accomplished incalculable good. The whole community appreciated his labors, and joined heartily in compensation. Of those received on trial nearly all were taken into full membership. Over one hundred were baptized at one time, eighty of whom were adults.

As Berea was a very intelligent and moral town, the seat of two colleges, and the spiritual condition of the church much above the average, there was but little of the opposition, such as the Evangelist had met in towns of the baser sort.

From the beginning Mr. Weber predicted a "big time." He had "never met so many people who would take hold and work as here." A special day of fasting and prayer was held, and daily the tornado grew in intensity and power.

"The pastor had for months been laying the foundation of an extensive revival. For over three weeks there were from twenty to one hundred and twenty-five at the altar crying for mercy. There would be a banker or shop-keeper, here a student, there a Sunday-school scholar, there a mechanic, there a drunkard.

"The weather was unusually wet, but the surging crowds that would wend their way to hear the Gospel indicated that God was there to save the multitudes.

"The congregation was alive, workers beseeching their friends to come and be saved.

"Neighbors who had been at enmity with each other for years became friends, and old men said, 'We never saw it on this wise before. It must be God, for man could not do such a work.'

"Ministers from other charges came, caught the fire, and went home to spread it."

The College faculty worked very hard, Dr. Cuyler and Dr. Nast leading by their example.

Nearly all the unconverted students were saved.

It was thought that there would have been a thousand conversions, could the Evangelist have remained. Salvation was not confined to the sanctuary. Some were converted in Mr. Weber's room; one man, while he was in his shop, sawing meat. People came miles in the mud and the rain on purpose to be saved.

One night the altar and ten seats were filled with seekers.

A student was asked to come and seek Jesus, but refused by saying, " I am afraid I can't hold." Brother Weber said, " Maybe you will not have a long time to hold out." He came, and the third night was gloriously saved. In a few weeks after his conversion, he received a letter asking him to come to Dakota. He came to the pastor, sorrowful, and took his letter, and one day while out on the farm and seeing a black cloud coming he ran for shelter under a tree, but, while there, the lightnings did their awful work, and he was found a corpse. We know not what a day may bring forth!

A woman, with a disease which was pronounced incurable, was here healed in answer to prayer.

Death speedily claimed another convert, — a young lady, but in Jesus she trusted and entered eternity triumphant through his grace.

Brother Weber continued to be pressed with calls from many places, and now felt that he must hasten to other fields which already were " white with the harvest."

God has given marvellous victory in the past; he will

continue to keep his trust in him, feeling that, "Surely, O God, through the greatness of thy power shall thine enemies submit themselves unto thee."

His next place of labor was Niles, Mich., where he aided Rev. A. M. Gould in a blessed victory for God and souls. Great success, but many adversaries. When the church was full at this place they "closed the doors," and many were turned away. Insults were hurled at the Evangelist on the streets, and boys would come to his window and belch their rage. Two hundred and sixty-five gave their names as saved.

His next point of attack was Harrison, O., a town contaminated with saloons, distilleries, and a Campbellite church, whose pastor indignantly refused to pray when invited at the revival meetings. Why is it that the devil and Campbellites often seem to equal each other in their opposition to Holy-Ghost revivals?

About the time the meeting was to close, they invited forty ministers to come and help destroy what the Methodists had done. Like the Indian that tried to stop a train by throwing his lasso over the smoke-stack of the engine: the Indian was crushed, but the train moved on.

The pastor was Rev. J. L. Glasscock, a college chum of the Evangelist's. He says that "the church was at the lowest ebb," that the prayer and class meetings were increased many hundred per cent. in numbers and spirituality, and that the pastor's salary was increased one hundred per cent.

Mr. Weber's father and mother were present, on one occasion, at this meeting, and for the first time heard their son speak. "Lou, Ida, Laura, George, and Cliff," all members of his family, "came to the altar and were saved by the power of God."

Several pastors, including him who now is Bishop Joyce, came out one night to help, but the Evangelist records what is usually true on such occasions, that, "instead of helping us, it did us harm, as the people looked at them instead of looking to God."

At the close of this meeting he worked a few days at Madison, Ind. About fifty had professed conversion when he abruptly closed the meeting, because the church "would not hold up his hands or do as they promised."

His next place of labor was Springfield, O. Dr. J. W. Bushong was pastor, and, under his labors, there had been a large ingathering of souls only a short time before. But, not satisfied, he, with his official board, invited Mr. Weber, and claimed, through God, another great victory. Between two hundred and three hundred professed conversion.

During this meeting, a man, eighty-four years old, felt strongly impressed to come from Indiana to Springfield. He knew not what for, but the desire grew so strong that he came. He was prayed for and converted, and now he says, "he knows why he came," as God saved him.

A young man in an after meeting said, "He hated the Methodists, and would not go to the altar if it would save him." In less than half an hour he was there, and soon converted.

A murderer in jail was visited during the meeting, prayed with, and professed conversion. Truly Jesus came to "seek and to save the lost."

"NOT TO-NIGHT."— A FEARFUL WARNING!

A lady came to the meeting in the middle of the week, and was urged to yield at once and be saved. She said, "Not to-night."

The next Sabbath she was buried. She died wailing, without God, her "not to-night" having driven his Spirit away forever.

Closing this meeting, June 1, Mr. Weber improved the next six weeks in taking needed rest. He revisited the scenes of past revival victories, and a part of the time was with his people at Preston, O., where he was building a house for his parents. Here he writes, "I am having joyous times with my dear ones," and "I talk to the men around me about this Jesus."

His soul, however, soon gets anxious for the activities of his calling, and he writes, "Glad the time is coming when I will leave to begin work again."

The camp-meeting season has again come, and the Evangelist prepares to meet his engagements under the azure dome.

July 10 found him on the camp-ground at Clear Lake, Ia. The meeting continued until the 20th, and was said by the managers to have been the best camp-meeting ever held on the ground. Between two hundred and fifty and three hundred professed conversion. Bishop Foss had been advertised for Sunday, but in his absence Brother Weber preached in his stead, and "fairly outdid himself in this effort, and produced a powerful effect on the audience."

When spoken to about his soul, a wag said to Mr.

Weber, "I came to see the monkey show." The Evangelist replied, "Here's the monkey, and he will pray for you." The wag ran away as fast as his feet could carry him.

Our storm centre of cyclone power in those realms of manifold tornadoes passed from this meeting to another at Big Stone, Dak., where several nationalities mingled. The following entrance, made in his journal when here, speaks for itself.

"Bishop Foss came to-day. I had to preach before him to-night. How hard it was to do that. But the Lord did help me. I shrank so much, it seemed I could not, but God helped me." This was a new ground, but between fifty and seventy-five were saved.

CRYSTAL SPRINGS, MICH. — ONE HUNDRED SAVED IN A DAY.

Crystal Springs is one of Michigan's oldest and most honored camp-grounds.

Here Brother Weber had been engaged to labor from July 5 to 14.

How God set his seal upon his labors at this memorable meeting, may be seen by the following report of the services by Rev. I. Wilson, which was published in the *Michigan Christian Advocate*, —

The meeting was conducted by our faithful and worthy Presiding Elder, I. Taylor, assisted by the devoted and successful Evangelist Rev. J. H. Weber.

The labors of the Evangelist were highly appreciated and greatly blessed to the people. He had charge of the morning prayer-meetings, followed nearly all the sermons with powerful exhortations, and preached every evening. His prayers, exhortations, and sermons made a deep impression upon all present. At first some were disposed to criticise, but the tide of holy feeling rose so high, and the spiritual power accompanying his services was so evident, that all inclination to criticise was quickly swept away. Brother Weber's secret of success and power for good cannot be understood, nor his work fairly judged, by attending one service. . . . If at first you are not impressed, go again. Notice his intense enthusiasm. See how he flies through the congregation like an angel of love, urging sinners to flee from the wrath to come. Look how penitents press to the altar and cry for mercy. Hear the shout of redeemed souls, and you will be constrained to cry, "It is the Lord's doings and marvellous in our eyes." The Evangelist fearlessly lifts up his voice like a trumpet against all manner of sin. Lukewarm Christians and careless sinners receive their portion in due season. He tells the ungodly that unless they repent and believe on the Lord Jesus Christ, the wrath of God is upon them, and he will banish them to hell forever. He sings and shouts to the great congregation, "Ye must be born again," until scores of souls feel the words of the Lord Jesus penetrating their hearts, and they are led to weep and cry for mercy.

Sin, and salvation through Christ, hell and heaven, are realities to him. These fundamental doctrines he preaches in the demonstration and power of the Spirit, and hundreds are converted to God.

The glorious results of Crystal Springs camp-meeting this year demonstrate the above statements. Not less than two hundred and fifty souls justified or sanctified to God. . . . At every altar service each day there were from twenty-five to seventy-five seeking pardon or purity. Niles district received a mighty spiritual uplift. The central idea of Christianity and the central doctrine of Methodism, "holiness unto the Lord," was kept prominently before the church, and we had a real Pentecost. Brother Weber led the people along the line of victory, from the beginning. . . . Glory to God for the great work done at Crystal Springs in 1884.

A PENTECOSTAL SUNDAY.

The Evangelist had never before seen such a day as the Sabbath at this meeting. At least one hundred were saved that day. Was there not joy on earth! And in heaven!

Brother Weber went from Crystal Springs to aid

in a camp-meeting at De Witt, Ia., where converting grace and sanctifying power went hand in hand.

This meeting, like some passed and others to come, receives but passing mention, as full particulars are not in our possession.

His next appointment was Decatur (Ill.) camp-meeting. This was a remarkable meeting, two hundred and fifty professing pardon, and as many more entire sanctification.

That Mr. Weber can receive blows as well as give them is seen from the following allusion to the pulpit utterance of a prominent preacher: "He struck me very hard, but it will make me a better man."

Tuesday, September 2, finds Mr. Weber again with his loved ones at home. He had been there but a few days, however, when he wrote: "It seems I'm getting so restless that I do not know what to do, I must go out and work for Jesus. The fire burns in my bones!"

So we find him with fresh strength again bearing the Gospel message to the famishing multitudes. During the balance of the year, he held meetings in Michigan, at Muskegon, Buchanan, and St. Joseph, closing the year in the midst of a sweeping cyclone at Geneva, O. Hundreds were saved in these meetings.

The following, from the pen of Rev. G. L. Cole, pastor of the Methodist Episcopal Church at St. Joseph during the revival there, gives some idea of the nature of Brother Weber's work at that time.

Rev. J. H. Weber of Preston, O., visited St. Joseph in the fall of 1884. His coming was attended with precious results. Over two hundred gave their hearts to Jesus, nearly all of whom united with some branch of the Christian church. We opened our meetings under what seemed to be very unauspicious circumstances, being just on the eve of the presidential election, but God was with us in mighty power, and we soon forgot all temporal matters in view of the weightier interests of seeking and caring for lost souls. Brother Weber is a workman chosen of God. His methods are peculiar to himself, yet mighty through God to the pulling down of the strongholds of sin.

His work at St. Joseph was not confined to the immediate results, but reached out to months and even years to come. His visits at intervals during my three-years pastorate proved a benediction to the church and whole community. May the dear Lord detain him here for many years to proclaim the terrors of the law and the unsearchable riches of Christ.

The dying moments of the old year, and the flying ones of the new, found Mr. Weber, as usual, upon his knees. The keynote of the success of his past life has been prayer. He will seek no better for the future. The first day of the New Year closed with twenty souls converted, the first fruits of another abundant harvest. The Geneva tornado continued to sweep on until between three hundred and four hundred were saved. "Jesus is doing the work, it would be a queer work if I did," writes the Evangelist. Rev. H. Webb, now Presiding Elder of Steubenville District, East Ohio Conference, was pastor. Referring to this revival, he says, —

The revival reached nearly all classes and ages in the town. The young men were reached, and gathered into the church in great numbers. The work was generally regarded as thorough and genuine from first to last. Brother Weber having some peculiarities, both of address and methods, served on one hand to attract those who had not been church-goers, and on the other to rebuke sin, in all its types and forms, with such boldness and plainness that the people were moved and brought to decision. His kindly manner, mingled with intense earnestness, made his services attractive and aggressive. He was loyal to the Methodist Episcopal Church, and pleasant in all his relations to the pastor, assuming no responsibility without full, frank counsel. . . . I believe that fully the average number that were received on probation graduated into full membership. I cherish nothing but pleasant recollections of Brother Weber's labor among us. I believe the divine approval was unmistakably upon it. My knowledge of his labor elsewhere served only to increase my respect and esteem. I shall continue to pray that added years may be given him, and similar victories attend his labors.

From Geneva he turned a deaf ear to many other urgent invitations, and, led by God, entered upon another campaign of warfare and victory at Bedford, O. Romanism was one of Satan's most active agents of tornado opposition here, but the cyclone might of divine power defied opposition, and caused the truth to triumph. From there he went to Cleveland, where, laboring in the different churches, he improved the balance of the winter. While here he was seriously sick, which crippled his public work, but, notwithstanding, when possible he labored on, and many during the winter professed conversion. To God be the glory!

For some time the Evangelist had felt a drawing westward, and, in response to an official invitation May 5, we find him at Rock Rapids, Ia., when he writes: "I am looking for a most wonderful time. It will come as sure as light is light." He was not disappointed.

On his way to Rock Rapids he had been detained over Sunday. Unexpectedly he met an old friend on entering the church Sunday morning, who insisted that he should preach. He did so, and "God did the work," and twenty-seven seekers came to the altar, twenty-four saved. He was pressed to remain, but must hasten on to Rock Rapids. Here the tide rose until the mayor, several county officials, and many business men were converted. One employé, when seeking, said to his employer: "I want to be a Christian, and if I cannot sell machines without lying and misrepresenting your goods, I give you thirty days to get another man." "Go on, Handy," was the manly answer, "and we will give you more wages."

Another said: "I was determined not to be converted under Weber, but I had to come and I am glad."

Writing of this revival, March 26, 1889, about four years after it occurred, Mr. I. K. Thompson, a business man, who was converted in this revival, says of it: "It was a work of love, and the effects of it truly have been wonderful, and are as visible now after all these years as then; with one or two exceptions, all are living up to their profession."

He attributes Mr. Weber's great success to his "private life and upright walk before God and man." The farewell service here was as enthusiastic as any that had greeted him in his own State, "several hundred people with a band of music escorting him to the depot," where he took the train to *Sioux Falls*, his next place of labor. While here the converts from Rock Rapids chartered a car, and came over *en masse*, "marched from the public square to the church, singing. Went down after the meeting, singing, and held an outdoor meeting." A sore-headed editor, who had been struck by revival lightning, sarcastically criticised this act, but as many of the most influential citizens of the place were among the number, his words were like leaves before a gale. Brother Weber was compelled prematurely to leave this place to meet another engagement, but not until over fifty had professed conversion.

At Sibley, Ia., the engagement just mentioned, about one hundred and fifty claimed salvation, among whom was one who had "been the champion among infidels of the town," and thus God gave his servant another midsummer revival. While here he "celebrated" July "Fourth" by attending a camp-meeting at Spirit Lake, where he was invited to speak, and "forty-three came forward," "fifteen saved." "It was God, not Weber," writes the Evangelist. The camp-meeting season having rolled around again, Mr. Weber is at his post. Invited again, as on the year before, to Crystal Springs, he is compelled to leave the West, and after a short visit home hastens to fulfil his promise.

"Not less than one hundred and twenty-five were converted and reclaimed, and at least one hundred and fifty were cleansed from all unrighteousness," making the number converted and sanctified the two years that he was there, five hundred and twenty-five. So writes Rev. I. Wilson.

Brother Weber's next field of labor was the camp-ground at Wilton, Ia., where he "saw people moved on" as never before. And between one hundred and fifty and two hundred were saved.

Closing his camp-meeting engagements, he again

begins work in the churches August 24, when he labors for the balance of the year at Strongville, Cleveland, Royalton, O., and St. John's, Mich., where success crowns his efforts.

The following are some of the incidents which occurred during this time, —

Wrongs made right. — At Strongville a man sought salvation but to no avail until he had gone and paid for a suit of clothes he had stolen from a storekeeper, and confessed to another man wherein he had cheated him, and *refunded the money.*

Lost fifteen pounds of flesh. — Another man while under conviction lost fifteen pounds of flesh.

One man was converted who had said he "would cut his throat from ear to ear" before he would yield.

A number who accompanied Mr. Weber on his recreative hunting tours were saved.

While at Strongville Mr. Weber went over to Berea and was ordained deacon.

At Royalton a man sought in vain for a number of nights, but "no light came." He "forgave a man whom he hated" and all was well. Truly "*If we forgive not men their trespasses neither will our Heavenly Father forgive ours.*"

At St. John's a "well-dressed" woman, when Mr. Weber knelt to pray for her, slapped him in the face and also spat in his face. He prayed, "Jesus, forgive her." That night thirty were at the altar, and soon after this woman, "under the greatest conviction," writes Mr. Weber, "wanted me to come and have a talk."

Truly said Jesus, "There is no man that hath left home or brethren or sisters or father or mother or wife or children or lands for my sake and the Gospel's, but he shall receive an hundred fold now in this time, houses and brethren and sisters and mothers and children and lands *with persecutions;* and in the world to come, eternal life."

CHAPTER X.

OVER THE OCEAN.—1886.

The Evangelist had long felt that for God's glory and his own good he should cross the ocean and learn lessons from Oriental lands that would enable him to still more successfully accomplish the great work which God had given him to do. Especially was he desirous himself to travel in

> "Galilee, sweet Galilee,
> The place where Jesus loved to be."

Preliminary preparations having been perfected, January 16 finds him at New York City on board of the steamship *Aurania*, his native land receding from his sight, and new and longed-for scenes about to burst upon his vision.

"Going out," he writes, "we passed every boat we came in sight of. Saw one vessel sunken; it looked sad. Another on the ground, with several boats attached to pull it off. So in life we see people, some on a sand-bar, others sunken, others passing all."

As usual Mr. Weber had his eyes open and pen busy, and gathered much valuable material, which of itself would make a very attractive book. It is hoped he may some day see fit to prepare it for the public; here we can give but brief mention of some of the many points of interest.

At London, Britain's great metropolis, he tarried for a time both on his going and his homeward trip. Here he visited many places sacred in history, and others full of interest because of present worth. Among them were St. Paul's Cathedral and Westminster Abbey, each magnificent beyond expression and replete with tablets and statues of the good and great; the far-famed British Museum sparkling with wonders as the sky with stars; the nation's great granary of gold, the Bank of England; the services of Spurgeon and of Joseph Parker; the Salvation Army in this the great centre from which that mighty movement sprang, and where marvels of God's grace, in the shape of souls saved from the deepest depths of sin, outvie the wonders of the outer world collected in the Museum. Also the grave of Bunyan, the Bedford tinker, who became by God's grace the world's teacher, his college the common jail; and last but by no means least, City Roads Chapel, which was built by John Wesley, the Father of Methodism, the mightiest movement of his century. Here our traveller had the honor of STANDING IN WESLEY'S PULPIT.

After his visit to this church he wrote as follows, —

It is not as spacious as I thought it was, a gallery is seen on three sides with a high pulpit up about seven feet out from the tribunal. In this chapel the mighty Wesley stormed the gates of hell. With solemn awe I ascended the pulpit and stood where he stood so often. Then I passed around to the rear of the church, where I saw the tomb of this most godly man. I took off my hat as a sign of obedience to such a man of God. O Jesus, let my days be like his, full of love for the church and souls.

stood by the side of the graves of Adam Clarke and Joseph Benson, two mighty men of God, whose commentaries speak if they have passed into the heavens.

From London he passed to giddy Paris, which he also revisited on his return. Her fountains, her museums, her palaces, her works of art by the great masters, and many other points of interest made tarrying here a delight, and as France was the birthplace of his father her attractions had a double charm to him.

"It would take many books," he writes, "to describe what I saw at Versailles."

Among many things mentioned in his glowing description of the French capital he says, —

Here are fountains, forests, drives, walks, flower-beds, statuary, with many varieties of trees, giving it the appearance of a little Paradise. I never was so charmed with a place as Versailles Palace and its gardens; but much of its history is sad and some of it shocking, but this is the way of all earthly places.

Thank God, in the Paradise fashioned by the Great Master Hand of the worlds, no sorrow, no unhappy recollections can ever come. I am going to do my best to go there.

Our desire to follow Mr. Weber in his travels increases, and as we hear him say, "Wish so often that my friends were along; get very homesick at times," we take in our imagination the same journey. We pass from Paris to Turin, Bologna, Brindisi, and reach Corfu, Greece, February 13. Here we take passage for Cairo, Egypt, which we reach on the 11th. In the midst of a terrible sea-sickness on this part of the journey Mr. Weber writes: "When I was so sick I would say, 'I will praise Thee; bless the Lord, O my soul; and all that is within me, bless his holy name.'

stood it better than if I had complained." Would that others might try the same remedy. Passing by many of the sights that lure us in Egypt, — the land where the "great Jewish lawgiver" was born, where Joseph served and reigned, where Pharaoh fought with God and was conquered, and whither Joseph, Mary, and the Babe divine took refuge, where once a mighty empire and an advanced civilization held regal sway, and which now is covered with antiquities that attest the glories of the past, — we will pass at once to

THE GREAT EGYPTIAN PYRAMIDS.

Alluding to his visit here, Mr. Weber wrote as follows: —

When part of the way up my head would whirl when I would look down; and then the Arabs began to talk about bakshish and to buy some old coins, and I looked at them roughly and said, "Let us go on." On we went and rested three times in the ascent, which was very fatiguing. Then in exactly eighteen minutes we reached the summit, and I said, "Praise God." Was given some water, and put on my coat, as it was very cool. The sight was one long to be remembered. The delta could be seen for miles with its feeding herds and working fellahin; the waving palms, the sandy desert, the Sakkarah Pyramids, the flowing Nile, the moving ships, the minarets on the mosques, the palaces, the flat houses, the lazy, sleeping Sphynx, were all calculated to stir one to the very depths of his nature.

Leaving Cairo and vicinity, we now pass through a town where the children of Israel made brick, and behold the land of Goshen, now, as then, a beautiful country with green fields and waving palms. We finally reach Port Said, and for the sake of such a companion and for the sights to be seen we are willing to meet the mad fury of the Mediterranean, as spiteful now as when in other days it stranded Paul, and so take passage on the steamer *Mars* for the long-desired land of the nativity of Jesus. During this part of the journey a storm burst upon the pathway of our voyager, which he describes in the following words, —

> The winds were blowing furiously, the boat was dancing like a chip on a mill pond, and few were ready for breakfast. On the deck men and women were pacing to get an appetite, but by the blueness of their faces and the haggard look of their eyes one could soon discover that they were almost ready to land. The time wore heavily, the storm increased, the captain had a look of uneasiness, and soon we were told that it would be impossible to land at Jaffa, as it was very dangerous, many having found a watery grave here. Discouraged, with a desire to put our hands on our stomachs and make a home run, the deck was cleared and all passengers had returned to their state-rooms. The waves increased, the ship leaked, the angry waters were dashing against her side; when the elements were loosed a more terrific blast came, yet the dinner-bell sounded; but not one of the passengers responded. It seemed the ship could not live in such an angry sea. The angry waves beat more furiously, the ship rolled as never before, when suddenly a gust came and the boat lay over as if to rise no more, then back she came; and now a scene took place that shall never be forgotten by those on board. The dishes were breaking, the glasses going to pieces, the sailors running hither and thither, the passengers frightened, and avalanche after avalanche of water pouring into the cabin; there were hand-bags, valises, clothing floating in the cabin, and consternation written on every face. "The boat has sprung a leak!" says one. There is a man clinging to the sideboard, another being dashed against the side of the ship, some trying to make their way across the room to get something to cling to. These are some of the joys a traveller has abroad. All that night and the next day the storm raged. Had the boat gone down with me, I believe I would have been with Jesus. About noon we cast anchor in the Bay of Acre.

Having escaped the threatened shipwreck, Mr. Weber landed at Haifa, Palestine, February 25, from the back of an Arab, as the passengers had to be thus carried ashore because of the breakers.

Putting up at the hotel, Mr. Weber went from there to visit at Mt. Carmel. The following is from his pen:—

We first visited the reputed place of the "School of the Prophets." Found many inscriptions on the walls in Greek, Hebrew, Arabic, and Turkish. The room is eighteen by twenty and about ten feet high, with a place for an altar. It is cut out of the solid rock. This might have been the place where Elijah really was.

Describing the scene on the summit, he says,—

There lay the restless ocean many hundred feet beneath; across the bay lay Acre. Then I thought of Napoleon being defeated, then that city laid in ashes. There were the hills of Galilee, there again Little Herman; yonder the modern style houses built by an enterprising colony of Germans, the green olive trees, the beautiful flowers decking the hill with rich beauty over the mountain. As I thought of that tragic scene of Israel waiting to see the Prophet of God match the enemy, what feelings of awfulness poured their fire in my soul.

Returning to Jaffa by boat that night, the next morning with seven others in carriages he set out for the Holy City. Passing through Kirjath Jearim, with its "castle-like gardens and vine-clad hills," and also through the "valley of Ajalon" where "Joshua commanded the sun to stand still," after a ride of eleven and a half hours, he reached the city which in sacred annals is famed above all others, the city towards which both the Jew and the Christian feel drawn by an attraction which at times seems well nigh irresistible. The Evangelist had learned many a lesson from the Holy Book, had sat reverently under the teachings of the holy prophets and apostles, had been following in the footsteps of the Holy Son, and guided by the Holy Spirit, and now, in the Holy Land and the Holy City, he will learn new lessons, never to be forgotten.

The people at present who inhabit the city resort to tricks innumerable to deceive people, and make what they can out of them, but despite all this there is much to remind of sacred incidents and persons.

To copy all that Brother Weber said or has written about this city would make a book of itself; we can simply follow him to a few of the many points of interest. Let us go with him as he visits the "Tomb of David;" the room that is said to be the upper chamber where "the Holy Spirit came on the one hundred and twenty, and the next day, that most wonderful sermon of Peter's from which the world vibrates to-day; the reputed palace of Caiaphas, the place where Peter denied Jesus." Mr. Weber says, "The Catholics have every sacred place that can be thought of to deceive the people." At the church of the Holy Sepulchre nearly all the events which occurred when Jesus was crucified are pointed out.

AT THE GARDEN OF GETHSEMANE.

The location of the garden is known, and to the sacred spot this man of agonizing prayer naturally wends his way. Concerning this place of holiest memories, and his thoughts when there, he wrote, —

Took a walk on the east side of Moriah in the Kedron. As I strolled along how my mind went out as I looked at the Garden of Gethsemane, to that awful night of our Lord. How the flesh pleaded, if it were possible, that the bitter cup might pass, but his Father's will, not his own, then his betrayal and death for you and me.

Again, —

With my Bible in my hand, I made my way to the brow of Olivet, read there of the awful night with the place really before me, and got more light, and saw more meaning in the Word, than ever before. After prayer and meditation, I passed through a low gate in the Garden of Gethsemane, which is walled with high walls, kept by monks; they have planted flowers all through the garden. There are eight very old olive trees which may be the original trees, but the time Titus destroyed Jerusalem, 70 A. D., all the trees were cut down, and these may have sprung up from the roots, or even may have been but very little trees. They look very old. There is no doubt that Jesus prayed and agonized some place near here. I took off my boots and hat, was overcome, and had to weep. I knelt down by the roots of one of those old olive trees, and prayed that I might be with Him in His glory, and that my dear friends, and the converts who were converted and who should be, should meet over there in heaven's golden land.

Now he is beholding the "valley in which the shepherds kept watch over their flocks by night," where "a small chapel is built, called the home of the shepherds. Here it was that the angels proclaimed a Saviour come, and sounded the glad tidings which vibrate from pole to pole." The Evangelist has devoted his whole life to the proclaiming of the same glad message. What wonder that his heart dilates with new rapture on this hallowed spot. Now he enters the church of St. Helena, at Bethlehem, the oldest church in the world, and now he nears the very spot of which our mothers sang, —

> Soft and easy is thy cradle;
> Coarse and hard thy Saviour lay,
> While his birthplace was a stable,
> And his softest bed was hay.

And finally he reaches the very place that marks

THE BIRTHPLACE OF OUR SAVIOUR.

I thought, he writes, of the thousands and even millions who have worshipped at the birthplace or Jesus. The grotto showing where Jesus was born is common property of the Greeks, Latins, and Armenians. The Chapel of the Nativity is thirty-eight by eleven, on the east end is a semicircle apse, and under the altar is a silver star, and on it, in Latin is, "Here Jesus Christ was born of the Virgin Mary." Near the star are suspended sixteen silver lamps kept continually burning, and in the grotto thirty-one; on the west, cut in the south side a little lower down, is a marble manger, with lamps suspended. My soul here bowed with my body in reverence to the King of men, the Prince of life. As I knelt, and poured out my soul to Him who is and was and ever shall be, my feelings overcame me, and I prayed and reprayed that in His kingdom I might worship with the redeemed of earth, and sing the song of Moses and the Lamb. Kissed the star seven times, once for myself, and the other for my mother, and five of my most loving boys.

The boys mentioned are some of those whom he is helping to educate for God's great work.

The American Consul, Hon. S. Merrill, aided him in many ways, and thus he was enabled at great advantage to see the sights and to study the ways of the people.

We regret that we cannot tarry with him longer at "David's well" and Rachel's Tomb, "the site of which is known," at Jericho the scene of Joshua's mighty triumph, the Dead Sea, the Jordan, where John baptized and Jesus received the baptismal rite, where Elijah ascended to heaven in the chariot of fire, and Elisha wrought marvels, and at Golgotha and other places sacred beyond expression to Christian hearts.

No mills, no cars, no wagons even: Jerusalem lacked

nearly all the advantages that civilization brings.
This, doubtless, is a part of her doom for rejecting
Jesus. Not only is the mark of God's displeasure
seen in this and in the scattering of the Jewish nation,
but the further awfulness of the meaning of those
words uttered at our Saviour's crucifixion, " His blood
be on us and our children," is vividly pictured at

THE JEWS' WAILING-PLACE.

Concerning this sad scene Mr. Weber writes, —

There were over two hundred Jews at their wailing-place. Many of these were women. It is here they come and weep over their doom, and ask God to avenge them. Some of them were sincere, and the tears would flow very freely. Was very much touched myself. Came near weeping to see how sad they were. What a sad lot they have. If they had accepted Jesus how changed the world might have been.

What a striking commentary on the Scripture.
"Then shall they call upon me, and I will not answer, they shall seek me early, but they shall not find me."

Mr. Weber visited the Mosque of Omer and many other places of deep interest; he observed carefully the customs of the people, now nearly the same as in Jesus' day and earlier; he met Willie Rosenzweig, a " nice, pure Syrian boy," for whose salvation he was greatly burdened, who afterwards was saved, and whom he has brought to America and who is now being educated in the Ohio Wesleyan College, Delaware, O. He made valuable collections of views of important points, garments worn by the people, olive wood, and other relics of the sacred land; and then on March 17, with a company of seventeen persons, he left Jerusalem.

From the sacred city the company journeyed to Ramah, where Samuel was born, and, as they moved onward through the Holy Land, paused at Beroth, and took lunch at Bethel, where Jacob had the wonderful vision. Here Mr. Weber "took a stone for his pillow and lay down and prayed, but did not see any angels." Riding on amid the ruins that greet on every side, under the wise leadership of Bernard Heilpern, a man thoroughly posted on every Scripture site that is possible to point out, and who gives Scripture, book and verse, as proof of every place, the company tarry for lunch at "Jacob's Well," the site of which is certain, where prophets, apostles, and Christ himself had been. They behold Mount Ebal and Mount Gerizim and ascend the summit of Samaria, where is "pointed out the prison and the tomb of the Apostle John." While riding along the plains of Dothan a caravan of camels was coming over the plains in the same direction also that the Ishmaelites were proceeding when the brothers of Joseph, who were feeding their flocks on this plain, being jealous of Joseph, sold him to them and they carried him to Egypt. God was with Joseph, and he will be with us if true to him.

NAZARETH, THE HOME OF JESUS.

Passing Mount Gilboa and Jezreel and Nain, where Jesus raised the widow's son from death, at about 4.45 P.M., March 21, the company reached Nazareth, the city of Joseph and Mary, and which in his childhood, youth, and young manhood was the home of our adorable Lord.

Went to the Franciscan convent, writes Mr. Weber, where we were shown the place where the angel announced to Mary that a child should be born. A beautiful altar made of marble marks the spot where Mary was apprised of the fact that she was to become a mother. . . . Went on the hill back of the city and had the finest view of Palestine there is around here. We could see over the plains to the Jordan, and the deep cut through which the river runs, and the Moabite hills as a background, then the famous Gilboa with Jezreel at its base; Little Herman with Nain and Shunem at its feet; Tabor towering far above like a cap rounded, covered with trees, and a convent on the top; then the blue Galilee hills with Big Herman way up in the clouds covered with snow; then, as we come around the circle, the hills and valleys produce a most pleasing effect, and as we come around the dark Mediterranean with its shores lined with yellow-looking sand, then the Bay of Acre and the Carmelite range uniting with the Dothan hills circling on to meet on the other end near Jordan. A most wonderful panoramic view it was. It was here that Jesus lived for twenty-five years, and then at last the people rejected Him. The brow or ledge from which they wanted to throw Him is located about two miles from the city.

Next visited was Cana, where Jesus turned the water into wine, and then Tiberias, and then a ride upon the Sea of Galilee, where Jesus and the apostles oft resorted and to whose waves He commanded, "Peace, be still," and they obeyed Him. They camped near Bethsaida, the former home of John, James, Philip, Peter, and Andrew, and, before leaving the vicinity, Mr. Weber "went to the Lake of Galilee and took a bath, gathered some shells and flowers, and also fished, but, like the disciples, 'caught nothing.' Saw many fish, but they would not bite."

On March 23 the company turned their steps towards Damascus, the city of which it is said that "Mahomet loathed to leave it, as it was such a paradise." Passing the place where "Saul saw the light and heard the voice from heaven," on the 27th they reach this beautiful queen city of the East, spend here a number of days in profitable research, then pass on to Beyrout, where Mr. Weber takes a boat for Smyrna.

> Stopped at Cyprus, he writes, where we landed and had a fine time seeing the town and the church, in which was a festival. This church boasts as having the tomb of Lazarus, who, as the guide said, "died twice." This may be so, as we read that the Jews were planning to kill Lazarus after he was raised from the dead, so he might have fled here. When one stops to think of the ancient glory of many of these places and their desolation now, how different the book of God seems, as in it we read about the judgments pronounced against them.

He visited Smyrna, where once was one of the churches of Asia Minor, of which it was said, "Be thou faithful unto death and I will give thee a crown of life," and where Polycarp was bishop, and where, when burning at the stake and offered freedom if he would recant, he said, "Eighty and six years have I served the Lord Jesus; and he has never forsaken me; I will not forsake him." From here he paid a flying visit to Ephesus, in other days second only to Athens in the fine arts and in culture; now a heap of ruins. Here it is claimed that Homer and Crassus both were born, and Alexander the Great, Anthony, Cleopatra, Augustus, and Diocletian have been here. Here is "a reputed tomb of St. John," and here Paul preached the Gospel for two years; and it was here that he laid his hands on John's disciples and they received the Holy Ghost. Here too was the great heathen temple of Diana. "The once proud Ephesus," writes our traveller, "is like a heap, and the place where her temple stood is a place for the frogs to serenade the weary traveller who is fortunate enough on a hot day to walk around and be hurried at a breakneck speed by a guide who simply knew nothing but to get his bakshish." From Smyrna we follow our friend to Athens, where he revelled among antiquities too numerous to name, among them "the prison of Socrates, where he drank the deadly hemlock," and Mars Hill that had listened to the eloquent of the ages, where Paul preached his immortal sermon, his text, "To the unknown God." From Athens he went to Corinth, where Paul founded the church to which two of his epistles are addressed, and then by way of Venice and Florence on to Rome, where Paul and Peter both preached and died the death of martyrs. During this trip the "inspiration" came, and he wrote the song "To Save a Poor Sinner like Me," No. 109 in his song-book, "The Evangelist."

At Rome Mr. Weber met Bishop Fowler and family, whose society he highly prized. Here and in other cities of Italy he visited the many places which always attract the tourist, and then by way of Lucerne and Interlaken, Switzerland, and Strasburg, Germany, he passed on to Paris and from thence to London. At London he purchased a

VALUABLE STEREOPTICON

with which to illustrate the lectures he was preparing on his travels. These illustrated lectures the Evangelist sometimes gives in connection with his revival meetings to the great delight of large audiences. It would take volumes to describe what he saw in all the places of interest visited, but through these lectures and the magnificent views accompanying them a person is made to feel their reality almost as vividly as if there.

Having, aside from the precious impressions received at Palestine, visited the chief places of interest on the continent and caught the inspiration that comes from viewing the works of the master painters, sculptors, and architects of the ages, Mr. Weber, on June 12, took a passage on the steamer *Servia* from Liverpool to his native land.

On his travels he had often done personal work with souls which was to bear lasting fruit. He had also composed a number of the sweet hymns that the people in his meetings have learned so much to love.

On his homeward journey through his words a man was

SOUNDLY SAVED,

and gave evidence of his conversion by saying, " When I crossed before, when a storm would come, I would say, 'Oh, if the boat goes down!' Now I sleep and say, 'It's all right.'"

Carefully preparing the discourses on the Holy Land, which he feels that God is calling him to give, and breathing the prayer, " Jesus, bless them to thy glory," time speedily flies, and, borne swiftly homeward by giant steam, he soon is in the midst of joyous greetings from waiting loved ones.

He had received the assurance, before he went, of a safe and prosperous journey, and such it had been.

Soon we shall see him, qualified as never before, in the midst of new scenes of revival victory.

CHAPTER XI.

TORNADOES — 1886-7.

During the closing months of 1886, Brother Weber labored at Algona, Eagle Grove, and Correctionville, Ia.

In each of these places many professed conversion, and

> "Heaven came down his soul to greet,
> While glory crowned the mercy-seat."

"Living holier than in any other time" in his life, no wonder that he was able to speak to threatening waves of revival opposition, "Peace, be still," and command their quick obedience. "Living in the light of Beulah land" and "with soul overflowing at times," no marvel that God delighted anew to use him as a centre of revival tornado power in the towns of this western State.

At Algona he writes, "It seems as if many more sinners are moved by fear than love." A statement ever true of most impenitents, but which many seem slow to comprehend.

Here, referring to his own experience, he further writes: "The devil comes, but finds nothing in me," and gives God the glory for such an uttermost salvation.

Concerning the revival at Eagle Grove, Rev. C. B. Winter, who was pastor of the Eagle Grove church at the time of the revival there, writes as follows, —

> It gives me great pleasure to write of the series of meetings held by Rev. J. H. Weber at Eagle Grove, Ia., during my pastorate of the Methodist Church of that place. For five weeks Brother Weber preached nightly and held afternoon meetings; while there was considerable opposition at first, the spirit of God finally prevailed, and the entire town was moved. The meetings grew in interest and spiritual power until there were over one hundred and fifty reclaimed or converted. During these meetings it was impossible to accommodate all the people who came to attend them, and often, after the main audience-room and lecture-room were filled, scores of people were compelled to return to their homes because the building was crowded to its utmost capacity.
>
> The character of those who professed conversion, and the remarkable stability manifested by the majority of them after the meetings were over, was a subject of great interest to me, and proved to be different from the general impression in regard to the after effect of great revivals.
>
> All classes of people, old and young, learned and illiterate, some of those holding positions in the best of society and nearly all the professions of life, were reached on this occasion. During the year quite a number of the probationers moved West, but nearly all called for letters. And the great majority of those who remained were received into full relation at the close of their probationary period. Many of them to-day are among the most active workers of the church, and two of the young men, we learn, are making preparation for the ministry.

God's people never get beyond their Master, where they cannot be tempted; Mr. Weber was no exception. In the midst of a great revival victory he writes, "What temptations I had to-day! It seemed that Satan was bound I should yield. God gave me grace." Tempted, but triumphant. Praise God, all through Christ thus may conquer.

Amid "regular cyclones of glory" the days of the old year swept by, and its closing days found the Evangelist in the midst of a blessed revival at Correctionville, Ia. At its closing hour, as usual, he was upon his knees, in praise for mercies past and prayer for those to come. During these meetings Mr. Weber "met a man who cursed and swore" at him. He knelt down and prayed for him.

His attack of the doctrine of purgatory "stirred up" the Romanists greatly, until some feared they would use violence, but God took care of His servant.

When he asked one woman to be saved, she shook her head. "So God will shake His head at you," he said, and left her "pricked to the heart" by the message God had sent.

At Eagle Grove he finished the hymn, "Go work in my vineyard."

One woman said, "How he does swear," because he used the words hell and damnation as they are written in the Bible. She was afterwards at the altar.

If others would warn more, Evangelists would not need to so much.

He says, "I talked to a banker, and then I asked him to pray to his God. Then I knelt down and he said, 'I will pray Quaker fashion.' Then I prayed Methodist fashion."

Mr. Weber was told that a man was coming to a service to whip him. The next night the man came, but, instead of trying to whip him, gave him a dollar, and said, "I believe you are a good man."

At Correctionville he heard a man swearing in a blacksmith shop, and "got down and prayed for him."

Amid such scenes the work of rescuing the lost went on. Sometimes it seemed as if souls were suspended by a single strand over a bottomless abyss, and that the powers of heaven and hell, with all their might, contended for their possession. Within the man whose destiny was being determined, appetites and passions, prejudices and propensities, joined with the hosts of hell to accomplish his final ruin, while reason, judgment, and conscience all were on the side of God and his salvation. The Evangelist led the hosts of God to victory; and many were the songs and shouts of triumph that here arose and found an echo in courts above, during the closing weeks of 1886. To God be all the praise.

Prayer and praise go hand in hand in revival work, and should all through life. Joshua *praised* until the walls of Jericho fell, and Elijah *prayed* until rain fell. Mr. Weber does both, continually, in darkness or in light. They seem to be the wings with which he soars from one great victory to another.

Concerning the tornado at Correctionville, where he closed the year of 1886, and began that of 1887, the pastor, Rev. Bennett Mitchel, formerly Presiding Elder of the district, writes as follows: —

The meeting was a remarkable one. The entire community was greatly stirred. The house was packed from the first to the last service. The devil raged. Men got mad. Some wanted to whip him, others to tar and feather him. Others stood aghast with mute astonishment, while many came to the Lord and were saved.

For the first week his preaching was directed to the church, and he scored Christian people almost unmercifully. This was fun for the irreligious. They greatly rejoiced while he exposed hypocrisy and denounced the sins in the church. They thought they never had heard such a preacher. But he suddenly turned his attention to them, and routed them with canister and grape. Some of them were maddened, some slunk away in shame, while many were subdued and brought penitently to the foot of the Cross.

In the congregation, men would threaten to strike him, when he would calmly look them in the face, and say, "You dare not do it, I am in God's hands," and then put his arms around them and pray for them. Women would threaten to spit in his face, but he heeded it not, and persisted in pleading with and praying for them.

In dealing with the perversely wicked, he was awfully severe, but to the penitent he was as tender as the mother to her infant child.

We visited every family in the town, and he prayed in nearly every home.

In some of these visitations very ludicrous things occurred. In one the father raged, gesticulated, and threatened, but Brother Weber held his ground, and said to him, "Sit down, and be calm; the devil is in you, that's what's the matter." But the man became still more wild and threatening, until Brother Weber knelt down to pray, then he fled from the room, saying, "You sha'n't pray with me." But he prayed. Presently the man came back and said to him, "I did not want to hear you pray, but I was going to ask Elder Mitchel to pray." Then we knelt down again, and I prayed, and Brother Weber responded in hearty amens. The man was partially subdued, and, as we left him, Brother Weber shook him heartily by the hand, and urged him to become a Christian, assuring him that he loved him, and would continue to pray for him. . . . Brother Weber had a wonderful influence over the boys and girls. They were strangely and strongly drawn to him.

The following June he was with me at a camp-meeting, and preached a most remarkable sermon on the parable of the prodigal son, full of tenderness and pathetic appeals to the wanderers. The congregation was greatly moved, and prodigals returned to their Father's house.

The visits of this eccentric but earnest and devout man will long be remembered, with pleasure and profit, by the people of Correctionville. The grace of God was certainly upon and with him.

Mr. Weber is a wonderful man. . . . He makes the people laugh, cry, mourn, shout and rage, but the mad ones all get in good humor before he leaves them.

At Correctionville, as in many other places, the

revival continued with power after the Evangelist had gone to his next appointment, which was

FORT DODGE, IA.

The fifth night of the meeting, the altar invitation was given, and fifty came, — twenty of whom professed to find salvation.

The minions of darkness, as usual, concentrated their opposition; but God came in power, and the place never before was so "shaken up." Tidings kept coming of the work still moving on with might at Correctionville and Eagle Grove, and this discouraged the agents of the devil and inspired the church. The usual means were here used, and the cyclone continued to sweep on in sin-killing, soul-saving currents, until over three hundred had professed conversion. The following are extracts from Mr. Weber's journal, when at Fort Dodge: —

Went out and was met by two men, who were very mad, and they began their talk, and I looked at them and told them they were what I told them the night before in a sermon. They got madder, so I fell on my knees in the snow, and began to pray, and they sneaked off.

The people are very enthusiastic Methodists here.

I asked the Father in Jesus' name to change the cold weather to warmer, and it is.

Over fifty came to the altar. I asked God for fifty.

The devil tries me, but I cling to the Lord all the same.

Gave F. E., who was converted yesterday, $2.50, to help pay his board.

A man was swearing in the barber shop, while I was in the chair, so when I was through I knelt before him and prayed, and said, "That is the way I pray to my God." It moved him very much.

The Holy Ghost must move them or they cannot be moved.

A man slipped up to me and gave me a five-dollar gold piece. No matter if I give, I am always rewarded by God. Amen.

Stayed up till nearly half-past eleven with three young men, talking to them about their souls.

Jesus, keep me holy and pure and like Thee.

Preached to a full house on "Full Salvation." Very many said, "I want it." Holy Ghost, give it to them. Amen.

The town is wonderfully excited about this revival, and many are very mad about it, but we trust in God's power, and move on and on and on.

Having a grand time hunting out here to S——'s. The father, mother, and five children have been converted at my meetings. I always have some one converted when unconverted persons go with me out hunting.

Monday, January 31. There has been no decline in the interest, but it has kept up to the very last. There were about forty forward this eve.

Closing at this date here, he next opened up at

CLARION, IA.,

where he at once was greeted by a "packed house, and many under deep conviction." In regard to the particulars of this, we will let the Evangelist continue to speak for himself.

February 3. Went out visiting the business men, who were all glad to see us, and I feel we made a favorable impression.

February 8. A most wonderful time, sixty came forward, and among the number were several married men and women.

February 9. Sinners are terribly mad all over town; they were saying everything, and even chalked "Fifty dollars a week" all over the sidewalk. The harder sinners fight, the harder will we pray.

February 9. Time bears us all nearer to the judgment. Oh, when it comes, what scenes and what sights by some. Others, a day of eternal joy and blessedness.

February 11. Many are very mad, and swear they will not come again. Yet they do come, and will come. The great trouble is, the truth fits them too close.

February 20. There must have been thirty forward this eve. I get invitations to come and help at other places very often.

February 24. Had a great meeting in the afternoon and evening.

March 1. There is a dance here this evening. They have tried everything in their power to get the converts to go. God will send something on the propagators of this dance. Had a most wonderful closing service. Many at the altar.

Shortly after the house of one of the main projectors of the dance burned down. Surely God speaks by judgments as well as by mercies.

This revival continued to increase in interest and power, until one hundred and fifty professed conversion.

Commending the converts " to God and the word of his grace," he bade farewell to Clarion, and on March 6 began at

SPENCER, IA.,

where with Pastor Brown for over three weeks he labored faithfully, and, as usual, the preaching of the Word was not in vain.

While here he composed the beautiful song, "I Long for the Fulness of Blessing," and also "By and By."

SIOUX CITY.

The place of Haddock's brutal murder was the next scene of the Evangelist's intense activities. His work there was during the trial of the reputed murderers. Pastor Glass labored earnestly with the Evangelist, and despite all contending influences much good was done.

While here, Brother Weber completed and sent off a lot of music for his song-book, "The Evangelist," which he was preparing as an additional aid in his great work.

A COUNTRY TENT-MEETING. — ONE HUNDRED AND TWENTY SAVED.

From May 24 to June 24, Mr. Weber was engaged in aiding Pastor F. E. Drake in a summer tent-meeting at Piero. Though in the country, and in "too busy a time," it proved a revival of great power. At this place he writes: "I have given over three hundred dollars since I've been here."

Thus the Evangelist labors on, opposed by Satan and his subjects, misunderstood by those who otherwise would aid him, but everywhere leading souls to the Saviour, and forming friendships which are to be eternal. Like a war-horse anxious for the fray, he rushes from one battle quickly into another, counting almost as lost those days in which he sees no souls redeemed.

CHAPTER XII.

MICHIGAN TORNADO.

October, 1887, found Mr. Weber preparing for a soul-saving tour in California. He had received a cordial invitation from Bishop Fowler to labor there, with the promise that he would use his influence to open the way and to aid him in the work.

He bade farewell again to loved ones, and took the train for his trip to the land of gold.

God, however, had a different plan for him. How our Father's plans sometimes surprise us both in their nature and the suddenness of their unfoldings!

An urgent invitation led him to stop off over Sunday at Marcellus, Mich. A protracted meeting was in progress, and he was invited to preach. He did so. It was the beginning of a mighty revival cyclone in Southern Michigan, the influence of which is still felt, and will be upon the shores of eternity.

Its currents were so strong that the Evangelist could not break away from them. His visit to California was postponed. "The Spirit suffered him not" as yet to labor there, but opened to him a great and effectual door in the Peninsula State. The same methods which had hitherto been so abundantly blessed were used with undiminished success.

"For seven weeks," writes Pastor Prouty, "the meeting sparkled so continuously with interesting incidents, that it would seem like breaking the chain to narrate anything in particular."

Over two hundred were saved, and many are rejoicing to-day that Brother Weber came that way.

A correspondent who knows whereof he affirms, Brother S. Cromley, writes, —

> A year has passed, and we think as many have proved faithful as usual after a protracted effort. . . . Brother Weber bears acquaintance; at first he seemed to repel. He is peculiar, but can be trusted to manage his own affairs. Some become his enemies at first sight. The mass love and respect him. He is fearless in all he says and does, getting at the very inner life of all his hearers. Is not afraid to attack the great abomination, the liquor traffic.

His labors ended at Marcellus, where next? The "world is his parish," and many open doors invite. Which shall he enter? Providence points to

WHITE PIGEON.

Mrs. Sophia McGowan, a member of the White Pigeon church, paid a visit to Marcellus during the great revival, and, coming home, at once agitated the question of securing the services of Brother Weber in that place. Jesus has said, "If I send my sheep forth I will go before them." She found that he had gone before her, and soon the way was prepared, and a cordial invitation extended to the Evangelist to "come and help."

Concerning this wondrous work one of the leading members of the White Pigeon Church, Prof. J. G. Plowman, writes as follows, —

On Dec. 11, 1887, Brother Weber began meetings at White Pigeon, Mich. The church membership was small but remarkably united and ready to support and uphold the leader in all his measures for reviving the spiritual power of the church, and securing the conversion of sinners.

The church was filled to overflowing night and day. It was no uncommon thing, too, for members to come ten or twelve miles, only to find the house crowded, and many others who, like themselves, were unable to gain admission. For seven weeks the meetings continued with interest unabated. The country for miles around was stirred as never before, and the question "What shall I do to be saved?" seemed to be agitating the people everywhere. The Spirit of God was manifested in mighty power. Not a single invitation to the altar was given without a response, sometimes fifteen or twenty seekers being forward at once. Two hundred professed conversion, of which one hundred united with the Methodist Episcopal Church. Nearly all of these are now good and faithful members. The church was more than doubled in membership and greatly strengthened in its spiritual power. The effects of Brother Weber's meetings among us are permanent and abiding, and the influence of this series of meetings, on the church and on the community, will go on widening we trust, to all eternity.

Sister McGowan, one of the elect mothers in Israel, at whose house Brother Weber made his home while at White Pigeon, and who has labored in a number of his meetings, says,—

There never was known in southern Michigan such a revival. For seven weeks he held the fort amid threats and slander. Men, women and children came to the Lord Jesus and were saved. Brother Weber brings a blessing wherever he goes. He is pure-hearted and kind, gives his money like water to those that are in need, as those who know him can testify. I have been in his meetings six months altogether, and have seen over thirteen hundred conversions. Some have asked me, "Where is the secret of his success?" I can tell you, *he is on his knees for hours* pleading with our Father, in the name of Jesus, to send the Holy Ghost to convict of sin, of righteousness and judgment.

I have seen him in the greatest agony for souls, and *he would not give up until he received an answer.*

Thus like Jacob he wrestled with God and like Jacob prevailed, and many in White Pigeon rise up and call him blessed.

Oh, may men who thus will stand between an angry God and angry people until their own souls "feel the shock of their dread warfare" continue to multiply until the glorious Gospel is proclaimed to every creature.

Genuine revivals spread like a fire in a pine forest, where the sparks fly from tree to tree.

From Marcellus the sparks flew to White Pigeon until that was ablaze, and from White Pigeon it spread to

BRONSON,

the next point where the Evangelist claimed revival victory. Rev. L. S. Matthews was pastor.

Scenes similar to those described in other places, yet varied by many local incidents, here occurred. One hundred and fifty-six professed conversion.

A great work, as usual, was wrought among the young people. Their bondage to the card-table, rink, opera, and kindred sinful amusements was broken, and the service of God's house was substituted instead. "Congregations more than doubled," "attendance to prayer and class-meetings increased threefold," and one year afterward it was said that only "five or six had gone back," the rest had "continued in the faith." Brother C. H. Compton says, —

The effect of Brother Weber's singing and songs was one of the marked features of his work here. His song "My Mother's Hands," as rendered by him here, seemed to open the fountain of tears in the audience, and more than half could be seen weeping whenever he would sing it. Although the dear brother has been absent from us months, yet we are singing his beautiful songs still, and our young people never tire of them. His lectures on the Holy Land were listened to by large audiences with deep interest.

The pleadings, the prayers, the hand-to-hand conflicts with the enemy, the tears of penitence and of joy, the songs of triumph and shouts of praise, all are marked on memory's pages to be read across the river.

The closing service was described as follows by Presiding Elder N. L. Bray, —

Yesterday was the most remarkable day in the history of the Methodist Church in this place. It was the occasion of our quarterly meeting, and also the closing exercises of a most extensive revival under the direction of Evangelist J. H. Weber. Over one hundred testimonies were given in the love feast in thirty minutes, and one hundred and forty partook of the Lord's supper at the close of the sermon. Following the sacrament, the door of the church was opened and twenty-two probationers were added to a list of fifty-six, making in all seventy-eight. Handshaking followed. In the afternoon a most impressive meeting for the promotion of Christian holiness was conducted by Brother Weber. The evening meeting can never be described. Scores of sinners were led to a decision in the interest of their souls. The probation list reached the number of ninety-five, with many yet to enter the fold. Pastor Matthews and his faithful flock are happy. Brother Weber is rejoicing in the conversion of about four hundred souls in two meetings on Coldwater district, and will commence his third meeting at Coldwater City on Wednesday of this week.

What if the three revivals mentioned should prove to be but the prelude to still greater victories? It may be that they will. It would be in keeping both with the character of the Evangelist and *the promises of God*. We will see.

THE COLDWATER REVIVAL — NEARLY ONE THOUSAND CONVERSIONS IN THREE YEARS.

Coldwater, one of the finest cities in southern Michigan, is the county seat of Branch County. Here is one of the most flourishing Methodist societies in the State. It is the head of Coldwater District and the home of the presiding elder, N. L. Bray, who was instrumental chiefly in retaining Brother Weber on the district, and to whose support much of his success was due. The pastor, Rev. W. A. Hausberger, was serving the second year, and had won the hearts of the people.

The year preceding Brother Weber's coming had been a year of great spiritual blessing, about two hundred and fifty professing conversion, and quite a large number also the December prior to his coming. His success in the fields mentioned and elsewhere led the Coldwater Official Board to extend to him the invitation to labor in their midst. The Spirit said, "Go," and as usual he was prompt to obey. Many thought that because the field had been so thoroughly gleaned in the revivals preceding a great revival could not be expected. The church Mr. Weber declared to be in the best spiritual condition of any he ever labored with. Having from the beginning the support of pastor, presiding elder, and official board, as at Berea, O., the Evangelist did not meet the opposition that sometimes appears in places of less piety. Almost immediately the work began and increased in interest and power to the end. There were times when a solemn awe hung over the city like the hush between the lightning flash and the thunder's crash. Waves of convicting power were followed by those of converting grace until scores had yielded to be saved. As is his custom, the Evangelist visited the shops and the factories and prayed with the workmen. He called at the cart factory three times. One of the employés says "that when he prayed it brought conviction to every man in the room, and when he arose many were in tears and soon were at the altar seeking mercy." In the midst of the meeting Pastor Hunsberger penned the following report to the *Michigan Advocate:* —

We are having the greatest revival that ever swept over the city, considering the brief time we have been engaged in meetings. Last year we were blessed with one hundred and ninety-seven additions to our church, as the result of special services, nearly every one of whom is faithful to-day, but, judging from present indications, we shall be blessed by nearly or quite double that number of accessions, through the present meeting. Rev. J. H. Weber is surely a man commissioned of God to do the work of an evangelist. He came to us but three weeks and a half ago, yet over two hundred and fifty souls have already professed conversion and scores of others are earnestly seeking Christ. The meetings seem only nicely begun. They are increasing in interest and out-reaching power from night to night. Yesterday (Sunday) was the greatest day ever known in the history of our church in this city. It was a day of weeping for joy and hallelujah shouts. No less than one hundred and thirty-three were received on probation and thirteen by letter. As fine a class of converts as I ever saw, made up of age and youth from the business, professional, and other walks of life. This raises our present membership up to seven hundred and fifty in all. Next Sabbath and the following Sabbath we expect to receive many more. Let all pray for Coldwater and especially for Brother Weber, who is so grandly and successfully leading God's people forward to victory.

A noted infidel came to the meetings, got under conviction, and was saved. A lawyer and his wife were both converted and are happy Christians to-day. The Y. M. C. A. and the other churches received many members from the fruit of the revival. At a meeting held especially for men one of them became so happy that he threw his book in the air and shouted aloud. The Evangelist, pastor, and others held meetings at the factory at the noonday hour. In this and kindred ways the lion was bearded in his den and victory achieved.

For three consecutive Sundays there were forty converted each day. The following from a correspondent to a Detroit paper speaks for itself : —

An incident which occurred at Coldwater on Thursday showed what a big heart has Weber the Evangelist. While at the depot, waiting for the train on which he was to leave the city, he noticed the City Marshal with a prisoner shackled to him. Inquiring into the matter, he found that the fellow was bound to Ionia for ninety days for striking a man. Weber had had some talk with him at the meetings before the trial, and had not heard of the result. He inquired the amount of the fine in default of which the prisoner was going to Ionia, found it was twenty dollars, put his hand down into his pocket, the fine was paid, and the man went free. Strong men wept at the affecting scene.

While laboring here Brother Weber was royally entertained at Brother R. G. Chandler's. Mrs. Chandler was present at the Board meeting when Mr. Weber was invited, and it is said that a proposition which she there made had much to do with his coming. It was here that her remarkable healing narrated elsewhere, in answer to Brother Weber's prayer, occurred. This became one of Brother Weber's "homes," and Brother Chandler and wife, by their presence at Quincy, Hillsdale, Adrian, and other places where he afterwards labored, did much to help in the work.

Time would fail to tell of all the incidents occurring.

The souls converted through the influence of his songs alone, only eternity can number. The work rolled on until over three hundred and fifty had professed conversion, a large proportion of which Pastor Hunsberger has received into full membership. He says, —

> The effect of the revival was to deepen the piety of the members, enlarge our congregations on the Sabbath, and increase the interest in and attendance upon the prayer services of the church. Indeed, the work was so deep, searching, and awakening that souls have been coming into the kingdom almost constantly since our brother was here, nearly four hundred being converted during the winter of the present year, two hundred and eighty of whom have united with the church, the largest revival in the history of the church. Some of the conversions were most remarkable, and Coldwater, because of these, will have reason to thank God throughout all eternity. It may be truthfully said that Brother Weber's coming to our city left an already prosperous church in a far more prosperous condition than ever, numerically, financially, socially, morally, and spiritually. He is, we feel, a heaven-commissioned minister of God.

The following incidents, mentioned by Presiding Elder Bray, illustrate some of Mr. Weber's peculiarities, and the last statement shows in what high esteem he is held by this evangelical sub-bishop, on whose district he has labored for nearly a year: —

> I once saw him walk from the pulpit to a pew, sit down on a gentleman's knee, and relate a conversation he once had with a roommate in college, while sitting on his room-mate's knee.
>
> I have often known him to buy dresses and other necessaries for poor and needy children, and many young men have taken or are taking a course in college through his generosity.
>
> On one occasion, he said to me, "*I will have success! I'll wear the knees of my pants out and tear a hole through heaven. God must come to me.*"
>
> "The kingdom of heaven suffereth violence, and the violent take it by force."

I saw him talk to a mother and daughter, at our camp-meeting, at which time the daughter slapped his face; he then turned the other cheek, and still continued to labor with them, until both mother and daughter went to the altar.

His singing has very much to do with his success. The songs fit the man and the man fits the songs, and wherever he sings them they are a marvellous power for good.

His lectures and illustrations on the Holy Land are very interesting and profitable. After paying him fifty dollars per week, there was money left in the treasury at every point.

I endorse Brother Weber, and would be glad to guarantee him the amount he demands in compensation for his labors all the time I may be on the district as its Presiding Elder.

The condition of the district when he first came, was at most points that of formality and death. About fifteen hundred have been converted during the two seasons of his labor with us, and my opinion is that his work had much to do with the great revival wave on the district during the past winter, through which two thousand have been saved.

We append the following testimony, as illustrating the convicting and converting power of the Spirit under Brother Weber's work. It is a letter written by a man who was converted in the Coldwater meeting. He wrote it in response to the question, "What led to your conversion?"

I can tell you what kept me out of the kingdom for many years, and I think the prayers of dear ones, now in the glory land, had much to do with my conversion.

I was brought up by praying parents. At the age of twenty-one I married a beautiful wife. Six months later I left her, for the gold fields of California. I there formed a partnership with a man, and we succeeded in making money, and my prospects were fair as I could wish. In 1854 I received a letter saying wife had the consumption, and if I ever saw her I must come home. I converted all I had into money, and was ready to start, when this partner took my money and left.

I found myself thousands of miles from a sick wife and not one dollar in the world. I followed this man many days over mountains and valleys towards the coast, till I fainted by a wayside inn. Two days later I came to myself, being nursed and cared for by these strangers.

In that room alone I bowed on my knees and took an awful oath to kill this man at sight. That oath was the one sin whereby I came near losing my soul. For often through all those years the Spirit came through the prayers of dear ones, and I felt that I could give up all but that one wicked oath.

Last spring I attended Brother Weber's revival services without any feeling, until the absence of all feeling frightened me. On the first Sabbath morning in April, while going into church, something said to me so plainly that I thought others heard it, "*If you refuse God your heart to-day, you will never be saved.*"

In thirty minutes I was broken down nearly a maniac. I was mad at myself, and nearly every one I saw, and left the morning service swearing I would never go back. Between the morning and evening service I walked many miles, trying to brace up, but grew more broken and weak every hour.

Evening found me in church. I never knew how, but at the first opportunity I started for the altar, saying, "*I must be honest.*" When on my knees the struggle commenced, for I surely felt like one enclosed in a great bell that shut out all light and all air, and was being drummed on by grinning imps from the infernal regions.

I then said to the Lord, I forgive my old partner, as I pray for forgiveness, and, wherever he roams, on the green old earth, I will pray for him! Then the burden seemed rolled away, and while I am not always on the mountain or in the sunshine, I am always in sight of the cross of Christ, and I praise God to-day that the blood is sufficient for the worst of sinners.

R. A. I.

Hundreds through eternity will thank God for the Coldwater Revival.

What if pastor and people, as is frequently the case, had settled down content with the first hundred conversions?

What if Brother Weber had said, "I cannot succeed there, because there has been so great a work done already"?

Oh, how often Satan cheats the church out of what might be great victories, because of her lack of faith in God and the agencies he has ordained for the salvation of the people.

May the success which God gave his servants on this victorious battle-field inspire to hundreds of similar triumphs until the world shall be redeemed from the power of the enemy, and Zion become a "praise in the earth."

CHAPTER XIII.

MICHIGAN TORNADOES CONTINUED.

Did you ever pass from a parlor adorned with beautiful paintings, fragrant with delicious odors, fanned by balmy breezes, and flooded with radiant light, into a dark, cold ice-house? If so, then you have some idea of the difference between the church which Bro. Weber left at Coldwater and the religious condition of

LESLIE,

the next place where the Lord led him to labor. The spirituality at this place was so low that for years the church had been back on their dues to pastors and on the benevolences of the church, and some of the leading members would attend picnics where dancing was advertised as a part of the programme of the day! It was considered one of the most hopeless fields on Albion District.

Believing " that all things are possible to God" and to " him that believeth," the evangelist accepted the invitation to work in this seemingly barren field, and at the close of the Coldwater revival began work here, with his usual assurance of victory. In a few days the ice melted, the darkness fled, and there was a general breaking down before God, followed by the "lifting up" which Jesus has promised to all those who humble themselves before Him. Nearly one hundred and fifty professed conversion, when, right in the midst of the revival, Mr. Weber's health failed and he was obliged to give it up. There are times when God has a course of discipline which He wishes to give His children in the school of sickness and of suffering; until that end is accomplished it is impossible to exercise faith for physical healing. It seems as if Bro. Weber at this time reached this point in his experience. When the lesson is learned, it will be as easy to believe for health and strength as for any other blessing.

At Leslie, the pastor, Brother J. Webster, had done what he could to prepare the way for the revival, and he writes that since then the "church has been improving right along." Sickness was unable to hold the evangelist long from his God-given work, and June 22, 1888, found him, with all his wonted zeal and energy, beginning, under God, another great work at

QUINCY,

Rev. E. L. Kellogg, pastor. This meeting was held in one of the tents of the Michigan State Revival Band, which Coldwater District had leased for the season. The tent was quickly filled to overflowing, and after a short but severe struggle, the powers of darkness gave way, and the revival tide continued to rise until, notwithstanding the heat, haying, and harvesting, the multitudes came for miles, and the meeting proved *one of the greatest midsummer revivals ever known in Michigan.* Two hundred professed conversion, most of whom united with the churches. "Many of the converts," writes Pastor Kellogg, nearly one year after the revival, "are making a very fine growth."

At the beginning of the meeting very many were greatly enraged because of the plain sermon Mr. Weber preached on "the sins of the flesh." Much house-to-house work was done by the pastor and the evangelist.

One of the boys converted in this meeting is being educated by Mr. Weber for the ministry. "Whole families" were among the saved. The roughs undertook to run the meeting and do as they pleased. When they refused, at the evangelist's request, to leave the ground, he put them out.

All classes were among the converted: business men, farmers, mechanics, factory employees, with the engineer and one of the foremen. "A drayman who could not utter half a dozen words without swearing got under such conviction that he could not sleep; so they sent for the pastor and he was saved. He had said he never would come to the meetings; but he came, of course, and is now one of the most earnest workers in the church." Such convictions and conversions attest the depth and genuineness of the work. May this grand midsummer victory inspire others to plan for a similar work, until such revivals shall become the rule instead of the exception.

While at Quincy Bro. Weber made his home with Bro. and Sister F. Barber. The following from them will be of interest as it gives a view of the inside life of the evangelist and of some of the secrets of his success as a soul-winner, —

Bro. Weber came to our house June 22, 1888, and was with us six weeks. Words cannot express what those weeks were to us. We shall ever think of them as among the most happy and useful of our lives. The advice and counsel he gave us we shall never forget. We have read the biographies of many devoted men and those we thought lived near to God, but it has never been our pleasure to form the acquaintance of one we believe lives as near God as Brother Weber. He trusts his Heavenly Father as a child would an earthly parent. He looks to God for everything, both great and small, not doubting but God will give him everything it is good for him to have, praising Him for everything, both good and bad. His time, when not calling with Brother Kellogg, was spent mostly in prayer and reading his Bible; spending hours at a time in his own room, praying. He would be so burdened for souls at times that he would scarcely eat or sleep. When at the table, eating and talking about the meetings, looking up to heaven, he would say, "Oh Father, in Jesus' name, send the Holy Ghost to the people." In other words, he would be praying while eating. When everything would look dark and we would begin to doubt, his faith was as strong as ever. He would say, "It's coming; I *know* it's coming," and then praise God for what He was going to do for us. He never attended evening service without an hour of prayer before going for God's blessing on the meeting. He would let nothing hinder him from his hour with God. We remember once, when friends from Coldwater, whom he was delighted to see, came only a few moments before his hour for prayer. He talked with them a few moments, then excused himself and went to his room. If one of us was sick he would pray for the Lord to heal immediately, and we believe that his prayer was answered then. He was always patient, loving, and happy, yet always ready to reprove sin in every form in anyone. The children love him dearly, and always pray for him. The other day Emma came to the house, crying as though her heart would break, because some child had said bad things about Brother Weber. We do not believe that any one could know him as well as we do without loving him. Those who know him best love him most. The people who were converted when he was here think there is not another man on earth like him. A great many sinners, some who were his enemies, say now that they cannot help but like him. We shall always thank God that He sent him here.

Oh, may the spirit of prayer here mentioned come upon God's workers until thousands like Mr. Weber shall, in Jesus' name, be able "to move the arm that moves the world."

From Quincy, Bro. Weber went with the tent to Nottawa, where God gave another blessed victory.

The time for the

COLDWATER DISTRICT CAMP-MEETING

has now come, and arrangements having been made, he now begins again his labors in the tented grove. We are indebted to the Rev. Thomas Nicholson for the following sketch of this gracious meeting,—

Bro. Weber led in the services at the Peninsula Grove Camp-meeting in 1888. This is the Coldwater District Camp-ground. It was the first year that an evangelist had been engaged. Formerly, the meetings had been conducted by the preachers of the District, under the direction of the presiding elder. The attendance this year, as shown by the gate receipts, was almost double that of the former year. The meeting was one of great power. Over sixty were savingly converted to God, while many entered into a higher life. Preachers and people alike were greatly blessed. Many went home to their respective charges to do better work for God than they had ever done before. One man was converted in the Union City meeting four months afterward, who testified that he had become convicted at the camp-meeting, and had no rest of soul until he found it in God at the altar of the church. The genuineness of this man's conversion was shown in the following: a week after his conversion, he went some distance from home to visit friends. One of these was a man of influence in the community, not morally a very bad man, but without God. As soon as he met him, our converted brother frankly said, "Well, Ed, I have got religion, and I wanted to tell you about it. It makes me happy. I believe I have done the best act of my life." "Got religion!" cried the other in astonishment, "*You* got religion!" "Yes," replied he; "Weber has been over to Union City, and I have given my heart to God under his labors, and I wish you would get religion too." No reply was made, but the man walked off visibly affected. On the camp-ground one man undertook to thrash Bro. Weber, and following him around the tent, did nothing but belch forth his profanity. He went away and tried to get a warrant for his (Weber's) arrest, but the justice showed him the foolishness of the action, and he desisted, only swearing that some time he would pound him. A few nights later, he yielded to the convictions of the Holy Spirit, gave his heart to

God, and sought out Bro. Weber's address. He then wrote to him, confessing his wickedness and imploring his forgiveness. Another old backslider, it is said, became so enraged at some of Bro. Weber's home thrusts, that he packed his tent and left for home. His family refused to go with him, so he went alone. While at home he became sin-sick. In the night he became so troubled that he thought he was at the point of death. He implored mercy, and promised God that he would go back and make his confession and serve Him better in the future. He came to the ground, only to find that the evangelist had gone that noon, so he told his friends how the Lord had followed him and he is to-day a living Christian. Many instances might be given to show the power of this work, and the peculiar freaks of sin, as developed under the labors of this servant of God.

Up to this time the evangelist's labors have been confined to the West. Will the gospel preached by him prove as mighty in the midst of the staid conservatism of New England as in the growing West? Read and see. Pastor W. A. Wood, with whom he had labored so successfully at Strongville, O., in '85, had removed East, and was now pastor at

EAST ROCHESTER, N. H.,

at which place he had arranged for Bro. Weber to come and conduct a revival meeting. He went at the close of the Coldwater Camp-meeting. His work there can best be described in the words of Pastor Wood,—

On the seventh of September, 1888, while serving as pastor at East Rochester, the Rev. J. H. Weber came to me again in his office as evangelist. The people with whom he was to come in contact were typical inhabitants of New England, conservative in the extreme, cool, always suspicious of change and disposed to walk in the good old ways.

We had just finished building a new church, and the first thing to be done was to raise the money to pay for it. In this work Bro. Weber rendered most efficient service, as he always does. We dedicated the church free of debt. This done, we went in for victory along purely spiritual lines. The same direct, pointed, pungent, searching, Holy Ghost preaching, that had swayed, like a tempest, his great audiences in the West, pricked the heart of sinners here in the East, alarmed the conscience and led all classes to cry out, " What shall we do to be saved ?" God's radical gospel in the hands of this radical servant had the same effect upon the conservative East that it had had upon the stirring West. Many were powerfully convicted of sin, converted to God and born into the kingdom. The most thoughtful persons in the community were clearly and consciously saved. There was one noticeable feature here which had not before come under my personal observation, viz., he was instrumental in God's hands, not only in securing the salvation of sinners, but also in inducing these same new converts to seek that holiness without which no man shall see the Lord. At the close of a powerful sermon, which he preached on "entire sanctification," the altar of the church was crowded with converts, who were seeking the fulness of the Holy Ghost, as a sin-destroying, soul-sanctifying power in their hearts and lives. Many times have I seen Bro. Weber rise to truly sublime hights of spiritual power. I regard him as one of those Spirit-baptized souls whom God has thrust out, to "warn of the wrath to come." He is emphatically a preacher of God's law. He proclaims the law with tremendous energy. He believes that the religion of Jesus is tremendously true. With him it is a fundamental principle that men have no claim upon God's grace until they have submitted to His law. Possessing a heart full of God's love, he yet vehemently asserts God's law. Delighting in announcing the whisperings of Calvary, he does not neglect the thunderings of Sinai. Rejoicing to portray the exceeding heights of glory, he fears not to declare the "blackness of darkness forever." While fervently depicting the beatitudes of heaven, he shuns not to declare the terror of hell. While triumphantly proclaiming, "He that believeth shall be saved," he hesitates not to assert, "He that believeth not shall be damned." May God grant him a long life in which to bring sinners to repentance, and "spread Scriptural holiness over these lands."

Having thus faithfully delivered the messages which God had given him, and garnered many precious souls at East Rochester, he closed his services there, and amid tearful farewells, hastened to Haverhill, where he at once began another successful series of meetings with Pastor French. These two meetings were a sort of parenthesis in his Michigan work, as he then returned to meet other engagements which he there had made. Wherever God leads he is glad to follow, and with this new seal upon his evangelistic work in the East, he is prepared to return, and with renewed energy press the battle to the gates. His first engagement on returning to Michigan was

UNION CITY.

The pastor, Rev. Thomas Nicholson, himself full of evangelistic fire, had planned for a thorough work and was ready to co-operate with him. We are indebted to him for the following mention of the meeting,—

Rev. J. H. Weber began meetings at Union City on Tuesday Nov. 27, 1888. He had been engaged at the Camp-meeting the previous August, and his work and reputation had been well discussed before his arrival. The church had a membership of one hundred and sixty-six. They were true and loyal, but many were cold religiously. The great difficulty in this town had been to get the people to attend week-night services. There was a numerous infidel element in the town, and considerable religious indifference. From the first night after Bro. Weber's arrival the congregations began to grow and soon the seating capacity of the church was tested. It will seat (when lecture room, etc., are thrown in) about seven hundred. It was comfortably filled night after night, and some nights the people could not get standing room. Added to Mr. Weber's searching sermons at night, there was a systematic visitation of the people in their homes during the day, made by him in company with the pastor. He remained four weeks. During this time one hundred and sixty professed conversion, and one hundred and seventeen united with the church. The meetings were continued after his departure, and one hundred more gave their hearts to God. The effect of the revival on the community was marked. The opera house did not pay expenses. Shortly afterward an attempt was made to revive the "skating rink craze," but it died within a month. It was stated on good authority that the saloons lost an average of fifteen dollars a day by the revival, and one saloon-keeper was heard recently to remark that his business hardly paid expenses any more. There was also a large increase in the church-going population, many attending who had formerly scarcely ever entered the house of God. Equally marked was the effect on the prayer and class-meetings, where the attendance was more than doubled. At the present writing it is stated on the authority of the pastor that every family in the church, so far as he can ascertain, has family worship.

The effect, moreover, on the church finances was good. The expenses of the meeting were easily raised, and the general interests of the church benefited. Many of the conversions were marked. Of course there was the usual number of persons who proved to be stony ground and thorny ground hearers: some of them were not seen after the meetings closed, but the greater part of the work was genuine, and the converted were valuable additions to the church. The sermon from the text "Are these things so?" was much enjoyed by the people and was productive of great good. Under the powerful directness of his preaching many of those who "had a name to live and were dead," were brought to life. The church at Union City continues in a revival flame.

The editor of the *Register*, a local paper, presumed to bitterly attack Bro. Weber through the columns of his paper. This led to the following communication as to the revival by a correspondent, who signs himself "A Baptist,"—

Rev. Thomas Nicholson preached to a large audience at the M. E. Church last evening.

Surely Revs. Weber and Nicholson are deserving of a great deal of praise for the good that has been done in this place since Bro. Weber first came here. Over two hundred souls have declared their acceptance of Jesus as their Saviour, many of them heads of families.

There was a jubilee meeting held at the M. E. Church yesterday afternoon over the souls that have been saved, and the voices of the young converts could be heard praising God in every part of the house.

Rev. Nicholson took up the work where Rev. Weber left off, and by the aid of the Holy Spirit is doing a grand work here; the meetings will continue another week.

Rev. Weber left many warm-hearted friends when he went away, notwithstanding the false statements in the *Register* concerning him. It is quite evident that that editor and those *prominent church members* have been wounded nigh unto death by some of the evangelist's shot.

I am not a member of the M. E. Church, but I have heard Rev. Weber preach a great many times, even before he came to Union City, and I thank God that there is one minister who dare stand up and preach the plain, unvarnished truth, just as Jesus preached it of old; and Jesus says, "Whoso shall offend one of these little ones which believe in me, it were better for him that a millstone were hanged about his neck, and that he were drowned in the depths of the sea."

Mr. Weber's only answer was, "I have seen the *Register* and read it. You can say for me, as Jesus says, 'Blessed are ye when men shall revile you, and persecute you, and shall say all manner of evil against you, falsely, for my sake. Rejoice and be exceeding glad, for so persecuted they the prophets which were before you.'"

Christ came not to send peace on earth, but a sword, and the sword mission ceaseth not until sin and all her progeny of crimes and vices have been destroyed. God wants more men who, like Mr. Weber, will, when He commands, no longer keep back their swords for fear of sinful men, but who, with the Word of God, which is the Spirit's sword, will pierce error, until "wounded she writhes in pain and dies amid her worshippers." Bro. Nicholson makes mention of the evangelist's closing service in the following words,—

Rev. J. H. Weber closed his labors here yesterday. It was a wonderful day. We raised the money for the expenses of the meeting in a very few minutes in the morning, and had money over to put in the treasury. Afternoon, and at the close of the evening service, we had a reception of probationers. One hundred and seventeen were received, and there are more to follow. They were drawn up in a line around the church, and the congregation passed along and shook hands with each one. It was a day of old-fashioned Methodism; shouts and praises and hallelujahs. There have been one hundred and sixty-six to profess conversion, and fully two hundred people have been blessed, counting reclaimed backsliders, those who are still seeking, etc. Brother Weber is a grand success and he will long be remembered in this city. We will continue the meetings over next Sabbath, which is our quarterly meeting. Then we shall receive ten or twelve persons from probation and by letter, and more on probation.

Praise God for revivals like this one, and many others mentioned in this book, which continue to "go on" after the evangelist is gone.

HILLSDALE.

Rev. G. C. Draper, pastor of the M. E. Church at Hillsdale, had, with the members of his official board, invited Mr. Weber to hold a series of services in that city. He had promised to come, and as soon as he could close at Union City he hastened away to new conflicts and, thank God, to new victories at that place.

Hillsdale is the county seat of Hillsdale county, and also the location of the Freewill Baptist College. There had been no general revival there for years, and a severe spiritual drought prevailed. The pastor, Rev. G. C. Draper, could not rest with this state of the church, and through his efforts Bro. Weber was secured to lead in a revival there. Bro. Draper, in his usual racy style, makes the following mention of Bro. Weber and the great revival which attended his work at Hillsdale, —

I first met Bro. Weber when I was pastor at Ovid. He came and preached one night. One night is not enough to know him. I did not like him, and thought I should never want him to aid me in a meeting. At this time he was laboring at St. John's, where he had good success. I lost sight of him. The next I heard of him he had gone to Egypt. I did not care if he never came back. From Ovid I was appointed to Hillsdale. I needed an evangelist. The presiding elder asked me how I would like J. H. Weber. That was the first I knew he was back from the East. I said I did not want him. In due time our camp-meeting at Coldwater came. I went. Brother Weber was there. When I came on the ground he was preaching. I stood and listened. I liked his preaching, and I liked him. Before the camp-meeting closed, I said to him, "You are coming to help me at Hillsdale." He said, "I am not." I said, "Yes, you are." He said, good-naturedly, "Perhaps you know more about my business than I do." "Well, we'll see. Remember, you are coming!" After the camp-meeting he went East. I wrote to him twice about coming. His answers were full of interrogation points, but not decisive. I finally wrote, saying, "You are a Dutchman, not a Yankee, and you never can be; so you might as well stop playing the Yankee by asking questions, and tell me when you will come."

He wrote, saying, "I will be with you December 27th." He came; the pastor and church co-operated with him, and there was a great revival. Four hundred were at the altar; three hundred and fifty professed conversion. Where twenty-five attended prayer-meeting now there are over four hundred.

We paid him $50 per week, which, it seems to me, is a small sum for one doing such a work; and when the meeting closed there was a balance in the treasury of $180, which is something unusual, as Methodist churches, like Methodist preachers, seldom have anything in the bank.

The difference between him and ordinary preachers is, that he dares speak against men who sign saloon bonds, rent stores for whiskey, and do similar things, and they do not dare to.

THE ADRIAN REVIVAL.

Like Elijah on Mount Carmel, the faithful pastor of the Adrian M. E. Church, Rev. C. H. Morgan, had earnestly prayed and looked for a revival. To him and his city the rising cloud, as in many other places, proved to be our evangelist, Brother Weber, and the blessing which God sent through him to Adrian was far richer than that which came to Carmel and the plain of Esdraelon in the days of the grand old prophet "of like passions" with us.

When the "cloud" first rose at Adrian some did not like its appearance; were frightened by the lightnings that leaped from it, and terrified by its terrific peals of thunder. The gospel gales that attended it were so strong that some feared that they would "do more hurt than good." Soon, however, the mercy drops began to fall on every side, and Adrian was in the midst of one of the most gracious showers of divine grace that she ever had been blessed with. Converting grace and sanctifying truth were presented to the people, and very many will praise God forever for Bro. Weber and the revival tornado of 1889.

The *Northwestern Christian Advocate* made the following mention of the beginning of the revival,—

> Evangelist J. H. Weber began at Adrian, Mich., February 7. Earnest preparation had been made by pastor C. H. Morgan and people. Now the work is taking on great breadth and power. Up to February 24, there were one hundred and sixty conversions, and the foundation seems but fairly laid for that which is yet to be accomplished. Dr. Morgan writes, "Bro. Weber is one of the most helpful of all the special workers in the church to-day. He is exceedingly thorough in searching out and correcting sin, both within and without the church, but withal in such fervor, love and winningness, that it results in a deep, wide and abiding spiritual uplift of the church and community. All southern Michigan is feeling the impress of his labors — first at Jackson, five years ago, and now during two years in many other places."

This report is supplemented by the following from Pastor Morgan,—

> The last report brought our revival work up to and including Sunday, February 24. Saturday, March 2, Bro. Weber experienced a serious attack of nervous prostration, and it became necessary for

him to take a week of complete rest. The work moved on without a break, there being three or four conversions each evening during the week of his absence. On Saturday, March 9, he returned from Coldwater, where he had found a resting place in the delightful home of Brother R. Chandler, largely restored to his wonted strength. The Sabbath following was hallowed by wonderful displays of the divine glory. At the morning service, the mercy and goodness of God, the peace and melting power of the Holy Ghost, the breath of prayer and praise, made an atmosphere in which every soul seemed to thrill and pulsate with deeper life. The Sunday-school was turned into a revival service, and there were many seekers. The evening congregation, occupying all the available space of floor, gallery, altar, pulpit steps, vestibule and isles, was swayed and awed by the truth, "Thou art weighed in a balance, and art found wanting." Experienced workers say they never saw so many people under deep conviction at one time as during this day. There were between thirty and forty conversions, making the total number, to that date, two hundred and fifty-eight.

The writer had the pleasure of being present a few days in this meeting, which was an inspiration to him.

He was especially impressed, —

1. With Brother Weber's faith and power in prayer.
2. With his plain, pointed, searching preaching.
3. With his tenderness toward the penitent.
4. His severity toward the hypocritical and persistently impenitent.
5. His power in personal appeal, very many being led to the altar by him personally.
6. His self-denying persistence in seeking out and pleading with the unsaved at the close of the service, sometimes remaining late and working hard after nearly all others were gone, and usually rewarded by seeing his subjects on their knees before they left. In this respect it might be said of him, as of Jesus, "He saved others, himself he could not save."
7. The clearness of his exposition of holiness.

8. The closeness of the tests he put when helping people to see whether they were in its experience.

9. His fearless rebuking of those, who, like Meroz, "came not up to the help of the Lord against the mighty."

10. His giving all the glory to the " Father, the Son and Holy Ghost."

The writer was present over Sabbath, March 16, and reported the meeting in *The Revivalist*, as follows,—

At this writing, we are at Adrian, Mich., where one of the most remarkable revivals in the history of Michigan Methodism is in progress, conducted by evangelist J. H. Weber. The whole city is stirred. Over three hundred and twenty have professed conversion. Many are seeking holiness. Conviction is deepening and the revival tide is continually rising. Every day is a climax to what has gone before. Saturday evening was a meeting of great power. Rev. Weber preached his characteristic sermon on " Fools." He had great liberty. Many hurried to the altar and ninteen professed conversion. After sixteen had been converted the meeting was being dismissed, amid the victorious praise of the people, when three more claimed the victory, and all united again in " praising the Father, the Son and the Holy Ghost." Sunday morning he preached the sermon on Sanctification that has been so blessed in other places. It was a clear and Scriptural unfolding of this great Bible theme. At its close hundreds arose, signifying their desire for the experience. Then Mr. Weber turned the whole church into an altar, and the seekers knelt to plead for the promised blessing. The number who claimed it is not yet known, but eternity will doubtless reveal a mighty work wrought in that solemn hour. The large church was literally packed in the evening, and numbers were unable to gain admittance.

" Why are you standing here ? " said a lady to a company who were standing without during the preaching hour. " We want to get in to the after meeting," was the earnest answer. The evangelist spoke with awful impressiveness from the rich man and Lazarus. Multitudes were deeply convicted ; many came to the altar, and sixteen professed conversion.

There were a number of seekers at the " Woman's meeting " in the afternoon, and the class-meeting, led by Bro. Chandler, of Coldwater, was honored by the Saviour's presence. Over three hundred and twenty have professed conversion, and the tide is rapidly rising. Another installment of sixty united with the church Sunday morning, and pastor C. H. Morgan and his excellent wife, abundant in labor, are rejoicing in the glorious victory, which, under God, is attending their ministrations. A number of Roman Catholics have been converted. Formalists are frightened; mockers are trembling; devils are raging; angels are rejoicing, and God is being glorified. All glory to His name!

It sometimes seemed as if angels and devils were really present, contending for the souls of men. The church and the city were one great spiritual battlefield where unseen powers met in deadly fray. Sometimes a ripple of laughter would pass over the congregation at some quaint saying of the evangelist, only to be followed by suppressed sobs, as a dying Saviour was held before their gaze, or feelings of unspeakable awe, as the realities of Death, the Judgment, and Eternity were presented.

One evening Mr. Weber, at the close of his appeal to the unconverted, asked all who would decide at once to give up sin and accept of Christ, to come at once to the altar and take his hand. At once, from different parts of the house, they began to come, and after taking his hand, kneeled at the altar, which soon was nearly filled. Surely the day of the Lord is near in the valley of *decision*.

If seekers did not get where they knew they were saved the first night, they were exhorted to keep seeking until they had the witness. Only those who could witness that they "*were sure*" they were saved were reported as converted; but over each of such the congregation, led by Bro. Weber, with uplifted hands, would say,

"Praise the Father, praise the Son, and praise the Holy Ghost." No one could be present at these meetings without being convinced that in a marvelous way God is using Mr. Weber to tear down the strongholds of sin and to build up the kingdom of His Son.

Mrs. Sophia McGowan, of White Pigeon, accompanied by ladies of the church, visited in the homes of the people during the entire meeting, and in this way very much good was done. The work continued to sweep on for more than six weeks, until the closing service, which is thus described by a correspondent of an Adrian daily,—

Sunday, March 31, was a day long to be remembered by the friends of Rev. J. H. Weber, it being the closing day of the reverend gentleman's services in the First M. E. Church of this city. The pulpit was beautifully decorated with flowers, and though the day was a stormy one, nearly every seat was occupied both morning and afternoon. The communion service in the morning was very interesting and impressive, as the altar was filled again and again with those who came for the first time to commemorate the death and sufferings of Him who said, "As oft as ye eat this bread and drink this cup, do it in remembrance of me." Fifty united with the church at this service and twenty in the evening, making a total of over two hundred since the meetings began.

At the evening meeting the church was packed to its utmost capacity, and many were unable to obtain standing room. After the usual song service, Mr. B. S. Barnes came forward, on an invitation of the pastor, Rev. C. H. Morgan, and read the following resolutions, which had been unanimously adopted by the official board of the church, after which Dr. Segur rose and wished to heartily endorse every word that had been read, and moved that they be adopted by the whole congregation, which was seconded by several of the brethren of the church, after which they were adopted by the vast audience rising to their feet. At this service Rev. Mr. Weber preached a very able and impressive sermon, taking for his text Rev. 6 : 17. At the close of the sermon a large number came to the altar and were converted. The total number of conversions to this date is four hundred and twenty-one, and the church will continue the revival efforts in regular and special meetings, praying and working for the conversion of many more.

Following are the resolutions, —

"As Bro. J. H. Weber has been laboring with this church for more than six weeks, and is now about to go elsewhere and work in God's vineyard, we, the official board of the First M. E. Church, deem it proper to bid him a hearty 'Godspeed.'

"We rejoice that his labors among us have been abundantly blessed of our Heavenly Father. We are devoutly thankful that our church has been quickened into new life. God calls for workers. There are always plenty standing by to criticise, but only those who are able to plan and to execute, only those who go forward at God's command, are needed at the front. Bro. Weber attacks sin uncompromisingly in all its forms. He has sternly preached to this people God's commands and His condemnation of sin. He has lovingly told the gospel story and pointed the sinner to the cross. Four hundred have been converted, and let us praise God for it. How such wonderful results put to shame the halfhearted! With added responsibilities, let our church be foremost in building up God's kingdom. Bro. Weber has not shunned to declare unto us the whole truth. He will now labor in other fields; therefore,

"*Resolved*, That we most heartily commend him to our brethren elsewhere, and pray God's blessing on his labors. Bro. Weber, we bid you 'Godspeed.'"

Thus in the midst of victory, such as Jesus gives to those who obey him, Brother Weber closed for the present his work in Michigan. As he passes to other places the prayers of thousands to whom his messages have been glad tidings of great joy will follow him, and doubtless many who here have been saved from sin will be the first to greet him when he passes to the saint's reward above.

INCIDENTS.

When the business men opened their doors one morning they found under them the startling Scripture, —

"PREPARE TO MEET THY GOD!"

An aged lady attended service in the beginning of the Adrian revival. She was a backslider, and was urged to seek salvation. Her answer was, "Not to night; I will some other time." Before the meeting was closed she was ushered unprepared into eternity. What a warning to the procrastinator!

"The presence of mind," writes a reporter, "displayed by Evangelist Weber last evening, towards the close of his sermon on 'Passion's Slave,' prevented what certainly would have been a panic in the Methodist Church. The house was crowded, and the blowing out of the safety valve on the boiler used for heating the house, caused a general commotion, but Mr. Weber commanded the crowd to keep their seats, and those who started out were ordered to 'sit down,' and the doors were closed to prevent any rush out. Mr. Weber started up a familiar air, and the congregation all joined in singing, and they then could not hear the noise made by the steam. When the excitement was over he thanked God for keeping them from all harm, and then asked the audience what they would do when they passed into eternity, if they were so afraid of a little steam."

One of the converts at Haverhill, Mass., feels called to the ministry, and Mr. Weber is helping him at school.

An anti-treating association of seventy members was formed in Adrian as a part of the result of Mr. Weber's work there.

Mr. Weber on one occasion gave $150 to pay the passage of a young man from Egypt, who comes to this country to study for the Christian ministry, and is now at Delaware, O., in school.

Two of the young men converted at White Pigeon are going into the ministry.

A TRAVELLING MAN CONVERTED.

At White Pigeon, Mr. Weber had large posters put up with, "*Are you saved?*" "*Are you prepared to die?*" printed in large letters upon them. These were placed in the stores, when in came a travelling man, and " Are you prepared to die?" caught his eye at the first. He said, " I'm thinking how to live instead of to die." At this he began to show his samples, but could not keep his mind from that poster, and would talk about it, and before he left the store he was converted.

FIRST MAD, THEN SAVED.

A son of one of the leading church members got under great conviction and refused to come to church. He had a very tender affection for his mother, and she entreated him, when he angrily answered, " Mother, if you don't stop talking to me about the meeting I will leave the house." They continued praying for him, when one night he sent word, saying, " Tell Bro. Weber to have a good sermon to-morrow night as I am coming to be saved." That night he came. Bro. Weber persuaded him to yield, and he professed conversion.

MR. WEBER WATCHED.

In order to ascertain for a certainty whether Mr. Weber practised what he preached and professed in regard to private prayer, a minister at one of the camp-meetings made up his mind that he would test him. He therefore went quietly to his tent in a time when he was not expected; Mr. Weber was on his knees. Another time, still more cautiously, he approached the tent so silently that he was unobserved, and slyly peering through a slit in the tent, again the evangelist was found upon his knees with his Bible before him. Thomas-like, he still craved further evidence and the third time he investigated as cautiously as ever, and the third time found Mr. Weber on bended knees with Bible before him, wrestling for victory. This same minister was with him for weeks in a revival meeting after this, and says he never went to his room but that they united in prayer before separating.

SUDDEN CONVERSION OF A BUSINESS MAN.

In one of the services at Coldwater, while the church was shaking hands, welcoming the converts— among them was the man's wife,— a business man got so powerfully moved on, that he jumped up and was converted, joined the church with his wife, and they both are good Christians.

WON BY KIND WORDS AND TEN CENTS.

Mr. Weber relates the following incident, which also occurred at Coldwater: "The Sunday-school superintendent reproved a little boy in Sunday-school, by making him stand on the rostrum during the school. The little boy cried, and after school I went to him and put my arms around him and spoke kind words, and gave him ten cents. He came, and was converted. I often win a whole family by kissing the baby, or giving the little ones a few pennies."

FRIGHTENED BY A PRAYER.

One evening, a man and some women misbehaved in meeting. The man was compelled to leave the church. This greatly enraged him. "One day," says Mr. Weber, "I saw him and he wanted to whip me, so I fell on my knees and began to pray for him, and he sneaked away."

PERSISTENCE WINS.

The following incident, which occurred at the Coldwater camp-meeting, illustrates the power of the evangelist's plain rebukes, and also his persistence in personal work with the unconverted. It is related by an eye-witness,—

"Mr. Weber was earnestly urging a mother to go forward. Mr. A—— said to me, 'If you don't take him away, there will be trouble. I don't believe it's right to urge people like that.' I said, 'It will come out all right, I think.' Mr. B—— said, 'If he treated me that way, I'd strike him.' He continued pleading with the mother, who was somewhat softened; but her daughter was with her, and when appealed to by Mr. Weber, answered very scornfully, and evidently was barring the way against the mother's going forward. He sharply rebuked the daughter in blunt, plain language, which made both mother and daughter very angry, and then abruptly left them. 'Weber never can do anything with them,' said the critics above mentioned. In a little while, however, he came, and with a voice and manner, as tender as a mother's over a dying babe, he earnestly pleaded with the mother and daughter to yield. Their feelings softened, their wills bent, and each then and there yielded to Christ; two more trophies won by the wisdom of the evangelist, to increase the glory of his adorable King. 'I give up,' said one of the critics; 'it beats me.' When he said that, he simply voiced the feelings of many who have watched his methods with eagle's eyes, but not always as honest as he in confessing their mistake."

MR. WEBER INTERVIEWED — HOW HE TREATS "REPORTS."

While Mr. Weber was at Adrian, a slanderous article which was written by an enemy of his revival work in Hillsdale, was printed and being circulated. A representative of the city press called upon him to see what answer he might wish to make. He was simply referred to a letter written by Rev. G. C. Draper, pastor of the M. E. Church at Hillsdale, which endorsed brother Weber without reserve.

Changing the subject, the reporter asked, "By the way, Mr. Weber, is there any truth in the report that you were once a minstrel man?"

"Why, no. Well, the fact is, I did do a little rehearsing once while a boy, but I never went into it. And, say, while I am talking, here is a letter I received from Coldwater, which asks me in all earnestness if I have been refused admittance into the M. E. Church in Adrian. Now you see how stories travel. And is it any wonder that I pay no attention to the lies told about me?"

"There are also many stories told about the large remuneration you receive."

"Yes, I get good money; and it's nobody's business how I use it. I sometimes tell people so, too. Here is a letter I received from a young boy at Delaware, Ohio.

He is a young Syrian about fifteen, and is attending college at Delaware. I brought him from that country myself, and am educating him. I have one boy down East, two out in Illinois, all poor boys, receiving their education through this money. Besides this, I am making a large collection of Oriental curiosities, which I intend making a feature of one of these colleges in the near future. This cannot be done for nothing, and you can readily see where my money goes."

Mr. Weber here showed us an account he kept of personal money spent on other persons, footing up some $1700.

"You held no services Monday, I see. Do you usually rest on Monday?"

"Oh, bless you, no. I go 'hunting.'"

"Go hunting! Why, what do you mean?"

"I have been in many of the workshops of the city, and I intend to visit them all, stores, factories, shops, residences,—everywhere, and make a personal appeal for the souls of men. That is what I mean by going a hunting. I do not shoot to kill, but to save."

A LETTER FROM HELL.

While at Adrian, Bro. Weber was the recipient of the following note, which is indicative of the feeling which Satan has towards him and the work he is engaged in,—

HELL, Feb. 22, 1889, OFFICE OF HIS SATANIC MAJESTY.

MR. WEBER: Dear Sir,—Your consignment of sinners received. Will place them in pit No. 549.

Your work is spoiling my business. You have converted a number of persons I had marked as my own. . . . I am prepared to make it hot for you should you ever backslide.

Yours, sulphurously, MEPHISTOPHELES.
51 Bob Ingersoll St., Hell.

CHAPTER XIV.

A LOVE-FEAST. — SUNSHINE AFTER THE STORM.

> Ye shall be witnesses unto Me. — Jesus.

> "Blest be the tie that binds
> Our hearts in Christian love,
> The fellowship of kindred minds
> Is like to that above."

Brother Weber, like Paul, has many children in the Gospel, and, like the converts in the early church, they love to receive letters "written in his own hand" by their spiritual father. He receives from this source a great multitude of letters, which express the pure and ardent love which the converts bear to him and to the Saviour who has rescued them from sin. A part of the reward which those who travail for souls receive is the love which those saved through their efforts will always bear towards them.

The following extracts from the correspondence mentioned speak volumes for Jesus, and the truths which he has commissioned his servant to preach. As they were written with no view to public perusal, names will not be given, but each extract is from an actual correspondent. May the truths witnessed to, by the power of the Holy Spirit, be burned into every reader's heart.

If some of them breathe a spirit of deep devotion towards the Evangelist, what wonder?

Is it not praiseworthy for the drowning sailor to remember with ardent love the man who periled his life to warn him of his danger, and bear him to the life-boat?

We will not insist upon "tickets for admission," but now invite the reader to a

LOVE-FEAST

among those who have been converted in Brother Weber's revivals.

Heavenly Father, we pray Thee, in Jesus' name, that thy perfect love may be shed abroad in every reader's heart, and that each testimony may be like a beautiful flower distilling its fragrance freely for all.

"HIS FOR LIFE."

"Praise the Lord, I am his for life. I am working for my Master night and day. I was over to the church last night until half-past eleven, praying a poor boy into the kingdom. After staying on my knees two hours and a half, he came out nicely, and is now singing for God, and so the work goes on. Twenty-five or thirty have been born again. How good the Lord is to me and you. I can now say I enjoy 'perfect love.' My heart and love are always with you. — 'Charlie.'"

WHERE TO GO WHEN TEMPTED.

"Jesus blesses me daily, and whenever I am tempted or in trouble of any kind I go to *Him*, and He helps me. Blessed be the name of Jesus. He is my loving Saviour."

The above is from a youth who feels led to prepare for the ministry.

A BANKER'S TESTIMONY.

"I will say, first, the unusual interest manifested by my friends touched me. I noticed that people in whom I had the utmost confidence testified to the reality of religion, that it made them happy, made them better, and enabled them to withstand temptation. I looked about me, and found the best people in the community were professors. I read history, and found the best men the world ever contained were believers. . . . A great many things stood in my way, most of which were removed by your timely visit to my office, and I resolved to become a seeker, went to the altar the second night, and was praying for light when you commenced to sing

"'Just as I am, without one plea,'

and a sweet-voiced little singer, S. H., who sat just in front of me, sang so sweetly, as I suppose angels sing, and I was melted. If I was to say what *one* thing more than another led to my conversion, it would be *singing*, coupled with your explanation of what constituted a Christian, and your definition of their duties." — J. W. T.

"IS MY NAME WRITTEN THERE?"

"My husband and I had been thinking for a long time about making a start, but the devil kept tempting us and keeping us back. When you came you had such a way of talking, explaining things, and singing, that we could not resist any longer. That beautiful piece, 'Is my Name Written There,' kept ringing in our ears until we made a start." — L. and J. R.

PRESSING AFTER PURITY.

" When I think of how good God is to me, and the blessing of your love which is one of the choicest He has bestowed, it seems as though the best efforts of my life would, indeed, be 'a present far too small.' O precious promise! 'Thou wilt keep him in perfect peace whose mind is stayed on thee.' I shall never rest satisfied until I have attained perfect purity." — J.

HOW AND WHERE.

"I can tell you how I was converted and where. It was a week ago last Sunday evening, at the church. You preached from '*Where shall I spend my eternity?*' I thought you had chosen a terrible text, but I am so glad it was the one you chose, for that evening I was brought to see how sinful I was. When I knelt down at the altar I said, 'God helping me, I will spend my eternity with the Saviour,' and every day I have been more thankful that I started." — N. C.

VICTORY.

"Some think because they try and live upright lives that they are safe, but no; I know that is the devil's teachings. He tried to *destroy* me. Oh, hallelujah! Jesus *saves* me, saves *me*. The prayer of a *righteous man availeth much*. The Lord has given me the victory over the devil and hell. That stubborn will is broken, pride is gone, and the fear of the people. The blood has been applied. My mission is to help win souls to Christ. You will remember me as the one who swallowed a quart of sunshine. I am not sad, but very happy." — E. W.

CONVICTED BY A CARD.

"After you departed, I picked up the card, and read these words, ' *Where will you spend your eternity?* ' These words brought me to seek Jesus, and spend my eternity in heaven. When I came to the altar they were singing, 'Just as I am,' when glorious light came into my soul, and I knew that the Lord took me just as I was, and washed my sins away." — L. J.

A TEACHER RESCUED FROM INFIDELITY.

"I never received any Christian instruction when a child, but had always accepted the Christian religion until after I commenced teaching. Then I was unfortunate enough to board with a family who were strong infidels. They had always a quantity of infidel publications around them. At first I had no inclination whatever to read them, but after a time my curiosity was aroused, and I commenced reading Ingersoll's lectures, thinking it could do no harm. But with the first book came the first doubt, and it was not long until I, too, said that this religion was not true. For about three years, I think, I never entered a church, or let a chance to sneer at the Christian religion pass.

"Last winter I was taken suddenly ill, one night in perfect health, and the next noon not expected to live from hour to hour. While I lay there so near to death I saw things in a very different light than I ever did before, and I said, If God ever lets me get well again I will become a Christian. I did so, and all my doubts are passed away, and now I have perfect peace and faith in Christ." — N. L. G.

A PROBLEM IN GAIN AND LOSS.

"I got to thinking, 'What have I to lose? what to gain?'

"I had nothing to lose but what man despised, sinner as well as saint.

"What had I to gain?

"1. The approval of God.

"2. The respect of my fellow-men.

"3. The happiness of my family.

"4. My own self-respect and a quiet conscience.

"This being fully impressed on my mind, I said, 'By God's help I will lead a different life; I will humble myself before Him, and go to the altar and confess my sins before God and man.' I did so, and I firmly believe He heard my prayer." — E. J. G.

AN INVALID COMFORTED BY A DREAM.

"Christ had been very near to me through the day, and at night it did not seem as though I was yet asleep, yet in some strange way, I know not how, it seemed as if I was sitting in my sick-chair in a large, deep valley where there were so many people, and there were great walls on all sides with ladders to ascend upon, and arches extending from one side to another, with these words in gilt letters: '*Whosoever will may come.*'

"I said, 'I will go and be saved,' and immediately I went or was taken up this ladder and reached safe ground. There were many others there, and each one was handed a burning torch. On the handle of mine was written, '*Let your light shine.*' By these torches we were to light those in the valley up out of the darkness to the place of safety. Some had their torches down at their sides, so that they were almost out. Others held them high, crying, '*Come, come!*' I was holding mine as high as I could and joining in the cry. Many were coming and many were slipping back after almost reaching the top. When I awoke, oh, what a sweet peace I realized, and what a comfort to feel that I was holding up the light. I am so thankful that I started when I did." — G. M.

SAVED FROM THE RINK AND THE DANCE.

"Knowing that there are hundreds who, like myself, are leaders in all that is wicked, it may help you to know how you first interested me.

"I went first to hear you out of curiosity; second, because I was infatuated with you, and the third time your earnestness so impressed me that I forgot all else, in listening to your subject, 'The Dance.'

"I saw you knew what you were talking about; everything looked different to me, and it made me miserable.

"As you know, I could not give up skating; but I was miserable until I did. During those days I hated you. You read me, but you did not think me sincere. Through you I found God. I love him. Is that not enough to make one happy? I want you to pray for me, for you know how much I have got to fight. I joined the church on probation, Sunday morning."
— M. J. D.

WOULD NOT STAND IN THE WAY OF OTHERS.

"The reason that I made a start was that some of my friends said that they would start if I would. I thought that I had sins enough to account for without causing others to go down to hell." — O. D. S.

A HAPPY THANKSGIVING.

"It was Thanksgiving eve. I had been to church, and when I returned I read a chapter and kneeled down to pray. I had said but a few words when it seemed as if the room was all lit up with a glorious light, and it seemed as if I could do nothing but say, 'Jesus, blessed Jesus.'" — D. M.

"SOMETIME IS NEVER."

"I feel that I must inform you that I am *saved*. I only regret that I did not become converted before the last evening you were here. It was then that the dark cloud was taken from before me, which was caused by your asking, 'Won't you come now and be saved?' My reply was, 'Sometime.' You then said, '*But sometime is never.*'

"I could wait no longer, and as soon as I reached home I opened my heart to God, and have ever since been walking in the light." — A. W.

"WHERE WILL YOU SPEND YOUR ETERNITY?"

"O Brother Weber, those were the words that touched my heart, and all that long, long night I kept thinking, Where shall I spend *my eternity?* Thank God I am saved. Oh, how glad I am to think I attended that meeting." — F. N.

"IS YOUR HEART RIGHT?"

"Your text was, 'Is your heart right?' During the meeting I kept asking myself, 'Is my heart right?' but it had no impression until I reached home, when I fell on my knees and asked the question. This time my sins all came up before me, and then I saw how far I had been from living upright. When I had come to church again I had made up my mind to give myself to my Heavenly Father. I did, and am so happy since then and love to tell what Jesus has done for me."— S.

WON BY THE PLEADINGS OF HIS WIFE.

"The sermon, '*Where will you spend eternity?*' together with the pleadings of my wife and other friends with a desire to serve God, led me to seek salvation, and, blessed be his name, I found it." — H. F. G.

CONQUERED BY CALVARY.

"The text 'For God so loved the world' affected me more than anything had done before. It seemed that it was spoken especially for me.

"I thought that if God made so great a sacrifice for me, even *me*, that it would not be best to disregard it, and as you were talking I felt that 'to-night is the time chosen by God for me to give my heart to him.'" — A. M.

SANCTIFIED THROUGH BROTHER WEBER'S SICKNESS.

During Brother Weber's sickness at Leslie, Mich., he was kindly cared for at the home of Brother J. G. Wilson, and his presence there, like that of the prophet in the home of her whose child was raised in ancient days, proved a priceless benediction. Sister Wilson writes: —

The Lord had service for him to perform in his illness, and made him a blessing to the entire household, who will cherish the memory of those days as hallowed. To me he became, after the severest criticisms on his manner, the strongest living witness of God's power to save a sinner, who will "look and live," that I have ever known. Praise God! He praised God and lived a "Now is the accepted time, now is the day of salvation" kind of religion. His life of praise and trust and service helped me to the foot of the Cross, where the Blood was applied and cleansed my heart. Praise God! I had for some time been seeking full salvation, and the day before Brother Weber left our home it pleased God, in answer to the united petitions of three — himself, Mrs. I. Glenn (mother of the wife of the author of this book, and at whose home it is written), and myself — to grant me the faith to claim the blessing. I will ever praise God that in His loving kindness and tender mercies He allowed this "child of a King" to be stricken and brought to my home that he might lead me into this "closer walk with God." No. 104 of "The Evangelist," "He cleanseth Me," expresses my experience.

WON BY KIND WORDS.

"What brought me to follow the footsteps of Jesus was your kind words. Such pleading would or ought to touch a heart of stone." — L. B.

THE TRUTH TRIUMPHS.

"Hearing you preach God's holy truth, and knowing it to be the truth, brought me under great conviction, and when you threw your loving arms around me and prayed, I was converted there." — C. H. G.

MOVED BY FEAR OF HELL.

"I was gloriously converted the night your text was '*Where will you spend eternity?*' I thought, Where will

I spend my eternity? How awful it would be to spend it in hell! I said to my companions, 'I am going to give my heart to the Lord,' and I did, and have been happier ever since." — A. S.

FATHERS, MOTHERS, WIVES, CHILDREN, TAKE COURAGE.

"The teachings and prayers of a religious father and mother have always been with me, and in later years a religious wife and child and Christian associates have all prepared me for the work God accomplished through your sermon of May 17 to 'Unconverted Husbands.' God bless you." — C. D. M.

"WENT OUT OF CURIOSITY."

"I went to church out of curiosity to hear Brother Weber. The text was, 'Is thine heart right?' I thought, 'No, my heart isn't right; I wish it was,' but had no thought of having it made so. Next night I thought, 'He don't believe what he says; guess he's been an actor; don't believe in any one saying they are saved; don't believe they know.' Next night went to a party, thought there was more fun there; the next, to the lodge, thought it was my duty to go there. The next week I thought it over and thought that Brother Weber meant every word. Was sorry that I had thought as I did. I now would like to go to the altar. A friend invited me and I went. I went twice, but all was still dark. I thought, 'It is no use for me to go, I shall never know.' Then I would think, 'Others have been saved; why not I?' I prayed God to show me some way that I might know. I said, 'I will be saved, I will give up everything.' All at once there seemed to be a light around me, and I saw as in a vision a straight, narrow path before me, leading upwards. It seemed as bright as if the sun was shining on it, and I felt so happy and at peace and said, 'Thank God, my heart is right!'" — J. J.

POSSESSED OF THE "PRICELESS PEARL."

"I can truly say, —

> "'I've found the pearl of greatest price,
> My heart doth sing for joy;
> And sing I must, for Christ is mine;
> Christ shall my song employ.'" — J. E. M.

WORDS FROM THE CHILDREN.

Mr. Weber believes the Bible teachings in regard to the conversion of children, and very many of them are saved in his meetings. Like a wise shepherd, he cares for the lambs and has a love for the young that amounts to a passion.

At the close of the evening service it is customary for a large bevy of boys to gather around him and escort him to his room. Many of them become earnest Christians, and quite a large number are preparing for the ministry. Judases, who sigh for the conversion of bags of gold; — and spiritual dwarfs, who are as ignorant of the Saviour's love for the children and His plan for their salvation as a snail is of Greek, sometimes sigh, "Nobody but children," when such are converted. But Mr. Weber praises God just as heartily for the salvation of a little boy or girl as for that of a man of "influence," whose hair is gray with years squandered in the service of the devil. Why not? The child brings all the bright years of youth and the golden years of middle life and places them upon the altar to be used for the glory of God, while the other brings only a blighted life and faded leaves. Our love feast would be incomplete without the voices of the young.

WANTS THEM ALL TO COME.

"I have always liked to go to your meetings, but since I have been saved I like to go a great deal better. I wish all the children in North America were in the service of the Lord, as I am. It is a glorious service." — E. J. D.

CONVERTED WHILE READING THE BIBLE.

"I went forward three times, but received but little light. I went home, and the most that attracted my attention was the Bible, so I got it, and N. said, 'I want you to read First John.' Before I finished it, I was, oh! so happy that none but a Christian could explain, and, thank God, I have had the happiest three weeks I ever experienced. And, Brother Weber, I thank you for the influence you have had over me, and God for the victory." — A. S.

"The first night I came, my cousin told me not to go, but the second night I went and found the Lord, and I never was so happy before, and I am going to keep on." — E. C.

HOW SHE FOUND JESUS.

"I will tell you how I found Jesus. One night you came to me and asked me to come to Jesus, but I refused to come; again a lady asked me, but I refused, and how bad I did feel.

"I went up to the altar twice, and the third time my heart told me I must go, and so I did, and how happy I felt that night; and, when I went home, I went to God and asked him to bless me, and it seems to me that I could sing the sweet songs that I have learned, all the time." — B. F.

BYWORDS AND BAD TEMPER ALL TAKEN OUT.

"I want to tell you that God saves me to-day. I cannot tell you the joy there is in serving him, but you know. . . . Before I was converted I used always to sing and play comic songs. I never thought of playing a religious piece, unless the preacher or some church-member would come in, and then it almost made me sick. Now, glory to God, I can play and sing them, and it don't make me sick either.

"Praise his name, I know I am changed. Mamma said she knew I was saved, because I came home from church and sat down to the organ, and began to play that good old hymn, 'Jesus. Lover of my Soul,' and she noticed the next day I did not use any bywords, or show my temper, for I am sorry to say I have a very bad temper; but God has taken the bywords and bad temper all out of me; and when things do not go to suit me, instead of giving way to my temper and slamming things round, I just look up to God, and pray, and He helps me out of all my trouble. Brother Weber, please pray for me, and remember I am one of your flock." — A. P.

"THE DEVIL AT A DISADVANTAGE."

"I don't think it was a sermon or anything of that kind that converted me, but I think the Lord got the advantage of the devil that was in me. I thank Him that He did." — C. A.

"NOW IS THE ACCEPTED TIME."

"It had been my desire to be a Christian, and now the time has come." — B. A.

A KISS THE KEY TO HIS HEART.

"The second sermon you preached I was there. The sermon did me some good, but when you came to talk with me, and kissed me, it opened my heart, and Christ and glory came in. Hallelujah for that! I now am happy in Jesus, and can praise His name every day. I owe you thousands of thanks." — E. J.

STARTED WITHOUT A PERSONAL APPEAL.

"When the revival meeting began, I thought it was my duty to go forward. No one said anything to me about it, and I was washed in the blood of the Lamb." — H. S.

SAVED AND GONE HOME TO HEAVEN.

The love which the little ones feel for Brother Weber, and the reality of their conversions, are both beautifully illustrated in the life and death of little Eddie H., who was converted and went home to Jesus, before he was seven years old.

His own mother writes tearfully as follows: —

We have just heard the call of the Master, "Suffer him to come unto Me," and our darling boy, our only child, has gone to Him who said, "Of such is the kingdom of heaven."

I am sure you will pardon me in writing a few things, in reference to Eddie, when I tell you how ardently he loved you. He was not a demonstrative child, never loud in his expressions of affection, hence it seemed almost strange to us that he was always ready to say, "*I love Brother Weber.*" He knew all those hymns you sang last winter, and not a day has since passed, unless he was sick, without his singing some of them. He would often stop suddenly to ask, "Where is Brother Weber?" Or to say, "Oh, I wish I could see Brother Weber." And in his little prayer he hardly ever failed to ask God to bless Brother Weber. You gave him some pennies, — four in all, — and he would not have them put into his bank, for he did not want them "mixed up" with his other money, so he folded them up nicely, in a piece of paper, and put them in his drawer, and every few days he would take them out to look at. . . .

Have you forgotten the night when it seemed impossible longer to keep him from going to the altar, and, with tears streaming down his cheeks, he was lifted over the crowd and given place among the seekers? He had little to be forgiven, and in a few moments he arose with a face radiant with joy. You took him in your arms, and, standing on a seat, held him up, so that all could hear his testimony, "Jesus loves me." To your question, "How do you *know* that Jesus loves you?" He replied, "I feel so good." I have never doubted the genuineness of his conversion. He was a Christian — a *child Christian*. . . .

His sickness was brief but terrible, — membranous croup. His patience, during sufferings indescribable, was indeed surprising. After one of his paroxysms of coughing and fearful struggling for breath, I said, "Mamma is doing everything she can for you, darling." He kissed me, and whispered, "I know it, mamma." A little while before he died, he asked his grandma to sing, "I've been redeemed." . . . With the dawning of October 28th, his spirit was released, and upon him broke the morning of an eternal day. — M. E. H.

May we each go home to heaven as triumphantly as little E., and may every child who reads this *live* as grandly as he *died*.

Many more testimonies of children and others might be given, as Brother Weber is constantly receiving such letters from all ages and ranks of society, but time and space forbid.

These witnesses clearly show, —

1. That Brother Weber's converts are converted to God.
2. That they have a definite experience.
3. That they do not feel like stopping until made perfect in love.
4. That they "die well."

For all of which let us "praise the Father, praise the Son, and praise the Holy Ghost."

Brother Weber believes that people should "sing *with the spirit*, and with the understanding also."

Most Evangelists need to take helpers with them to lead the song services.

Mr. Weber, however, himself is able to lead the people in this most delightful and profitable service, and does so with thrilling effect.

The compiler of his song-book, "The Evangelist," and the composer of many of the pieces, he is able in a wonderful way to impress the Gospel truths therein upon the congregation.

The songs of this book, as Presiding Elder N. L. Bray has said, "are especially adapted to the man, and the man to the songs," and much of his success is due to the singing.

Nearly every one buys a book, and then ALL are exhorted to sing.

The contrast between these services of song and that of a select few mechanically chanting to a musical accompaniment is as great as between the ringing laughter of a happy child and the chatter of a parrot, or between a living man and a corpse.

All phases of the Gospel are sung, and often

commented upon by the Evangelist in the song service.

Every service is opened promptly at the appointed time by the announcement of No. 93, the Doxology. Tune, Duane St.

Praise is always comely, hence this tune is always appropriate.

If the people are faithless and disheartened, "A Rain of Salvation is Coming," No. 83, composed by Mr. Weber himself, is sure to inspire hope and courage.

The song "My Mother's Hands," which the Evangelist has composed, and dedicated to his own mother, has touched thousands of hearts, and so melted them that they were prepared for the blessed Gospel seed, and fitted to meet in heaven precious mothers who have gone before. His songs "I want to be like the Saviour," and "I long for the Fulness," are both sweetly and touchingly expressive of the state of those who, "hungering and thirsting after righteousness," are panting to be filled with all the fulness of a Saviour's love.

The hesitating procrastinator trembles as the words of No. 20, "Too Late! Too Late!" attended by a spirit of prayer, are actually *sung into his soul*, and he is made to feel that to tarry one more hour means too late forever.

To the contrite penitent his songs "To Save a Poor Sinner like Me," and "Sinner, Press Your Way to Jesus," come as a sweet and healing balm.

The Christ-like yearning of the Evangelist, and his tender sympathy for the lost, find expression in No. 114,

"Some Mother's Child," which can but move wherever it is sung.

> "At home or away in the alley or street,
> Wherever I chance in this wide world to meet
> A girl that is thoughtless, or boy that is wild,
> My heart echoes softly, 'Tis some mother's child.
>
> And when I see those o'er whom long years have rolled,
> Whose hearts have grown hardened, whose spirits are cold,
> Be it woman all fallen or man all defiled,
> A voice whispers sadly, Ah, some mother's child.
>
> No matter how far from the right she hath strayed,
> No matter what inroads dishonor hath made,
> No matter what elements cankered the pearl,
> Though tarnished and sullied, she's some mother's girl.
>
> No matter how wayward his footsteps have been,
> No matter how deep he is sunken in sin;
> No matter how low is his standard of joy,
> Tho' guilty and loathsome, he's some mother's boy.
>
> That head hath been pillowed on some tender breast,
> That form hath been wept o'er, those lips have been pressed,
> That soul hath been prayed for in tones sweet and mild.
> For her sake deal gently with some mother's child."

No. 104, "He Cleanseth Me," makes mention of his own "cleansing" by "faith" in the blood.

> "I sought for this blest cleansing
> Not many years ago,
> The blood that cleanses from all sin
> Now makes me white as snow.
>
> *Chorus.*—Hallelujah! now it cleanseth,
> It cleanseth even me!
> Hallelujah! now it cleanseth,
> Thro' His blood I am set free.

> It came by faith in Jesus.
> As soon as I believed,
> I took him at His blessed word,
> Then joy and grace received."

These and other pieces, both the words and music of which he has composed, prove wonderfully popular with his audiences. The tunes are easily learned, and in a little while are being sung on the streets, in the shops, kitchens, on the farms, and in the homes of the people.

Many is the wanderer first won by the more than magic power of these heaven-inspired hymns.

Aside from these, "The Evangelist" contains the cream of old and modern hymns, so that there is no lack of variety, but something always at hand suited for any stage of the meeting.

Concerning the value of this collection of revival songs, a pastor says, —

> One Sunday night I took along the copy of your book that I have, and, after the introductory exercises, began my preaching by singing No. 29. The Lord blessed the singing to the conversion of a lady.
>
> The Lord used another of your songs at one meeting for making a very solemn impression. It was, "How Will You Stand in the Judgment?" No. 51. An awful solemnity fell on the audience; it seemed as if the people scarcely dared to breathe.

May the heart of every reader be tuned to sing the blessed songs of Zion here below, and then unite with the countless choir before the throne in the song of Moses and the Lamb.

We close this chapter with one of the hymns from "The Evangelist."

CHAPTER XV.

SERMON.— ENTIRE SANCTIFICATION.

SERMON delivered by the Rev. J. H. Weber, in the Methodist church, at the city of Adrian.

In 1 Thess. v. 23, 24, you will read these words, "And the very God of peace sanctify you wholly; and I pray God your whole spirit and soul and body be preserved blameless unto the coming of our Lord Jesus Christ. Faithful is he that calleth you, who also will do it."

Now, I am sure there is not a person in this congregation this morning but that will admit that Adam and Eve, who were created in the image of God, were perfect. And as Adam and Eve were perfect, God used to come down in the garden and walk with them, talk with them, commune with them; and there they enjoyed His favors and His smiles. But the time came when the serpent came in the garden. God had said, "Of every tree of the garden thou mayst freely eat; but of the tree of the Knowledge of Good and Evil, thou shalt not eat of it. For in the day that thou eatest thereof, thou shalt surely die." So this serpent, the old devil, injected within the first parents the desire for the Tree of Life; for he said, "You know that when you eat thereof, that you will become as God, wise." So the tempter tempted Eve until she ate, and she gave to her husband; and after they had sinned, transgressed God's law, God came down for His usual walk in the garden, to commune with them, and He looked around and He found no Adam there. And then He called out, "Adam," and He found him away yonder in the bushes. And the Lord said, "What are you doing here, Adam?" Well, yes — he began to make excuses. Don't you know that just as soon as a man sins he becomes a sneak? It is wonderful how sneakish sin makes us. Holiness makes men as bold as a lion. So they were driven out of the garden, and man became a sinner. Oh, I am so glad that the seed of woman has bruised the serpent's head, and that if we will we can be perfect with God.

Now, turn in your Bibles and we will read some of the words of the Lord. Turn to Gen. v. 22, 24, "And Enoch walked with God, after he begat Methuselah, three hundred years; and all the days of Enoch were three hundred and sixty-five years." So you see he was sixty-five years old when he was sanctified, when he was made perfect. In the twenty-fourth verse we read, "And Enoch walked with God, and he was not, for God took him." Then again in Gen. vi. 9, we read, "These are the generations of Noah. Noah was a just man and perfect in his generation, and Noah walked with God." There are two men who were perfect and walked with God. Again, let us turn over to Gen. xvii. 1, "And when Abram was ninety years old and nine, the Lord appeared to Abram and said unto him, 'I am the Almighty God, walk before me and be thou perfect.'" There is another man who walked with God seventy-six years. Glory be to his name! Oh, I am so glad that we have these examples of walking with God.

And then, again, if you will turn to Lev. xix. 2 you will read, "Ye shall be holy, for I, the Lord thy God, am holy." Again, let us turn to Deut. xviii. 13: here is a verse that has done me more good on the subject of sanctification than any other verse in the Bible. Let me read it to you. "Thou shalt be perfect with the Lord thy God." How glad I am that my Father said that I will not be perfect with man; for, had God said unto me, "Mr. Weber, you must be perfect with man," I would have said, "Lord, your own Son could not be perfect with men; for they said, 'He hath a devil,' they called Him the prince of devils, they called Him all sorts of names." But when I read in this precious Word of God that "thou shalt be perfect with the Lord thy God," oh, it fills my soul with glory.

Now, sister and brother, you will never reach that stage in this world that you will be perfect with man; but all God wants in perfection is your love, your obedience, and your choicest heart's desire. And as long as I walk perfect with God, no matter what men may say about me, no matter what fault they may find with me, God looks upon me as being perfect. Let us again turn over to Josh. iii. 5, "And Joshua said unto the people, Sanctify yourselves: for to-morrow the Lord will do wonders among you." Glory to His name! Sanctify yourselves, set yourselves apart, be a peculiar people! Be a holy people, and I will do wonders among you.

I have not got time now to stop and tell you about the judges, about the kings, and about the great men and women that lived and walked with God, but I want you now to turn over to Job i. 1, "There was a man in the land of Uz, whose name was Job, and that man was perfect and upright and one that feared God and eschewed evil." Do you know he had a holy terror for a wife, but he would not curse God and die, as she said to him. He would have been a fool if he had. All his property taken from him, his children died, his wife forsook him, his friends pointed the finger of scorn at him, the devil had power to take and afflict his body with boils. Oh, what a wretched-looking creature he is! See him! But the last verse in this chapter of Job says to us, "In all this, Job sinned not, nor charged God foolishly." There is another man that walked with God.

Now I want you to turn to the Fifty-first Psalm, "Have mercy upon me, O God, according to thy loving kindness; according unto the multitude of thy tender mercies, blot out my transgression; wash me throughly." A lady one time thought I did not know what I was saying, maybe I do not sometimes; but she wrote me a little note and said, "Mr. Weber, you said, 'Wash me throughly,' and the Bible says, 'Wash me thoroughly.'" Poor, ignorant woman, she did not know any better, so I did not blame her. You will find out that all English versions of the Bible read, "Wash me throughly"; all American versions read, "Wash me thoroughly." That is just the difference. I gave my Bible to a preacher, and I said, "Please read this." And he said, "Wash me thoroughly from my iniquities." I said, "You better go to school and find out how to read;" he said, "Why?" I said, "Look here, that don't say 'thoroughly,' but it says 'throughly.'"

Now, I tell you I like that word "throughly" best. Why? I have a jar, and I have it sealed; I hand it to the servant girl and I say to her, "I want you to wash that thoroughly." All right; she takes and washes it all on the outside and it is nice and clean. I get it and I say, "Have you washed it thoroughly?" And she says, "Yes, sir." And I just take and unscrew the lid and I smell inside. Phew! "Why," she says, "it is thoroughly washed." But I say, "Now wash it throughly." And that is just the way with David. He wanted God to go right through him. You see, if God goes through you that takes the inside, the outside, the top side, and every side. Glory to God! So I like that word "throughly." It is God going right through me. Say, if God goes through some of you folks he will find quite a lot of dirt and filth on the inside. That is so; is it not? "Wash me throughly from my iniquity; cleanse me from my sin. Against thee and thee only have I sinned and done this evil in thy sight; that thou mightest be justified when thou speakest, and be clear when thou judgest." Seventh verse, "Purge me with hyssop and I shall be clean; wash me and I shall be whiter than snow."

Now you know as well as I do that snow is not pure white. For instance, you ladies say to the children, when the pumps are frozen up, "Go out and gather mamma a big kettle of snow." The children go out and fill the kettle clear up. You then put it on the stove and melt the snow, and you find out that the snow that looked so white was not pure white, for you find some of the heavier settlings at the bottom, and the lighter settling on the top. The consequence was, you said that that snow was not pure white. But now, how will I get snow pure white? Why, I will just take that snow yonder and melt it, then I will take and skim off the top, and put it through a strainer of very fine cloth, and then take and freeze that water, and from that what do I have? Snow whiter than snow. Some of you folks need freezing over, it seems to me. And I tell you, if you will get frozen over, my brother and sister, you will get whiter than snow.

Now, justification as we read here in Isa. i. 18, " Come now, let us reason together; though your sins be as scarlet, they shall be as white as snow." That is justification. David here, in the Fifty-first Psalm and the seventh verse, says, " Purge me with hyssop and I shall be clean; wash me and I shall be whiter than snow." Then in the tenth verse he says, " Create in me a clean heart, O God; and renew a right spirit within me." Ah, he wanted a heart from sin set free, he wanted a heart pure; he wanted a heart holy, he wanted a heart sanctified of God. And just as soon as he got that kind of a heart, what does he say? " Then will I teach transgressors thy ways; and sinners shall be converted unto thee." Glory be to God for that!

I asked a preacher down at Coldwater when David was called a man after God's own heart. He said, " After he was sanctified." I said, " You do not know what you are talking about." Well, he said, " I do, Mr. Weber." Well, I said, " You don't, for I want to say to you that nine-tenths of the preachers tell you that David, after he was sanctified, was called a man after God's own heart, and it is not so." There was an infidel who said to me one day, " David was a pretty man for God to call him ' a man after his own heart.' Why, if he had committed that sin in these days we would have put him in the penitentiary; and that is the man you hold up." Do you know, brother, when David was called a man after God's own heart? If you don't, I will tell you. Turn over here in your Bibles, to Acts xiii. 22, and you will read, " I have found David, the son of Jesse, a man after mine own heart, which shall fulfil all my will." Again, if you will look in 1 Sam. xiii. 14, you will find that it was when David was a little boy, out yonder tending his father's sheep, before he had been anointed king, that he was called a man after God's own heart. So that stops the mouths of infidels.

Now, I have not time to linger and talk to you about Isaiah and Jeremiah and Ezekiel, and some of the minor prophets, but I want you to turn now to Matt. v. 8, " Blessed (that means happy), blessed are the pure in heart, for they shall see God." Again, in the forty-eighth verse, " Be ye therefore perfect, even as your Father which is in heaven is perfect." Do you suppose my Father would say to me, " Be ye perfect." if I could not be? I want to say to you, I would not worship that kind of God. I believe in the God who said to me, " Be ye therefore perfect even as I am perfect," that it is possible for me to be perfect with God. He did not say, with man.

Let us turn over to John xvii. 17. The Lord Jesus

is here making a prayer, and in his prayer he says,
"Sanctify them through thy truth; thy word is truth."
Do you suppose that the Son of God would have
prayed for His disciples to be sanctified, if they could
not be? Do you suppose that the Son of God, who
was just about to go on Calvary's rugged cross, would
pray that prayer, "Sanctify them through thy truth,"
if it were not possible? No, no, no!

Again, turn to Acts xxvi. 18. He is speaking to
Paul here, and He sends him out on a mission, and He
says to him, "To open their eyes, and to turn them
from darkness to light, and from the power of Satan
unto God, that they may receive forgiveness of sins."
That is justification. And if I were to say to you, I
am going to give you my knife, you would not look
for something else, would you? So he says here,
"And that they may receive forgiveness of sins, and
inheritance among them which are sanctified by faith."
Let us turn over to Rom. vi. 11, "Likewise reckon ye
also yourselves to be dead indeed unto sin, but alive
unto God through our Lord Jesus Christ." Now, he
says, "reckon." Count it so, believe it so, and it will
be so. "Let not sin therefore reign in your mortal
body." And fourteenth verse, "For sin shall not have
dominion over you." But glory be to God, Brother
Damon, that we shall have dominion over sin. Oh,
how glad I am that God says, "Sin shall not have
dominion over you." Bless the Lord.

Again, let us turn to 2 Cor. vii. 1, "Having therefore these promises, dearly beloved, let us cleanse our-
selves from all filthiness of the flesh and spirit; per-
fecting holiness in the fear of God." Again let us

turn to 2 Cor. xiii. 11, "Finally, brethren, farewell." You see, they were in the Lord now; he calls them brethren; and then that benediction he offers and says, "Be perfect." Again let us turn to Heb. xii. 14, "Follow peace with all men, and holiness, without which no man shall see the Lord." 1 John iv. 18, "There is no fear in love, but perfect love casteth out fear."

Now, then, we have seen by these Scripture promises that sanctification, perfection, holiness, entire consecration, fulness of the blessing, are one and the same. I do not care so much what the people call it; some call it "second blessing," some prefer to call it "baptism of the Holy Ghost and fire," and some prefer to call it "Fulness of Blessing." Get it and then just live it, and you will be all right. Do you know I never saw a young convert opposed to holiness. It is some of you old backsliders that oppose holiness, do you know it? It is some of you who have been living in sin all your life, who oppose holiness. No truly converted man will ever oppose it. Just as quick as you get to be a kicker against holiness, put it down that you are backslidden. Let us go back to the text again, 1 Thess. v. 23, 24, "And the very God of peace sanctify you wholly, and I pray God your whole soul and spirit and body be preserved blameless unto the coming of the Lord Jesus Christ. Faithful is he that calleth you, who also will do it."

When I started out I said there was not one in this congregation but what will admit that Adam and Eve were perfect; but as David says, "In sin hath my mother conceived me; behold, I was shapen in iniquity."

So, then, here is a little child. That little child is born in the world with sin in it. But the atonement of the Lord Jesus Christ provides for the perfection of that child; if he dies before he reaches the years of accountability, that child goes right in the presence of God, perfect. But just as soon as that little boy or girl yonder learns right from wrong, learns to disobey, learns to lie, learns to do evil, just so soon that little boy or girl becomes a voluntary sinner against God, and, as a voluntary sinner against God, that boy or girl is responsible before God. Now, then, he says, if we confess our sins, He is faithful and just to forgive us our sins. Then that little boy or girl must get down, and say, "Father, in the name of Jesus, forgive me my sins." Now, when he becomes pardoned, all of his actual sins are forgiven him. But still that hereditary sin is within him. For justification is cutting off the tree by the roots, and sanctification is going down and getting the roots all out. So, then, I confess my sin, and God is faithful and just to forgive my sin. That is, my actual sin. Now, my hereditary sin, I must ask him, and believe him, and have faith that if I say "Father, in the name of Jesus, cleanse my hereditary sin," that God then comes and sanctifies me, and washes me, and makes me pure, and makes me a fit temple for the Holy Ghost to dwell in. Who, then, would oppose holiness? If you do, I tell you it is holiness or hell! For God says that without holiness no man shall see God. Some churches teach that a man receives holiness just before he dies; but I read in my Bible here about Enoch receiving it three hundred years before he died, and he walked and talked with God for three hundred years and lived perfect.

The Roman Catholics have a purgatory, for they say that no man can go in the presence of God, who is not pure and holy, so that they have yonder a refining process in purgatory, to get men holy. But, oh, I bless God that you and I can be made perfect in this life, if we will, for He says we can. If we confess our sin, He is faithful and just to forgive us our sin and to cleanse us from all unrighteousness. That is, my hereditary sins. And I pray God now, "That the very God of peace sanctify you wholly, and I pray that your whole spirit and soul and body be preserved blameless unto the coming of the Lord Jesus Christ. Faithful is he that calleth you, who also will do it."

Now, my brother, do you want to be sanctified? Do you object to asking God to cleanse you from your hereditary sin? If you do, you better ask Him, first, to pardon you as a sinner. Glory to God! I have not told you what this man or that man says; I have told you what God says; and if you have any fault to find, you find it with God, for here is his word. Now, then, my brother and sister, do you enjoy this state of grace? One says, "I am afraid to acknowledge it, for fear they will expect more of me." Expect more of you? God says, if we walk in the light, as he is in the light, we have fellowship one with another; and the blood of Jesus Christ His Son cleanses us from all sin.

Oh, sister, if you don't walk in the light of God, you are not even justified. You have the light this morning; you must go on to perfection, or else go to hell! One or the other, Holiness or hell! Glory to God, I am going to take holiness.

Do you want this state of grace? Do you want to get where you can give up your business and go to prayer-meeting? Do you want to get where you won't be a kicker in a revival-meeting, because they do not preach just to suit you? Do you want to get where you just love to worship God? Where it will be just joy to serve the Lord Jesus Christ? If you do, this morning ask the Father, in the name of Jesus, to sanctify you wholly, and He will do it. Be careful now, do not say that you have entered into a state of grace unless you have. Every one who believes you are sanctified, stand upon your feet. Don't stand up unless you know. Don't stand up unless you know it; be honest, and if you have it, God bless you.

Now, how many of you want it? stand up! Everybody wants it in this house. Everybody wants to be sanctified in this house. Glory to God, look at this sight this morning! . . .

Now, I want every one of you to get right down on your knees where you are. Now, my brother and sister, you ask the Father, in the name of Jesus, to cleanse your hereditary sin. You were saved as a sinner, but you are not saved yet from all your sin. Now say, Father, in the name of Jesus, sanctify me wholly, make me pure, cleanse all my hereditary sin, and cleanse me and purify me and make me holy now. He will do it. Now, you must believe Him when you ask Him; for He says He is more willing to give the Holy Spirit to them that ask Him than parents are to give good gifts to their children. Ask Him now, don't be afraid; ask that your joy may be full. Ask Him now. Father, in the name of Jesus, we come to praise Thee, that the people are hungering and thirsting after righteousness, and Thou hast said, "Blessed are they that hunger and thirst, for they shall be filled." O God, in the name of Jesus Christ, sanctify these boys and girls, these fathers and mothers, these loved ones, just now. I believe! I believe! You have asked Him now, in the name of Jesus, to cleanse your hereditary sin. That places you before God, perfect. Now, walk and live and be.

> "Lord, I give my all to Thee,
> Friends and time and earthly store,
> Soul and body Thine to be,
> Wholly Thine forevermore."

Glory be to Jesus! Angels are looking with glad faces to-day. Let us give our praises to God.

CHAPTER XVI.

HOW TO HAVE EVERY PRAYER ANSWERED. — SERMON ON PRAYER, PREACHED BY REV. J. H. WEBER AT THE FIRST METHODIST EPISCOPAL CHURCH, ADRIAN, MICH.

If you will open your Bibles, and turn to 1 Tim. 2: 8, you will read these words: "I will therefore that men pray everywhere, lifting up holy hands, without wrath and doubting."

There are two kinds of prayer that are represented in this book, the prayer of the child of God and the prayer of the sinner. It is the prayer of the child of God that we especially want to speak about this morning.

With everything in this life you will find a condition, and you see that the very text itself suggests a condition to successful praying. The first condition in our text then is, "I will that men pray everywhere, lifting up holy hands." Now, it means something to lift up holy hands. James said, "Cleanse your hands, ye sinners! Purify your hearts, ye double-minded!" So, then, the first thing God wishes us to do, when we come to Him, is to get these hands of ours clean; and it means so much to lift up holy hands. How can you lift up holy hands before God, if you go forth into this world, and men see by your actions, by your walk, by your conversation, by your contact with humanity, that these hands of yours are unclean? The world has a right to expect of you and me clean hands. Suppose they see a man just as anxious and grasping, just as penurious and as little, stooping to just as low things as the men of the world will in the tricks of trade, in the tricks of the various walks of life — if they see that you stoop to these things, and do the very same things that they do, they like to say. "That man is no better than I am," and they have a right to judge thus. And when you say lifting up holy hands, it means a great deal. It means, my brother, that if you make a church subscription that you are to pay that bill, as much as you would pay your grocer or clothier, or the dry goods man. I have known Christian people before now who were in the church, and who pretended to lift up holy hands; one, for instance, giving a church subscription to build a new church; they were very enthusiastic, and they put down their names for thus and so. It was put in the hands of the committee, and that committee was given power to act and do as they thought best. They changed the plan; perhaps they changed something that was not in the original plan, and thought it would be best; and before now, do you know, I have known those who were Christians, those who called themselves, at least, Christians, who would go back on their subscription and say "I won't pay it." Now, God cannot bless anything of that kind at all. Then again, I have known others who have gone into the church, and they have subscribed so much for the preacher's salary. The stewards have gone out and made the assessment, and when the time came to pay, he would not pay it. Why? The preacher began to preach real plain, and it began to cut right and left; he began to hew to the mark; you were guilty and you said he preached that sermon especially for you; and you went home like spoiled babies and went to finding fault, saying this thing and that thing and that other thing, and when the time came for you to pay your church subscription for the preacher's salary, instead of paying the ten dollars you subscribed, you paid, perhaps, four or five. And then you stayed away from church. And then you call yourself a Christian. Do you expect God can prosper a man who will do that? No, sir. You cannot lift up holy hands and be a successful Christian, my brother and sister, unless you do as James said, "Cleanse your hands, ye sinners!" Then again, how can a man be a successful Christian who does not give God one-tenth? The Bible word is one-tenth, and I dare say there are not twenty people in the house that give one-tenth to God. He says, " Ye have robbed me of tithes and offerings," and it is so. Do you know if the church of God to-day were living up to her high privileges in Christ Jesus, and were giving like the old Jew did — and you all know that the Jew of old gave one-tenth; the sacrifices were many and the approbation of God was sent; his smiles were on every hand, and Israel prospered, and the land brought forth, and everything they laid their hands to was successful, and they prospered and went on and Israel stood before the nations as no other nation in the world. Now, then, my brother, if you do not give one-tenth to God, you are a robber. " Ye have robbed me." And, oh, how many Christian people, who call themselves Christians, who try to palm themselves off on God as Christians, do not give God one-tenth! Now, I believe that if a man would give God one-tenth, that He will do just as He says He will do here. For instance, He says, "Honor the Lord with the first fruits of all thine increase; so shall thy barns be filled with plenty, and thy presses shall burst out with new wine." So it is to honor God. He says, "Honor Me and I will honor you." But if you sow sparingly, you will reap sparingly; if you sow abundantly, you will reap abundantly; so God says. And if you will just take and read Deut. 28, you will find that my Father says, if you will keep His commandments, and His commandments are, one-tenth of all thine increase, then He says, "Blessed shalt thou be in the city, and blessed shalt thou be in the field; blessed shall be thy basket and thy store; blessed shall be the fruit of thy body and the fruit of thy cattle, and the increase of thy kine and the flocks of thy sheep." Just to think of it. If you will take that and honor God. You must not expect God to prosper you if you do not do as He says you are to do. You remember in the first Psalm — let me just read it to you; wonderful, is it not? "And he shall be like a tree planted by the rivers of water, that bringeth forth his fruit in his season; his leaf also shall not wither, and whatsoever he doeth shall prosper." Think of it!

Now, then, don't you know, my brother and sister, that if you don't honor God, as sure as God is in heaven He will not honor you. I heard of a man, one time, who said, "I want to honor God, but I cannot give one-tenth, because I am in debt." That is just the way to get out of debt. What would you think if you should go to your grocer yonder, saying to him, "Well, I cannot pay you because I am in debt"? You owe Jesus one-tenth, just as you owe the grocer yonder. One-tenth belongs to God. It came from God; everything is His; the cattle on a thousand hills. Possessing all things, He will grant all things abundantly, or else He will take them away from you. And I believe the reason so many of you people are poor is because you do not honor God with the first fruits of all your increase. I am sure of it, because God says so.

Well, "lifting up holy hands." A great many people, if they had it to spare, would give it to God, but they will not make any sacrifices at all. Look at that widow yonder in the temple. She only has a little, and she drops it in yonder, and Jesus said, "She hath cast more in than they all." Why? She is there in her poverty, she is there in want, but she honors God. And I will venture to say that God just opened the river of prosperity before that woman, and that incident has come down, and will go down, as long as time shall last in this world, and the hundreds, perhaps the thousands, that the rich men dropped in were never noticed at all. See, I have a friend up in Hillsdale who only earns five dollars a week, and he has a wife; but he says, "Mr. Weber, I must honor God with one-tenth," and every week he goes down in his pocket, and takes out fifty cents and gives it to God. He says, "Mr. Weber, my wife complains sometimes, and she says, 'Now, husband, we ought not to do it;' but, Bro. Weber," he said, "I am going to be a whole Christian; I have been sanctified; I have given my wife and myself, my home and my tools and my property, and everything I have, to God, and one-tenth belongs to Him." And do you know, that man is prospering, and I tell you it will not be long until you see that man getting rich. I have some friends down in the country below Bronson, and after they heard this sermon, they said, "Now, Bro. Weber, we have been Christians, but we have not prospered as we might have prospered had we honored God. Now we are going to honor God with the first fruits of all our increase; we are going to give God one-tenth." And he told me he never had such a successful year in all his life, and never made so much money; and, do you know, that that man and every one of his children and his wife, and everything that is about him, is consecrated to God.

Now, if I were a farmer — I tell you I would be a city fool in the country — but I will tell you how I would farm. I would get down and say, "My Father, in the name of Jesus, let the Holy Ghost show me what I shall plant in this field." I would find out; and if the Lord told me to put onions in that field, as much as I hate onions, I would put onions in that field; I would fill it up with onions. First, I would take and plow it, and then harrow it. Then I would go into the middle — you might go into the corners of the field — and I would get down and say, "Father, in the name of Jesus, sanctify this seed I am going to put into this ground." Then I would put it in. And then, again, after I had the seed in, I would go into the field and I would pray and ask God to water it with the rains of heaven and bless it with the sunshine of His love, and prosper the fruit that I had put in; and then every day, around my family altar, I would pray for my cattle, I would pray for my crops, I would pray for my stock, and I would pray for my family; and I believe that when the time came, that I would have an abundant crop.

And then I would not be as mean as the man I read of one time. He had a great cranberry marsh, and it ran out; there were just a few cranberries the year before, and he said, "I guess I will give that cranberry marsh to God the coming year." All right. Well, the coming year, there was never known such a crop of cranberries as was found on that marsh. He went down and looked at it, and he said, "I never saw such a crop in my life." He said, "It is too much to give to God; I will not give it to Him." He was like that old negro and his boy, who had been out on an island where they had found a great treasure, and they were coming home in a boat, and while they were in the boat a storm began to rage, and the waves began to dash and splash in the boat, and the old negro got down in the boat, and said, "Lord, if you will take me over to the other side, I will give you half I have got." Well, the storm kept on; in fact, it increased all the time, and the poor fellow thought he was going down every moment, and he got down again, and he said, "Lord, if you will take me over, I will give you all I have got." He was almost like another negro that I read about at another time. He wanted to get very humble, and he thought the way to get humble was to go alongside a great big stone wall; and he prayed and said, "Lord, throw down this wall on this black man; throw it on me and kill me and crush the life out of me." There was a man there who heard him pray, so he just took a piece of a brickbat and threw it at him, and it hit him, and he said, "Lord, can't you take a joke?" This was about the way with this other colored man who was in the boat. Then his boy said, "Papa, I would not do that;" and the old man says, "Keep still; when we get over there we won't give him nothing." This is about the way with a great many people. "O Lord, if you will just bless me, if you just prosper me, I will give you one-tenth;" but about the time that the one-tenth is to be given, it is, "aught is aught, two is two, and there is nothing coming to you." All goes down. Can you expect to be successful that way? Can you? No, sir. God does not prosper men that do that way. You cannot lift up holy hands. You must lift up holy hands if you are going to have every prayer you put up answered.

Suppose I, as a farmer, put in a crop of corn. Well, I pray over it, just as I said before. If, for instance, I fed that corn yonder to the hogs. Supposing I have one hundred hogs and the time comes for me to market them. I pick out, not ten of the runts, — I pick out ten of the fattest and the very best, and then I would take the money to God and say, "Lord, here it is;" and I would not use a cent of it. I would be afraid that I would be a thief. Why, if you steal from God, it is just the same as stealing from men; and if you do not give to God one-tenth, you are a thief. So the Lord says here, and I believe just what God says.

"I will that men pray everywhere, lifting up holy hands." Lord, it belongs to you; I will give it to you. Why, I heard of a man out East, who every year used to give one hundred dollars to the missionary cause, and he was a prosperous man. But the year came around and he was taken sick. He had been such a good man in the mill, and he did so much for the mill, his employers concluded they would pay him all the same while he was sick. They kept on paying him a long time, but he continued sick, so they said, "Well, we will continue him on half-pay," so they gave him half-pay. And every year the steward came around for one hundred dollars for God, and they got it. He had saved quite a little money, and he used up that. Then the mill men said, "Well, we cannot afford to pay a man who does not work for us," so they stopped altogether; and the little money he had was about used up. And they came around again, and he had two or three hundred dollars in the bank, and he was still sick, not knowing where to get the next dollar. The stewards came around, and he put down one hundred dollars. The people said, "It is wrong." The pastor came to him and remonstrated and said, "You ought not to give it." But he says, "God says for me to give it." Why, they said, "You will starve." "No," he said, "My Father will prosper me; He will give to me. I am His child and He has promised to take care of me." After he had paid the one hundred dollars, in a few days after, a great, long envelope came from some attorney. One of his rich relatives had died and left him an immense fortune. So God provided for him.

I tell you, my brother and sister, you honor God. Why, if God told me to take every dollar I had in my pocket, everything I have, I believe I would go, and I would give it to Him, and I know that my Father would take care of me; He says He will.

Now, then, first condition: Lifting up holy hands. Second condition: Without wrath. Now, you may be able to give one-tenth; perhaps you do give one-tenth and you have prospered; but oh, my brother, how about the wrath? Are you jealous of that sister? Are you jealous of that brother? Have you wrath in your heart against that sister, because she does not live as you think she ought to live? Because she has been put at the head of the missionary society, and you have not? Because that man was made trustee, and you were thrown out? Because that one was made a class leader, and the class taken from you? Ah, my brother, we are to have no wrath. Have you wrath in your heart against that business man yonder, who is in the same business you are in? Do you pass him by and not notice him? Have you wrath in your heart at that sister yonder? Have you a great high fence built between you and her? Do you say to your little children, "Don't you speak to that neighbor's children there!" Do you talk about your neighbor so? If that is in your heart, God says, it is of the flesh. And you know as well as I do, as I quoted it to you in Galatians, that God Almighty has said, "They that do these things shall not enter the Kingdom of Heaven." Now, I have seen Christian people, that is, professed Christian people, before now, they have had all the characteristics, it would seem, of thorough Christians, but they had that contemptible thing in their hearts, wrath. "I will that men pray everywhere, lifting up holy hands without wrath." There is that sister who talked about you. She tried to ruin your character; she tried, as it were, to keep you out of your position. She lied about you. Now, are you to have wrath in your heart against her? No, no, no! Why, do you know the meanest man that lives in this world, the man who has done the most against me, tried to tear down my character, tried to tear down my reputation, tried to tear down, as it were, the work of God that I am trying to build up, do you know I could fall at the feet of the worst enemy I have and, if it would save his soul, I believe I could lick up the spittle at his feet; for I pray for my enemies, and try to do good to them that spitefully assail me. And that is one reason that when they try to get me into a paper controversy I say, "No, I will leave it with God." God says, "Vengeance is mine, I will repay, saith the Lord." Then, again, he says, "The triumphing of the wicked is short." And sometimes I have seen men spread themselves, it would seem as though they were about to cast me overboard and kill me, and I have just put my reputation, I have just put my character, I have just put everything I had into God's hands, and I have said, "Sink or swim, survive or perish, Lord Jesus, I am Thine." And that is one reason that you see that the work of God goes right on. I tell them I am the moon. You remember the story I told you about the moon and the dog. The dog used to bark at the moon, but the moon did not mind it at all; the little dog died and the moon went right on. I am the moon, bless the Lord. Going right on, working for the glory of God.

First condition: Lifting up holy hands. Second condition: Without wrath. Third condition: And doubting.

But that is one of the most difficult, one of the hardest points that it is possible for people to get hold of. I have known men to give one-tenth; I have known them to profess the blessing of entire sanctification. Yesterday, there was a minister up to see me. He does not belong to our church, he belongs to another church; we were talking, and he said, "Brother Weber, if you only touched on our lines." I said, "Well, you cannot tell me a sin you denounce that I do not. You tell me one I do not denounce, and if I do not denounce it, my name is not Weber." Now, we have been talking about experience, etc., but let us take the thirteenth chapter of Corinthians and read it over, and in the seventh verse it says, "Beareth all things, believeth all things." Now, I said to this minister, "You were down at Quincy holding meetings for about six weeks; you say that you are entirely sanctified of God; that you believe God. Now, if that had been so, you would have turned that town upside down, and they did not have a single conversion scarcely; so you do not believe all things, don't you see?"

So my brother and sister, God says that he that doubteth is like a wave of the sea that is driven by the wind and tossed. Let not that man think he shall receive anything of the Lord. Doubting? Oh, yes, I get down like that old woman and I say, "Lord remove that mountain," and I get up the next day in the morning and look for it, and the mountain is there. It is just as I expected. Don't believe it, don't believe it! Better believe, my brother and sister, that this roof will cave in; better believe, my brother and sister, that your very life shall be taken, than disbelieve God. For my Father has said that "Whatsoever ye ask in My name, I will give you." Now, we have just found out "I will that men pray everywhere, lifting up holy hands without wrath or doubting." Now, my hands are clean; I give God one-tenth; I do not owe these store-keepers; I pay my honest debts; I have no wrath in my heart; I do not doubt God. Now, I am just in a condition to pray. Before I was not in a condition to pray. Now, then, I will get down to pray; so I will say, just as Jesus said, "Father!" Why? Jesus says, "My Father is greater than I." Now, we will see how we have to pray.

Now I want you to take and turn in your Bibles and notice very carefully the fourteenth chapter of John and the sixth verse, and the last clause, "No man cometh unto the Father but by Me." Now again, I want you to turn over to Romans, five, two, "By whom also we have access." Now, I want you to notice that word "access" especially. "Access!" Now, turn over to Ephesians, two, eighteen, "For through Him, we both have access, by one Spirit unto the Father." Notice the word "access" again, please. Ephesians, three, twelve, "In whom we have boldness and access." Now then again, I want you to turn back to the sixteenth chapter of John and the twenty-third verse. "Verily, verily, I say unto you, whatsoever ye shall ask the Father in My name." The twenty-fourth verse, "Hitherto, you have asked nothing in My name." Why? Why, Jesus Christ was not an intercessor yet; He was not a mediator between God and man yet. But at the time He became intercessor, the day when He became mediator; in the twenty-sixth verse he says, "At that day ye shall ask the Father in My name." Now, let me see. Through Him we have access; by whom we have boldness and access. "No man cometh unto the Father but by Me."

If I want to get in the presence of God at the very opening of my prayer, what shall I do? "Verily, verily, I say unto you, whatsoever ye shall ask the Father, in My name, He will give it you." "Hitherto, ye have asked nothing in My name; at that day ye shall ask in My name." Now, how will I pray? At the very opening of my prayer, "Father, in the name of Jesus. Now I am right in the presence of God. I go on and pray and pray, don't you see, Bro. Morgan. I am not near God yet. Most all people will end up their prayer and say, "For Jesus' sake." You cannot find that in a prayer in the Bible; I defy you to do it. A young man said to me, "Mr. Weber, why not say, 'For Jesus' sake.'" Because the Bible does not say so in a single prayer. It says, in the name of Jesus. Now, it is going to be hard for you, older Christians, to unlearn what you have learned; you will go on praying just like you have prayed before; but if you will take this simple way that God lays down here, and every time you pray, say "Father, in the name of Jesus." Now I am right in the presence of God. "Now, what do you want, my child?" Ask not, as some ministers say to ask, largely; that is not in the Bible at all; but ask that your joy may be full." Now, let me see. Let us turn over to the fourteenth chapter of John, the twenty-sixth verse. "But the Comforter, which is the Holy Ghost, whom the Father will send in My name." Now, then, I have a son who is unconverted, or a husband unconverted, or a friend unconverted. I get down and say, "Father, in the name of Jesus, convert my husband." No, sir. You will not dare to pray such a prayer as that; you cannot find that in a single prayer in the Bible. Why, I have heard people get down and say, "Oh, God, convert everybody in this town." If I believed that God could convert everybody in this town, Bro. Morgan, and would not do it, I would rather be a mean, little, contemptible infidel. Jesus said, " I pray not for the world," and I do not propose to do it. But I will give you a little prayer that is infallible.

But you say to me, " Mr. Weber, are not all things possible to God?" No, they are not. God cannot make the parallel lines on this book meet; I defy Him to do it. God cannot create a yearling in a minute; He might create an animal a thousand times larger, but in order to create a yearling, how long must it live? A year, must it not? If He could not create a yearling in a minute, can God create a dry watermellon? It is impossible. Now, there are things which are impossible with God, and it is just as much impossible for God to convert you, sinner, unless you are willing, as it is for God to create a yearling in a minute.

But now, I am going to give you a little prayer that is infallible. But, Jesus says, the Comforter — that is the Holy Ghost,-- whom the Father will send in My name. Over here in the sixteenth chapter of John, beginning at the seventh verse, we read, " Nevertheless, I tell you the truth; it is expedient for you that I go away, for if I go not away, the Comforter will not come unto you, but if I depart, I will send Him unto you, and when He is come"— Who? The Holy Ghost — "He will reprove or convict the world of sin and righteousness and of judgment." Now, I have a husband, I have a son, I have a friend; how will I pray? "Father, in the name of Jesus, send the Holy Ghost to convict him or her of sin and of righteousness and of judgment." And that prayer is infallible. I tell you, all the devils in hell cannot thwart that prayer. The Holy Ghost can convict them whether they will be convicted or not, but the God of the Bible cannot convert them, if they do not want to be converted. Right here, sinner, let me say, if you are damned, and you go to hell, with all the weeping devils and howling fiends in hell, it will be because you want to go. So, therefore, I never pray and ask God to convert a single man or woman, unless they stand up and come to this altar, or say to me privately, "Bro. Weber, I want to be converted, I want to be saved." Then I can bring a blessing down, by prayer, into their soul.

Now, brother and sister, are you going to pray like you used to pray? If you do, you will just be that same little bit of an insignificant Christian that you have always been. But if you will say, "I will pray as the Bible teaches me; I will lift up holy hands without wrath or doubting, and I will begin at the opening of my prayer in the name of Jesus,"— every man and woman I have ever seen, who kept that up, and has practised that, I have always seen them to be purified, and to be such Christians as they never were before. Now, I will leave it with you. What will you do? My Father, in the name of Jesus, let the Holy Ghost rivet it on our hearts. Sanctify it, Father, to thy glory. Father, we do praise Thee, that Thy Holy Spirit in the name of Jesus, is coming to the people, to point out, to tell them, to show them the way to our Lord Jesus Christ. Now, Blessed Father, just as we are, help these dear, precious fathers and mothers, to go home and pray as the Bible teaches them. Amen.

CHAPTER XVII.

MR. WEBER'S EXPERIENCE AS TOLD IN HIS MEETINGS.

There is generally a great deal of curiosity exhibited when it is announced that I am to tell " How the Lord converted me, a Roman Catholic."

People often say, "What nationality are you, Mr. Weber?" Some think an Irishman, some a Dutchman, and some one thing and some another. I will give you my parentage, and you can judge for yourself.

My father was born in the province of Alsace, in the possession of the French government at that time; and my mother in that good old Buckeye State, Ohio; and I was born in Cincinnati, O., so now you can judge for yourself.

I inherited my Catholicism from my father's side, as his father was one of those wool-dyed Catholics. With him that which did not point to Rome was not anything. My early teaching was "that all Protestants would surely go to hell, as they did not belong to THE CHURCH; no matter how good they were, they surely would be lost."

I could see no difference in the other boys with whom I played, as they acted just as I did and the rest of the Protestant boys, and why they should be lost I could not understand. My grandfather, called one of the very best Romanists, would lie and get drunk; my father, with the rest of us would drink beer, and Sunday afternoons go to a hilltop resort kept by one of my uncles, and there spend the rest of the day drinking and dancing. Well, if this was religion, and I could go to heaven and do thus, it seemed queer to me.

In my early life, I had an ambition to become a rich man. I knew to become a rich man a boy must begin young; so I would save my money or borrow it from my mother, and go out during vacation, and sell matches, fans, or brooms: one day, when offering brooms for sale in a saloon, I said, "Mister, don't you want to buy a broom?" He said, "No, but I want to buy you."— "What do you mean?" I said. Then he told me he wanted me to come and tend bar in his saloon. My heart just leaped for joy, for now I could become a business man. I went home in high glee, told my proposed offer to my mother, but she objected; being a spoiled boy, I pleaded, and persuaded my father to go down and see the man, and I was sure they would let me go. When we arrived at the saloon, I said, "Here it is, pa," but he passed by; he seemed in deep meditation. I think something like this passed through his mind: "When I married, like all Germans, I liked a glass of beer, and now I am its slave, drink and kindred vices are bearing me down, and now to put my innocent boy on the same road I cannot." Then I began to plead with him to go in and see the man. At last I prevailed. The man received us with open arms and said, "I want your boy." When we reached home my ma and pa conferred with each other, and decided I should go to school, but I cried and tore around, — a spoiled boy, you see, — and said, "Now, when I want to work you won't let me."

When Monday morning came, I was up bright and early, and ma said, "Joe, I want you to go to school," but I said, "I am going down to try it anyhow." When I arrived there, I was so small that he had to build a rack about eight inches behind the counter, so I might deal out hell and damnation to the people. This is one of the blackest spots in my life, and did I not read in Isa. i. 18, "Come now, and let us reason together, saith the Lord; though your sins be as scarlet, they shall be as white as snow," I could never stand before a congregation and preach. Oh, the depths of God's love and forgiveness! My father had come home from the war worse than when he went in. The habit of drink had now completely overcome him. My poor mother, heart-broken and sad, decided it would be best for them to move away from Cincinnati; my grandfather had died, and left father considerable, and it was fast being spent in the saloons, so they bought a place in Hamilton, O., and thither they went; but I remained at Cincinnati. My father found associates there, and soon was being lost in drink again. I being the oldest boy, my mother yearned to have me near her, and she wanted me to come home and live. Then I said, "Mamma, I am such a big boy, and you need my help; if you will get me a job, I will come home." So a job was procured at the paper-mill.

Before this time, I was not very bad, I cannot remember of ever having sworn; but here at the mill and the place in which I lived I became acquainted with some very bad boys and men, who taught me many bad habits.

We organized a minstrel troupe, and soon I became an expert dancer, and could dance — songs and dances, jigs, clogs, etc., and was going on the stage. I told my mother about my project, and she said, "If you go I will send the strong arm of law after you, and put you where the dogs won't bite you." I did not want to go where the dogs would not bite, so I desisted. Oh, if every mother would put her foot down and say, "I am boss."

Then I persuaded my ma to buy me a violin, and soon I became proficient enough so I could play at dances.

I want to tell you I know all about dances, I have been to the highest and lowest. I am often asked, "Is there any harm in a select parlor dance?" You might as well ask me if there is any harm in stealing. I've seen the purest led forth by one of these lepers of society, whose bosom swells with lust to ruin the fair; I've had them come to me with their plans, by which they might lead that pure, innocent daughter of yours to obey their lust, and bring her disgraced to her home. Why, the chief of police at New York say six-tenths of the fallen women of that city say, "their first step to ruin was from the dance," and then you Christian people have dances at your home. Shame on you! it will be shame when you get in the presence of God!

After having labored in the paper-mill about two years, I then went to work for the Cincinnati Ice Company, who were running a branch office at Hamilton, O., and there fell in with worse company than ever, — now saloons and breweries were my haunts, and I learned to love the drink more and more, and sometimes, I am sorry to say, — I drank till I would reel! This continued till about the time the crusade opened their fire on the saloon. One evening, when going with the boys to hear Carl Schurz speak, I drank a glass of beer and it made me sick — thank God! — and I vowed a vow never to touch it again; and promised the boys five dollars if they saw me drinking. The boys laughed and said, "We'll soon have five dollars to go on a spree." I still continued to drink whiskey till the following March, and abandoned it forever. This was the beginning of a new life. Praise God!

After having labored for the ice company four years, I engaged with Peter Heck to learn the trade of carriage trimming, and remained with him about six months.

The exposition was going on at Cincinnati, and I concluded to go on a visit there. While there I saw an advertisement, — "Wanted, a boy, who has had experience in carriage trimming." So I went to the carriage factory on Freeman Street, near Lincoln Park, and met the proprietor, James Curry, who engaged me. I went home, glad of the chance, and told my mother, who sighed and wanted me to remain home. Often she would approach me, and tell me something she heard about me, and, boy-like, I would deny it. Now, to go to Cincinnati, and there, perhaps, fall in with a rougher class of people, no wonder she did not favor the plan.

I told my employer a lie, to get released. I'm sorry for it now. The time came for me to go. My valise packed, my mother's arms around me, and I must go. The tears streaming down my cheeks, we parted, and my mother cried, " My poor boy is lost." When about half a square from home, I raised my eyes to heaven, and there prayed and said, " Lord, help me to be a better boy." That prayer, I believe, was heard. Praise God!

I went to Cincinnati, and if ever a person tried to be a devout Romanist I tried. No Sunday ever came unless you would see me wending my way to the Bank Street Romish Church. When I would behold these poor people agonizing in the same manner I was; bowing before images, anointing themselves with holy water; yet going away with sorrow and sadness, and the load of guilt on them, my poor heart would yearn for relief, but none came. Day after day my heart would cry out, " Oh, that I knew where to find Him !"

One Sunday, being lonesome and troubled, I wended my way over the Rhine, amid the saloons, dance halls, and variety theatres. Hearing the patter of feet of the ballet dancers, I went in and ordered a bottle of mineral water. Before, these things charmed me, but now my heart yearned for something better. I did not remain there long, and went to the Washington Park. and, while there, I saw a large crowd gathered under the arch that extended from the exposition building to the art gallery in the park. So, curiosity attracted me to the crowd, and, while there, I cannot remember the text or a particle of the sermon, but when they began to sing, " Almost Persuaded," the music charmed me. I was riveted to the spot. The minister lined the hymn, and when he reached the last verse and the last four lines, he read, —

> "Almost persuaded, now to believe;
> Almost persuaded, Christ to receive."

Still, I was not moved much. Then he read, —

> "Almost cannot avail,
> Almost is but to fail;
> Sad, sad that bitter wail,
> Almost, but lost!"

When he said "Lost," I never had anything to pierce my heart through as this did; it seemed as though a dagger pierced my heart; and, for a moment, I quivered, but with lightning thought I raised my eyes to heaven and my heart to God, and said, "I will not be lost, I'll be saved." And as if tons of weight had been lifted, my burden was gone, my sin-sick soul free. I was enraptured with joy indescribable. The song went on, the meeting dismissed, but still I stood transfixed, riveted to the spot. The preacher — Joseph Emery, City Missionary — came and asked me to go to the Christian Association. Then the tears streamed down my cheeks.

I started for my home. The sun shone with brighter brilliancy, the grass looked greener, the faces of the people seemed different, my soul was filled, I was free. Praise the Lord!

That night I went to the Y. M. C. A., was met by the boys at the door, and given a royal welcome, and a book to sing.

After the sermon the invitation was given for all to hold up their hands, who wanted the prayers of God's people. My hand was up, and they gathered around and prayed for me; but all this time I did not know what was the matter with me. I asked the boys "when there would be another meeting like this." So they told me to come down Wednesday evening. I could hardly wait till the time came. Wednesday evening found me there, and they took me to St. Paul's Methodist Episcopal Church, corner Smith and Seventh Streets. Dr. C. H. Payne was pastor. The power of God was among the people, and at the close an invitation was given to all those wanting the prayers of God's people to rise. I stood up and soon they gathered around me and began to pray. The more they prayed the happier I got, but still I could not imagine what made me so happy, so I said, "What is the matter with me?" and they told me I was converted. I shouted, "Glory to God, I'm saved." I went home and began telling the people what Jesus did for me.

The following Sunday I went to the Christian Association building, expecting to find a Sunday-school, but, to my disappointment, I found it locked.

The following Sunday I said, "Maybe they have a Sunday-school at that church where they told me I was converted."

As I arrived there I found two men — Thompson and Wolf, class-leaders — going into the church. I inquired if they had a Sunday-school, but they said. "No, we have a class-meeting." A class-meeting — I did not know what a class-meeting was, but consented, and was shown into a small room with a row of chairs on each side. I took my position near the door, so that if it did not suit me I could go out. They gave me a book and we sang, and then all knelt and they prayed for me; so my fears began to subside. The class-leader read, and then exhorted each to speak, and my turn came, so I jumped up and said, "I'm saved!" and sat down. The leader at its close asked me to come again, but I said, "I won't have to be a Methodist if I come?" He answers, "No, no." Thank God, it was not long till I wanted to be a Methodist, and I'm a Methodist from my head to my feet.

I began to long for an acquaintance of my youth, so I renewed old friendship with one of the boys whose mother was a good Christian. He purposed a walk, and when about a half square from his home, whom should we meet but this Mr. Thompson, the class-leader, who was very glad, and said, "I want you to teach a Sunday-school class." When we arrived at the mission school we found hundreds of little street Arabs gathered, who howled and stormed around — a queer sight for me, who had been a Romanist, where order prevails. I was given charge of a class of boys to keep them quiet, so I began to act, when one boy pulled my coat and another squinted at me. Knowing that order was heaven's first law, I took one of the boys and set him down pretty hard, so much so that the other boys began to fear lest they would be treated the same. Mr. Thompson insisted I must take a class. I said, "I have no Bible." A Testament and a Teacher's Journal were given me, and now I was to become a Sunday-school teacher. That week I studied and prayed over my lessons, but when Sunday came I forgot the entire lesson and could only tell the boys what Jesus did for me. God helped me to win my boys, and ere long, with presents, pennies, and a visit to their parents, their little hearts were won for Jesus. Soon I must go and help them in the street meetings, where we were hooted and sometimes had dead animals thrown at us.

My relatives, hearing I had become a Protestant, sent for me, and then ridiculed my religion and said, " You will go where all the crazy Methodists go — to the lunatic asylum." I accepted a position on the road to travel for a firm, and was gone about six months. Hearing Moody was in Chicago, I visited his meetings, received a special blessing. Came home and found my mother needed winter supplies, and gave her all my money but enough to pay my fare to Cincinnati and two weeks' board. I felt a call to the ministry, but used to put it off by saying, " Lord, I am too ignorant and cannot go to school; I have no money."

Yet this spirit followed me, and one Friday afternoon alone in my room, when my money was all gone and nothing to pay my board, I knelt and said, " Now, Lord, I want to know if you want me to preach; I want to know by you giving me a sign — something I can see and feel with my hands." I seemed to hear a voice say. " Well, what shall I give you?" — " Lord, lay a piece of money before me in the space of a week," I said. Many times I would get up and look all around the room, looking for the money; then when passing along the street I would see the sun shining on something and would soon discover it was a piece of tin or glass. Yet my faith was, if God wanted me he would surely send the money. My relatives long before had become reconciled, and I went to my aunt and told her my circumstances, and she invited me to her home. This was Wednesday eve. I told her I was going to the Methodist church at Mount Auburn. Rev. W. W. Case was pastor then, and that evening was receiving probationers from the recent revival. After the dismissal, while speaking with a young man and telling him what Jesus had done for me, I lifted my eyes, and there, about twenty feet off, beheld two shining objects on the floor. My whole life passed before me in a panoramic vision, and such scintillations of God's glory as I never beheld before; and when I picked up these two shining objects, — they were two bright pennies, — as if they had been polished by angelic hands in glory, I gave them to the pastor and started home, the stars in their course seemed to sing, the air buoyed me up, and when I arrived home my aunty beheld my face, which must have shone like a mirror, and said, "Why, Joe, what is the matter with you?" I told her my prayer and the finding of the money, and she exclaimed, "You must go to school." The next morning I saw my pastor, Rev. H. B. Ridgeway, but received no encouragement from him; but I determined to go to the Ohio Wesleyan University, at Delaware, O., that fall. That night I asked God for a job, got his assurance, and told my aunty in the morning, "I was going to get a job." She said, "Where?" — "I do not know, God is going to give me a job." She gave me a little money to buy a lunch, but this I gave a poor beggar by the library and stayed there till about four o'clock, and went to Emmerson & Fisher's carriage factory, corner John and Findlay streets, and asked for a job, and they said, "We want good; sober men." When I told them I was a Christian, they said, "So much the better." On the following Monday I went to the factory, but my bench was not ready. On Wednesday began work, and soon was getting as much as the foreman in the shop.

When the Saturday evening came I asked the boys if they paid off this evening. They said, "No, on Monday." When going home I said, "Lord, I have no money for Sunday-school to-morrow." The Lord seemed to say, "Have I not provided for you before? can I not provide for you again?" I had not gone ten steps until I found money for Sunday-school.

That fall I started to school at Delaware, O., and remained there from 1877 to 1881, making my own money and giving away one-tenth and more to God.

I joined the Central Ohio conference in the fall of 1881, and was appointed to Lima, O.; and when going to Lima I found between eight and nine hundred dollars in my bank account ahead after having paid my own way through school. I found three appointments, but this did not keep me busy, so I took up another. The fruits of this year were over two hundred conversions, two new churches, and the repairing of another, besides going away and helping in three other meetings, having between one and two hundred more conversions. All this time, I felt the call to the evangelistic field. My presiding elder did his best to retain me on his district, but in 1882 I withdrew from the conference to go into my life's work. These years God has honored my poor labors with His divine seal, and many thousands have been converted and sanctified, and God has helped me to give away over eleven thousand dollars for the education of young men for the ministry, colleges, poor preachers, orphans, churches, and the benevolences of the church. To God be all the honor and glory, Amen. Do not think I have not made mistakes since I believed, but many times have I grieved the Spirit of God and done that which I ought not to have done, but these all have been forgiven, and I am saved by his precious blood. Amen.

CHAPTER XVIII.

SECRETS OF HIS SUCCESS.

"The secret of the Lord is with them that fear him." — BIBLE.

THE word "luck" is not in the Bible, neither is it in the true Christian's vocabulary. *Success*, however, is promised to the Gospel and to all who yield themselves completely to its truths.

What looks to men like failure is often in God's sight the highest success. Stephen's dying speech looked to be a stupendous failure, but proved in its results the most successful revival sermon ever preached by mortal man.

The success of the Christian worker is governed by certain fixed and changeless laws.

He succeeds, not by a persistent effort to win success, but by meeting the conditions upon which God has promised to give it.

Just as men live, not by being determined to do so, but by conforming to the laws that govern life.

The wonderful success which has attended Brother Weber's work to many is an unexplained mystery. It evidently is not due to birth or college drill or human eloquence.

That victory should follow victory for years in succession, and that in some of the most desperately wicked places, and often in the presence of a church membership, a large proportion of which was unconverted, in a few days or weeks hundreds should profess conversion and show it by their lives, does seem marvellous; and it is no wonder that it is attracting the attention of those who would be "wise to win souls," and that such seek to know the secrets of this God-given success.

A glance at the factors which enter into it is all that can here be given, but it is hoped that by this many may better know the man and catch the inspiration which seems to be the mainspring of his marvellous career.

The research has strengthened the writer, and it is hoped that its perusal may prove as "grapes of Eshcol" to all who read.

It is a source of rejoicing that we are *not compelled* to seek the records of the promoted to find deeds of apostolic power and examples of genuine Methodistic zeal, but that in such men as this Evangelist Pentecost and the early days of Methodism are being repeated in our midst.

Contact with Brother Weber and a close scrutiny under advantageous circumstances into his life and work convince me that the following elements have much to do with his wonderful success: —

His Positive Experience. — He is converted, and knows it. It was a change as from a dungeon to a palace.

He preaches the "Witness of the Spirit" in a way that makes the faces of fathers and mothers in Israel shine with rapture; and causes Mr. Half Hope and Mrs. Guess So, to tremble like aspen leaves.

Mr. Formality and Mr. Hypocrisy often, over this, grow furious with rage.

Rev. Mr. Lost His Experience, who once was a saved man but now is spiritually dead, cautions him not to be so "positive," that "it is enough to let his life tell it," and that he "always has his doubts about people who are so positive in their professions of religion." The Saviour who rescued Mr. Weber from the clutches of popery is just as able to deliver him from "false brethren" among Protestants, and so on he goes —

> "Telling to sinners round
> What a dear Saviour he has found."

He usually takes two nights in each revival meeting to tell his experience, and then salts many of his sermons with it. In one of his unique afternoon talks he put this point this way: "God gives it to me, and if I kept it it would get stale. I give it to you, and he gives me new."

He is a Man of Prayer. — He prays not "for Jesus' sake," but "in Jesus' name," and at once gets audience with God. He says that for one hour before appearing in public he would not leave his place of private prayer, should his own mother call for him.

I listened to prayers that fell from his lips at Adrian, that in pathos, power, and unctuous eloquence were equal to ten thousand synods of ordinary "addresses to the Supreme Being." It seemed as though I had never heard any one pray before.

He writes of a camp-meeting where many were present who came for "novelty or pleasure." It seemed at first as if the "recreationists" were to win the day. "The walls were like granite." He went to his tent and "prayed by the hour." In answer, "Soon a wave of salvation came, prostrating everybody." "Hundreds lay on their faces with tears at the awfulness of God, and many were saved and sanctified."

Thus prayer prevailed. Take courage, Brother Faint Prayer, and henceforth persist until thou too shalt prevail.

His record of New Year's was, "I spent the old year out and the new year in on my knees."

When he left his home in Ohio for Jackson, Mich., he told his folks that if the ministers would stand by him *his bones would bleach in Jackson before he would leave with less than five hundred conversions.*

At Fort Dodge he asks for "warmer weather," and it is given. For "fifty souls at the altar one evening," and they come.

During the Coldwater revival the Evangelist was entertained by Mr. and Mrs. R. G. Chandler.

While there their family was exposed to the measles. Mrs. Chandler was attacked with congestion of the lungs and was rapidly sinking. While in this condition, one morning, the family physician said, "You are now coming down with the measles, you are a very sick woman, and this will go hard with you."

The children were greatly alarmed. Mr. Weber, with his great, sympathetic nature, in a moment took it all in, and said with an assurance born of his mighty faith in the promises of God, —

"*Don't you worry; mamma is not going to have the measles, for Brother Joe is going to pray for her.*"

This was at about nine o'clock in the morning. As in the days when Jesus was on earth, faith triumphed, disease was rebuked, and she herself witnesses, "At noon I was sitting up, and before the day closed I was well."

Is Brother Weber alone in possession of this key of prevailing prayer? No, thank God, others have it, and all may have it who will *abide in Christ*, for unto such, and such only, it is promised.

He Aims to Hit. — All of his sermons have a "Thou art the man" ring to them. His listeners, like those of Jesus, "perceive that he speaks of them." He said in one of his sermons, "When I climbed up the old monument at Bunker Hill I remembered what the great general said, 'When the enemy gets near enough for you to see the whites of their eyes, then shoot.' I don't preach for fun, I always shoot at something and always shoot to hit, and, as I said last night, if you don't like it just get up and go out. . . . I am not here to please people. I do not tickle your ears. I want to tickle your heart, so that your heart will get right before God. . . . I am not a-going to talk about the instability of Peter, but I am talking about you, and *you, and* YOU."

He is Full of Faith. — He will not for a moment entertain the idea of a "failure" or a "small victory," or "moderate success." The devil must be routed, and he believes from the first that this will be accomplished, *and it is.*

When he began work at Jackson, Mich., where eight

hundred professed conversion, in the beginning, though "the church was in a very low state of spirituality, and the signs of life were few," and to others all seemed dark, yet to him the "prospects were bright as the promises of God." To the amazement of all, the very first night of the meeting, with the church like a spiritual ice-house, he *announced that there would be from five hundred to one thousand conversions.*

Doubting Thomases and fearful Peters, and they were many, said, "*It cannot be*," "But," to use his own words, "there are no impossibilities with God. Many were the hindrances. New trials came up daily. Some hills seemed too high to scale, but faith in God helped those hills to be valleys; and those stones that seemed unsurmountable were only stepping-stones to higher regions of faith in God. The Beulah heights would glisten, and then the people would rejoice, but soon a dark, dense cloud would envelop us, and so intermingled were the glories and the darknesses that at times we were lost in the fog. But Jesus found us every time, as a shepherd findeth his sheep. Faith in the power of God conquered all obstacles. Hundreds went away, many nights, who could not get access. For weeks the altars and front seats were flooded with penitents, until over eight hundred were enrolled on the list that testified that they were saved."

He is in Dead Earnest. — This trait of Mr. Weber so impressed a racy reporter, who came to criticise him at Muskegon, that he wrote as follows: —

There is not a lazy bone in his whole frame; and, while his manner of conducting a meeting is often amusing and even ludicrous to the ordinary mortal of this every-day world, there is a strong evidence of sincerity and earnestness in his work. . . . He will labor so hard with sinners that great beads of perspiration will roll down his face. His method can be best illustrated by his own language : "Suppose," said he, "that my house was burning, and a neighbor should come slowly up to me, and still more slowly drawl out, 'Mr. W-e-b-e-r, y-o-u-r h-o-u-s-e i-s b-u-r-n-i-n-g !' I would be so indignant that I would say, 'Let it burn.' But suppose a man, full of zeal and anxiousness, should come rushing up, and yell, 'MR. WEBER, YOUR HOUSE IS ON FIRE !' I would rush to the rescue." And he showed how he would rush, by jumping over the altar-railing.

During his meeting he is all over the church. One time he is in the pulpit, and another, down on the altar, and again, among the audience, — speaking, pleading, hand-shaking with the people, begging them to stand up and be saved. He told how he himself, snatched from the slums of Cincinnati, had been made to stand upon his feet aright. "Oh, if you only knew from what vice and degradation I have been rescued," says Brother Weber, "you would not wonder why my soul is red-hot with zeal for the young men of your city."

His burning zeal is a quenchless fire, that soon causes a mighty conflagration wherever God calls him to labor. It scorches terribly Brother and Sister Lukewarm and Professor At Ease in Zion, but it often wakes them up from the death sleep into which they are falling, and then they are thankful. Large numbers of the Iceberg family, including some high in ecclesiastical position, have been melted by it.

It is an earnestness born of the Holy Ghost. The kind of earnestness that in all ages has led men to defy fire and flood, human opposition and Satanic might, only that they might please God and win souls. It is "the old religion revived with energy, and heated, as if the minister really meant what he said."

He is Humble. — If he makes a mistake he confesses it. He can sit and talk wisely of the "mysteries of the Kingdom," or roll on the floor in boyish glee with the four-year-old. If men revile him, and they do by word and pen, he prays for them.

When at Quincy he mistook the character of a person, and the mistake of the head led to a mistake in practice, which threatened to seriously embarrass the work. As soon as he was convinced of this, with tears of sorrow he made both private and public confession; the people were touched by the act, and the work went on with power. God save us from the Peacockism that will not own and confess a wrong. He believes and practises the principle that "it is our business to get down, and God's to lift us up," and God honors him in it. His statement that he would be willing to "stand on his head," or "climb a greased pole," *if thereby he could save a soul*, expresses his willingness to humble himself to any depth, only that God may use him to His glory. Cold critics sometimes censure him for these "inelegant" expressions, but they forget that both Paul and the prophets said things even more "inelegant;" and that Mr. Weber, in these terms, simply means what Moses did when he pleaded that his name might be blotted from the book of life if only rebellious Israel might be saved; and what Paul did when he said that he was willing to become "accursed" for the salvation of others.

This Evangelist has proved, with other brilliant stars that now shine in the constellation of soul-savers, that before "honor is humility." All who would arise to similar heights must first sink to similar depths.

Deacon Pride and his wife, Miss Haughty and **Mr. Vanity**, will probably, with pleasure, allow contempt to curl their lips and knit their brows at such an Evangelist. But either here or at the judgment they will be humbled in the dust.

He puts the Ministry above everything else. — Many enticing voices invite him to turn aside, but he heeds them not. With Ezekiel he feels : —

> "I had rather stand
> A Prophet of my God, with all the thrills
> Of trembling that must shake the heart of one
> Who in earth's garments, in the vesture frail
> Of flesh and blood, is called to minister,
> As Seraphs do, with fire — than bear the palm
> Of any other triumph."

He employs Plain Language. — He calls Sin, Satan, and Hell by their Scripture names. He uses plain English, — so plain that sensitive, silken-eared people often are "shocked" by it, and which falls harshly on the ears of some good people who have allowed themselves to adopt a vocabulary composed of Latin and Greek derivatives.

The laws that govern expression are such that when a person becomes so in earnest as to forget himself, he almost unconsciously uses the language of childhood. I think this is true in nearly all persons who have not, by the severest discipline, placed themselves where acquired expressions have become a "second nature."

As Mr. Weber is always so in earnest in the pulpit that he is oblivious to self and all minor matters, he naturally adopts the plain language of his youth.

Thus all of his hearers, from the street Arab to the doctor of divinity, from the little child to the hoary head, are able to clearly understand him. This is one of the most important secrets of his success with the masses.

He speaks to them in their Own Language.—Many candidates for the ministry, while in school, acquire a vocabulary that the masses do not use or understand. It becomes a "second nature" to them, and because these expressions are clear to themselves, they do not stop to think that they may be "an unknown tongue" to nine-tenths of their audience. So they go through life shooting over the heads of the people, and wondering why they don't succeed, and " why they are not appreciated." They put the Gospel kernel into nuts that half of their hearers cannot crack, and then wonder what is the matter.

The best remedy for this trouble is a baptism of the Holy Spirit and of *common-sense.* " Brother —— speaks much better when he is surprised and has no time for preparation," was the criticism of a parishioner of one of the most refined of modern ministers. The cultured few might not have indorsed the criticism, but nine-tenths of the congregation doubtless would have echoed a hearty *Amen.*

Other things being equal, Rev. Peter Plain Speech will draw and hold people ten to one against Dr. Big Words.

Many grand books and sermons are sealed secrets to many because of the violation of this law of common-sense.

Jesus used simple language, and it is wise to follow in His steps. Otherwise people feel, after listening to pulpit efforts, as a parishioner did at the close of a sermon by his pastor, who was a learned divine. Mystified, instead of edified, he was heard to pray, "*O Lord, send us a man who don't know so much.*"

Scholastics sometimes defend themselves, in this unscriptural practice, by saying that they "cannot furnish brains for their hearers."

Paul compared this class of speakers to "barbarians." See 1 Cor. xiv. 8-15.

He perseveres until the Desired End is reached. — Although some of his work has been in places that from a human standpoint seemed well-nigh hopeless, yet to him it was settled that victory was coming. And he "held on" until the clouds burst and the copious showers fell. His meetings usually last several weeks. To an Evangelist who plans his work to remain but a week or two in a place, he said: "That is just what the devil wants of you."

"*If* there is victory, matters will be so and so," said one in his presence.

"No *ifs*," said he; "that we are sure of, for God has promised it."

This indomitable determination to succeed has much to do with the end reached. He is at his best when the heavens are darkest. "How long do you expect to stay in Adrian?" asked a "knight of the pencil," who was sent to interview him in the midst of strong opposition at Adrian. "Oh, six, seven, or eight weeks," was the determined answer, and he stayed until decided victory had come.

Thousands of revival battles are lost, because Zion's soldiers get discouraged, and retreat on just the verge of what might have been a sweeping victory.

He has Tact.— He plans to get the crowds out to hear him. He understands that one of the lawful ways of getting attention is to ring the door-bell of curiosity. So by announcing novel themes, such as "Fools," "Sneaks," etc., by thoroughly billing the town, and by a thousand appropriate surprises, he moves upon the curiosity of the unconcerned until they come to his meetings, and then they "cannot stay away." Jesus and the apostles, through the miracles that they wrought, and the novelty of the new doctrine, got the ear of the public; but new circumstances demand new expedients, and if the Gospel-bearer is wise he will utilize them.

A correspondent of the *Fort Wayne Evening News*, referring to this feature of Mr. Weber's work, wrote: "Peculiarity wakes up the sensibilities, and curiosity brings out the people; they hear the truth, get interested, and look beyond the watchman through Christ to God, and get their sins pardoned, and become heirs with Jesus Christ."

He preaches against the Sins of the People.— Card-playing, dancing, worldliness, public wrong, and secret sins are all rebuked. His plain preaching does much to aid in drawing the crowds, and then pierces them with conviction as with an arrow. A reporter of his wonderful revival at Berea says: "The prime mover was Rev. J. H. Weber, whose marvellous success as an evangelist has given him a national reputation. All admit his wonderful power. He is intensely earnest. He delivers his blows direct from the shoulder. When plain language can make a point, plain language is used. He works upon the reason, imagination, sense

of fear, and the emotions. . . . His facial expressions
and bodily action help to hold the attention. If a man
has a weak point, Mr. Weber will find it."

He warns vehemently of an Eternal Hell. — He believes in a literal hell, just as awful and eternal as
the Scripture portrays it. This stirs up infidelity
terribly, but many "flee from the wrath to come."
It has been truthfully said of him, "He preaches a
whole Gospel, dwells largely on the doom of the
damned, the trickery of the devil, and the deceitfulness of sin." His portrayals of the condition of the
lost are at times awfully vivid and impressive. Rev.
Post Mortem Probation is very nervous under his
preaching, for he sees all his sermonic essays utterly
ruined. Though his auditors, like the criticising editor
of the *Sioux Falls Leader*, may climb up on the pedestal
of their "intelligence" and "culture," and aver that
"harping on hell" is grating to their refined sensibilities, and that the "good Christian-thinking people who
attend those meetings have no particular belief in a
literal hell fire," and that "this legend has been long
since exploded," and that the speaker should be "dignified," and "talk of the love of Jesus, and not the
damnation theory," yet Mr. Weber keeps right on like
Jesus, Wesley, and Finney, in declaring the truth just
as it really is. The hostile criticism is so much free
advertising, which simply helps to increase the surging
crowds, who, deep down in their hearts, believe that the
Evangelist is right.

He loves the People. — He understands what tragical
peril awaits the sinner, and as a friend he faithfully
warns him. Such expressions as "I love the people

here so I hate to leave them," are frequent in his journals. Though sometimes vilely misrepresented, he "loves his *enemies*," and prays for them, as Jesus taught.

He is very Liberal. — He was in youth possessed of a benevolent nature, and during the years the stream has become a river. He shows his love by what he does. He is educating several young men for the ministry, and has so aided in securing collections for the Ohio Wesleyan University that one who speaks for it says, "If the university had a few more such friends as Mr. Weber, it would not be long before we would have everything we want." He gives as the Spirit directs wherever he goes; in one place twenty dollars, in another two hundred dollars, and in another place he scatters money as he sees that it is needed. I understand he has given away between ten and eleven thousand dollars in eight years. If those who criticise the sums received by him would but consider the way that they are expended, their voices would at once be hushed.

The People soon learn to love him. — Love begets love. From boys and young men whom he has rescued or aided he receives hundreds of letters, full of the most endearing language that exists. When laboring at Adrian, he received the following verses from Hillsdale, that breathe the spirit that thousands feel for him: —

> "For thee we wish for all that's best
> And nearest to thy heart;
> That no dread care may pierce thy breast
> With sorrow's cruel dart.

> That sweetest peace may still be thine,
>   With faith and truth together;
> That with thy bark it may be fine
>   And never stormy weather.
>
> That flowers may round your path entwine
>   *As fair as those we send you;*
> And every blessing, friend, be thine,
>   And all good gifts attend you."

The demonstrations manifested when he departs for the next field of labor or returns to an old one show that one of the secrets of his great success is the fervent love which he wins from those among whom he works.

He is Punctual.—Everything is done on time. This may seem a small thing, but many have failed for life because they so esteemed it. At the instant the bell ceases to ring, "Praise God, from whom all blessings flow," begins to chime. "From the time he begins a service to the end, he allows no drag, no tedious sermon, nor over-long prayers, but all life, sparkle, briskness. Business is his style."

He is a Love Slave to the Bible and the Biographies of Successful Evangelists.—His Bible is marked from cover to cover, and each mark has a meaning. On his knees, with the Book of books before him, he receives much of his theological training. The spirits of Knox, Wesley, Whitefield, Edwards, and Finney seem to hover around him, and the perusal of their lives has been his recreation and delight. I have seen him kiss and caress the Bible with an affection that seemed thus to overflow as naturally as the gushing of a fountain.

He honors and co-operates with the Pastors with whom he labors.—In all his journals I find no expressions but of respect and love towards the pastors with whom he works. Rev. I. R. Henderson, in a report to the *W. C. Advocate* of the Findley (O.) revival, in which five hundred and thirty were converted in four weeks, truthfully says, " The Evangelist has the good sense of allying the pastor as prominently as he can to the revival and the converts."

He secures the Pledged Co-operation of the Official Board of the Church.

He is a Foe to Formality. — Church forms, like Israel's brazen serpent, have to be "broken up" to keep the people from worshipping them. Although Mr. Weber " has a sweetness of spirit that wins," and " a passion for saving souls, that seems almost all-absorbing," yet that very passion makes him feel that the ice of formality in which they are freezing to death must be broken. So, as one has said, " his manner is largely dramatic, toppling over many of the old customary proprieties of the pulpit. People in dead earnest seldom stop to think much of these proprieties or heed them in other situations of life, and why should they in the pulpit? This breaks up old rut-lines of thought, in which people are apt to plod unconcernedly along, and starts them on a new track, much to their spiritual benefit." In all ages formalists have been the most violent opposers of aggressive revival work, and he who would win must, like Mr. Weber, be wise to outwit them in Jesus' name and by His power.

He sets the Church to Work. — " Go out, brother; go out, sister; don't leave three or four of us to do all the work," he may be heard to exhort, if the workers hang back during the invitation service. Leroy A. Belt, in a report of him in *The Advocate*, says that "he has the power to set others to work and inspire them with the idea of doing something for Christ." Success without that power is impossible. If a general cannot inspire his soldiers to fight, defeat is certain.

He not only sets Others to Work, but Himself leads in the Battle. — An old associate of his, Rev. J. L. Glasscock, who had passed through a blessed revival with him, speaks advisedly when he says, "Brother Weber is a skilful general in managing a church. Every member is pressed into service or made to feel he has come very far short of doing his duty." As a general leads his troops, so he *leads*, not *drives*, his workers. The following, from his journal, illustrates the way that much of his time outside of meetings is improved. "While out to-day, visiting, we found a lot of strangers who were visiting. Got to talking to them about Jesus, and three of them broke down. Prayed with them, and one was converted. Praise God!" Again, "Brother Woodworth and I have been out seeing the business men and inviting them out to church. We even went into saloons and the lowest dives. How nicely we were received by all!" Some very ludicrous things sometimes occurred during these calls, illustrating the Evangelist's eccentricities. The following appreciative notice of Brother Weber's personal work is clipped from a secular paper: "Rev. J. H. Weber is having crowded houses at the Methodist-Episcopal church. On Sunday night hundreds of people could not get in. Mr. Weber's success is largely in visiting people during the day and inviting them to come to church. This is a pointer for the ministers of our city.

Get acquainted with the boys. A hand-shaking minister as well as politician seems to meet with success." Thus from "house to house," in the inquiry meeting, and at the altar, he says by word and example, "Come," and soon he has a band of earnest co-laborers.

He utilizes the Power of Sacred Song.— Himself a composer and author of "The Evangelist," a Gospel songbook which is fast growing in favor, he understands well how to utilize this power with the people.

He gets the People to Sing.— Some trace their conviction and others their conversion to this source. He leads the singing himself, interjecting remarks to rivet special points, and in this way gets quickly a mighty grip on his audiences. This service, like the others, is never allowed to drag, but keeps step to the tornado velocity of the entire meeting.

He persistently presses Personal Invitation.—At the close of the sermon, he often dismisses the congregation and keeps only those who are saved and those who wish to be. He thus gets rid of a large counteracting influence. Then begins personal pleading, and all whose hearts are in the work assist. Thousands have thus been won. This is an important factor in his success. He has personally led thousands to the altar in this way.

He is Thorough.— Rev. A. J. Nast, reporting the Berea revival, wrote to the *Western Advocate* as follows: "Mr. Weber is an emphatic believer in the old-fashioned mourners' bench. He insists on a thorough work and the doctrine that a sinner may know his sins forgiven, cautioning seekers against professing salvation when they are not fully satisfied." Often at the altar he will say to the seeker, "Do you know your sins forgiven? Are you *sure* that they are?" Unless they answer "Yes," they are not reported converted, but encouraged not to think they are, but *to seek until they know it.* What a lesson for shilly-shally workers who are more anxious to count converts than to save souls!

He practises New-Testament Fasting. — I find in his journal such statements as the following: " Have been having a fast day here all day; I did not eat all day till this eve." That day "his soul was filled," and "many came to the altar."

As near as I can learn, none become proficient in soul-saving who ignore the Saviour's teaching in this particular.

He is Fearless of the Threats of Man. — Often Romanists, saloonists, and hypocrites are furious in their rage, and, as their brethren of old, stir up "fellows of the baser sort" to threaten deeds of violence. This was true at Spencer, Ia., concerning which he wrote, " A lot of roughs followed me home this eve. Some were afraid they were going to tackle me. I would not be afraid of a whole town full of those sneaks. They know that God is with me. If God will be my friend, I am safe anywhere!" Truly has it been written of him, "He is bold and fearless in his attacks upon sin, it matters not when or where he finds it."

Only the brave soldier wins the battle in any warfare.

He adapts himself to People and Surroundings. — He is a child with children, a young man with the youth, and sympathetic with all whom he hopes thus to win.

He reaches a child through a top or doll, a young man through his books or business, parents through their children, and thus he studies to find avenues through which he can successfully reach people. In a good sense he seeks to become "all things to all men," and thus wonderfully succeeds in winning many. All cannot be Webers, but all can incorporate in their lives the great principles that have given him success.

He takes Systematic Exercise. — To succeed largely as an evangelist, a strong body is a necessity. He has been well endowed by nature in this particular, and by proper relaxation and exercise he seeks to keep it at its best. One day in each week he usually takes for this purpose.

With Bishop Taylor he believes that the minister should *rest* from his labors one day in seven. Many workers, by ignoring this principle, purchase to themselves premature decrepitude and failure, when they might with strength have been shouting pæans of victory.

A reporter of Lake Side camp-meeting, where he was engaged to conduct the services, mentions his work in the following words : —

"He has wonderful power. The secret of his success, which is great, may be found in a few things characteristic of the man through the blessing of God.

"*a*. He is neat in appearance.

"*b*. He is natural and humble.

"*c*. He has a good education and is a fluent talker, with an abundance of common sense.

"*d*. His tact is marvellous, always ready, never at loss for a new surprise or measure.

"*e*. He sings well; is a good timist and often leads the thousands. He believes in his ability to succeed.

"*f*. Has strong faith in God and the Gospel. Preaches the latter. Pays no attention to the new schools of theology; calls sin *sin*, and hell *hell*.

"*g*. Utilizes older and wiser heads, whom he often consults.

"*h*. Perpetrates surprises continually; keeps alive the curiosity; is at times tragical; is a good actor, but does not know it."

Through the Prayer of Faith he often heals the Sick. — This works on the curiosity of all who hear of it, to see a man who can through God do such deeds, and the fact that such "signs" attend his ministration to many clothes his messages with superhuman power. At Akron, Ia., "The banker Bready came to the parsonage, and we prayed that God might cure him, as he had been sick from his birth, and immediately he was made well and shouted." Again at Sioux City, "Had several healed by prayer." At Fort Dodge, Ia., "Ed Thompson's mother, who came to church, but fainted, and who has been very sick, and the doctors could not help her, was gloriously cured to-day. We prayed for her, and laid on hands for healing."

He shouts Victory before the Walls fall. — One of the leading workers at Quincy, Brother F. Barber, says: "When everything looked dark, and we would begin to doubt, his faith was as strong as ever. He would say, 'It's coming, I *know* it's coming,' and then praise God for what He was going to do for us." He begins every service with the doxology.

His Past Victories give him and the People Confidence

for Coming Ones. — This feature is apparent in the following notice of his meeting at Marion, O.: —

"He commenced at once to assail the strongholds of Satan, and showed immense strength as a besieger, and proved himself master of the field, for long before his bugle ceased calling the advancing host, when he had but half exhausted his store of ammunition of powerful argument, reason, and logic against the weakening foe, Satan declared himself an unconditional prisoner, and the prisoners and deserters came by scores and hundreds to beg mercy and forgiveness." Every victory, if rightly realized, is a stepping-stone to another, and what was true at Marion has been many times repeated.

He is sometimes bitterly Persecuted. — "The devil, as usual, is very mad," is no infrequent statement in his journal. "Crank," "hypocrite," and kindred epithets are often bestowed upon him, and many are the "threats" that he has encountered. He treats them all as a steamship treats the spray, and the spirit in which he does it shows the people that he has something which his enemies have not, and so Providence hitches Persecution to the revival chariot, and compels him, like a captured slave, to draw the Evangelist on to victory. Glory to God for such a King!

He is Eccentric. — Not an affected, sickening eccentricity that comes from aping others, but that which comes from being filled with the Spirit and led by God. Finney said: "I never knew a person who was filled with the Spirit that was not called eccentric." "Deviating from usual practices," is Webster's definition of the word. All who would be and do like Jesus must be in this sense of the word eccentric. This leads Mr. Weber to do many things that make remarks, and thus helps him to get the attention of the people. The following incident mentioned elsewhere is an illustration. "A man was swearing in the barber-shop, while I was in the chair, so when I was through I knelt before him, and prayed and said, 'That's the way I pray to my God.' It moved him very much." Again, "I took an old man by the hand, and forced him to the altar last night; this eve he was so happy!" His life, like Finney's and Cartwright's, is replete with such incidents. To imitate him would be apish, but to possess the piety that will obey God at all hazards is to court success.

Brother Weber is entirely Consecrated. — He gives himself " without reserve to God."

He does not rest in the Consecration, but claims the Baptism of the Holy Ghost. — The following, from his diary, points to this blessed phase of his experience. "My soul was filled with the glory of God. Praise His name!" Again, "God did baptize me to-day with the glory of God. My soul was full!" Again, when at Clarion, Ia., "Went over to the afternoon meeting, and got a baptism of the Holy Ghost. I prayed about one hour." If Jesus and the apostles and Wesley and Finney and such men must need this inducement to do their life work, how foolish for any to rush on without it!

He not only receives the Baptism, but testifies to the Gospel's Keeping Power. — So that he can write, " Jesus keeps me daily."

He believes in being "led by the Spirit." He expects God to guide him in all things, through the teachings of His word and an entirely consecrated judgment, under the light of the Spirit. His appointments — where he shall go, how long stay, whom he shall aid, and all — are held before Him who has promised to "guide by his counsels," and held there until the needed guidance is given. "Jesus, map out where thou wouldst have me go," is his humble prayer as he looks to Him who cannot err for direction.

When the official invitation came urging him to work immediately at Jackson, he says: "I took it in prayer to God, and the way seemed so plain that I said, 'I will go.'" Much of his success is due to this guidance.

He continually craves and receives New Manifestations of God. — "Oh, for more of the Holy Ghost," is the breathing of his soul. Faber's prayer fittingly expresses his feeling.

> "With gentle swiftness lead me on,
> Dear God, to see Thy face,
> And meanwhile in my narrow heart
> Oh, make Thyself more space!"

He preaches Full Salvation. — He presents it from an experimental and practical as well as doctrinal standpoint. He says concerning his own experience at this supremely vital point, "I was sanctified at college the first year I was there. It came while I was praying with some colored people."

While his great mission seems to be to call sinners to repentance, yet he realizes the relation of the sanctifying baptism of the Holy Ghost to revival work.

He wisely seeks to avoid the error of pressing holiness upon backsliders, and aims first to bring the members into a clear justified relation to God, where they will want perfect love. Then he puts the light of entire sanctification before them, and "presses them to expect it now and by faith," as the Scripture and church so plainly teach. One of his heart prayers is, "Jesus, keep me pure and holy."

The *Michigan Advocate* report of Crystal Springs camp-meeting, where Brother Weber was in charge and over two hundred and fifty were pardoned or sanctified, states that the "central idea of Christianity and the central doctrine of Methodism, 'Holiness unto the Lord,' was kept prominently before the church, and the result was we had a real Pentecost." In a recent sermon on sanctification he says, " I never saw a young convert oppose holiness; it's you backsliders who do that."

"Who, then, would oppose holiness? If you do, it's holiness or hell."

I had the pleasure of hearing the sermon above mentioned. It swept away prejudices and ignorance like a Niagara and was attended by a wave of melting power.

This element of success of the Evangelist, though among the last mentioned, is by no means the least. May God make him a Hamline, Palmer, Inskip, and Watson combined, to help "reform the continent and spread Scriptural holiness over these lands."

He gives God All the Glory. — In relating the victories that God gives him, whether by tongue or pen, he frequently adds, " I give God all the glory for it." Those who know him best believe he does. At every conversion, at his request, the whole congregation with him lift their hands towards heaven, and triumphantly and adoringly repeat, " Praise the Father, praise the Son, and praise the Holy Ghost."

While this is being repeated, waves of power will frequently come, and others will be convicted and converted, and then, amid the waving of handkerchiefs and the shouts of the saints, new praise will arise to the triune God.

It has been truly said by Rev. I. Wilson that " Brother Weber's secret of success and power for good cannot be understood, nor his work fairly judged, by attending one service; you must hear him day after day, and go with him through a protracted service, to appreciate his work and the remarkable success that crowns his efforts."

We trust that every reader will avoid the folly that some have fallen into of imitating the personal peculiarities of this prince among soul-gleaners, but will carefully, prayerfully, and persistently seek conformity to all of the great principles mentioned which are at the foundation of soul-saving success. If this chapter emphasizes one thing more than another, it is that this success does not depend chiefly upon birth, natural endowments, or school culture, but upon unswerving fidelity to the word of God, the Son of God, and the Spirit of God.

Scholastic attainments, like the possession of muscle and of money, may be of great value, but if they be substituted for the Spirit's baptism, which Jesus taught was the crowning qualification for life's great work, infinite harm is done.

It is a sad fact that Christian colleges and men high in ecclesiastical position, in lectures and other instructions, by emphazing other qualifications of true manhood and barely mentioning this or perhaps passing it in silence, are stabbing Jesus in the house of His professed friends, and are filling pulpits with men who are intellectual giants but spiritual weaklings, where God demands that there should be men who will preach the Word in *demonstration of the Spirit and with power.*

The success which God gives such men as Moody, Harrison, and Weber is a standing rebuke to all who are directly or indirectly, by unduly exalting scholasticism, depreciating the "gift of the Holy Ghost."

CHAPTER XIX.

"TO WHOM SHALL WE LIKEN HIM?" — CLOSING REMARKS.

It may not prove profitless to trace some of the correspondences between Mr. Weber and others of the same evangelistic lineage, who have sounded the Gospel trumpet in this and in other centuries.

He is unlike Noah, in that his efforts appear much more successful; yet he resembles him in that his own family have confidence in his religion. Since his conversion, his entire family, with the exception of his father and one sister, have turned from Catholicism and "entered the ark." The father is standing at its entrance, and his sister is awakened.

In his deliverance from death in infancy, he reminds us of Moses; also in that the burden of his mission is the rescuing of captives from bondage.

Like Joshua, he is dauntless, aggressive and full of faith, daring to echo the shout of victory in the defiant presence of Jerichos and giants, as well as to sing praises after their surrender.

Like Isaiah, he has a glowing enthusiasm, vivid imagination, and the readiness that is ever saying, "Here, Lord, am I, send me, send me."

He has, like Jeremiah, a special mission "to root out,

and to pull down, and to destroy, and to throw down, to build and to plant." He is like him, also, in that there are seasons of which he can say, " His word was in my heart, a burning fire shut up in my bones, and I was weary with forbearing and could not stay "; and in that he often has a burden of soul for the people, such as led Jeremiah to say, " Oh, that my head were waters, and mine eyes a fountain of tears, that I might weep day and night for the slain of the daughter of my people!" In prevailing prayer he reminds us of Elijah on Mt. Carmel, and his meetings are suggestive of the testing there of the religion of Baal and of the living God.

Like Elisha he was called to minister in holy things from secular employment.

As with Ezekiel, God has against his enemies "made his face strong against their faces, and his forehead strong against their foreheads. As an adamant harder than flint." Thus, like him, he is enabled to deal crushing blows against the sins of the day, and at the same time, without injury, receive any blows that may be returned. His descriptive powers also remind of those of Chebar's prophet.

Like Daniel, he weighs great men in " God's ballances," and fearlessly declares to them His messages. Regardless of men's pet and set ways of doing things, and emphasizing the Scripture Gospel of repentance, he, probably in this respect more than any other evangelist, except it may be Jones, resembles John the Baptist.

Like the apostles, he forsook all to follow Christ, and like them, were it not for existing protective laws, would doubtless meet a violent death.

Like Paul, he was converted suddenly. He says, " I

did not know I was under conviction one moment before I was saved. As soon as I saw the light, I accepted it."

Rescued from the Church of Rome, like the evangelistic reformers of the Reformation he is zealous in exposing its errors.

In his burning zeal for souls, his scorn of all opposition and his love for sacred song, he seems akin to Wesley, while his "magnetic" influence over a congregation, and his multiplicity of public services, are suggestive of a Whitefield.

Himself receiving blessed baptisms of the Holy Ghost like Finney, with him he is a mighty power in personal persuasion and appeal, and in "holding on" to God and man until revival victory comes.

In profligacy before conversion, and fearlessness, fervency and evangelistic success afterwards, he resembles the sainted Summerfield.

In the discouragements he met when first beginning Christian work, he reminds of Moody; also in his fearless presentation of the Word.

A part of Hyde's description of Thomas Harrison, whose fame fills the land, applies fittingly also to Mr. Weber. "His eyesight is keen; no movement in any part of a great congregation escapes him. His wit is ready; he knows as if by instinct how to answer a question, how to encourage a movement, and how to quell a disorder. Yet he is immensely inferior to what he is doing. No wit nor wisdom nor speech of his is equal to what is done in his presence." His sermons, delivery and mode of conducting a meeting are such, that he has been frequently likened to this successful evangelist. Their converts, when properly cared for, are reported " to be among the best workers in the churches."

His battle cry of " Victory or Death " seems like the echo of the voice of that prince of Baptist evangelists, Jacob Knapp.

As with Peter Cartwright, he is richly endowed with " muscular Christianity," which he once utilized by kindly pitching an abusive editor out of his room.

Like General Booth, he feels " like a man on a rockbound coast strewed with wrecks, on which the struggling mariners, unless rescued from the shore, were certain to go down beneath the raging surf."

Like Evangelist Sam Jones, he feels of the great success that God has given that "it only makes me love my Saviour the more, who has been so good to me and who has done so much for me." He is also like him in his keen insight into human nature, the flashes of wit that sparkle in his sermons, his kindness of heart, and in that " he makes all his studies and plans contribute to the one work of saving men from sin." Also in his liberality often " giving nine tenths of all he receives to the needy."

While we see in Mr. Weber the striking resemblances to the great men mentioned, yet there are, of course, points, also, of dissimilarity. Points wherein he excells them, and others, doubtless, where he falls below. Having compared them singly, we will now glance at some particulars in which he is like them all.

They all are enigmas. When we contrast their weaknesses with the mighty work that God does through them, we are bewildered. It is true, however, that the shortcomings of such characters are, like the spots on the sun, lost in the brilliancy of the shining of their graces, gifts and works. Perfection in love all may attain to, but absolute perfection, none but God. As Whittier has truthfully written,—

> "No perfect whole can our nature make,
> Here or there the circle will break;
> The orb of life, as it takes the light
> On one side, leaves the other in night."

The following, which the "Quaker poet" also wrote of Whitefield, is doubtless true of all except the Son of God,—

> "So incomplete by his beings laws
> The marvelous preacher has his flaws;
> With step unequal and lame with faults,
> His shade on the path of History halts."

Remembering that "God hath chosen the weak things of this world to confound the mighty," we suppose that though the evangelist may be both saved and sanctified, yet, in common with all saints, he still is "compassed with infirmities" and liable to err.

Like all others who, as he, have succeeded in so great a degree, he has repeatedly "shocked" hypocrites, formalists, and other disguised enemies of the King, by his plain words and plainer illustrations.

Some have sought to find flaws in all of them, Jesus not excepted. Like them, he acts independently of the opinions of censorious fault-finders, and fearlessly riddles the traditions of men and customs of society that are contrary to the teachings of Christ, even though thus all earthly supports are alienated. The authority and sustenance of such men are not from below. Their bread shall be given and their waters are sure.

Like them all, he is misunderstood, and sometimes slandered, reviled and otherwise persecuted, by the leaders of sham "society."

He also reaches the masses with his messages, gets a hearing and sends it home with such energy that it will never be forgotten. Captious critics, as with them, carp at the way he sometimes does it, but he is too busy to be bothered by their bickerings. At their faces, like others of his illustrious line, he rebukes men of their sins; and when they condemn him for severity in so doing, they arraign the prophets, Whitfield, Wesley and all who have been true to their message from on high.

As with all of the worthies mentioned, great crowds attend his ministry, and God crowns his labors, as theirs, with success, such as will more vividly appear throughout the ages of eternity.

Like theirs, his converts do not *all* " hold out." A large proportion of them do, but sometimes they have to be left with teachers who are unable to lead them on unto holiness. Sometimes they are starved to death on the husks of " scientific " sermons, or are " amused " or " entertained " to death. Some are " shallow earth " and others "stony ground" hearers and others like the seed that " fell among the thorns."

It was so with Jesus' ministry. Some thronged Him for the loaves and the fishes, but when He gave them a real spiritual talk, "many of his disciples went back and walked no more with him." Paul lamented sad backsliding among early converts, and Wesley takes up the same wail. Probably as large a proportion as usual of Mr. Weber's converts remain firm.

With all the other bright stars in this wonderful evangelistic cluster, God cares for and protects him, and will continue so to do, if faithful, amid the perils of this life, the swellings of Jordan, the throes of dissolving nature, the scenes of the Judgment Day and through the cycles of eternity.

To Him be glory forever! Amen.

Like all of those mentioned, his most eloquent eulogiums will be after he is dead and gone. Then, as with them, when the "mists have cleared away," his work for humanity will be better appreciated than during his life. As he sometimes says when criticised for giving merited praise, "The world needs more 'taffy' and less of 'epitaphy.'"

Closing Remarks.

To comprehend all the results of his evangelistic work would be as impossible as to number the stars in the heavens.

Through his agency God has put in motion influences that will vibrate throughout eternity.

It is thought that twenty thousand have professed conversion in his meetings. He has the knowledge of twenty-five young men converted in his meetings who are going, or have gone, into the ministry. There are doubtless many more whom he knows not of. The church debts that have been paid and buildings erected, the believers perfected and backsliders reclaimed, and the service for God rendered by his converts on earth and their successes on the shores of eternity, no tongue is able to tell.

Bro. Weber's life, in a marked manner, shows that it is the highest wisdom to hearken unto God rather than unto men. Not that human counsel should be entirely ignored, but secondary. "If any man lack wisdom let him ask of God."

Had he listened to his well-meaning advisers, and remained in the pastorate instead of heeding, as he did, the Spirit's voice, the probabilities are that through his agency only hundreds would have been saved where now there have been thousands. Instead of becoming an evangelist whose worth in the church and in heaven is reckoned by the souls he has rescued from the pit of sin to shine in Jesus' crown, he would probably have been but a divine whose greatness the people would have measured by the number of cents in his salary.

Is it possible to conceive of how he could have made more of his life than God is making of it in the field to which He has called him? The following words of another, slightly altered, seem very fitting when applied to him, and may be a stimulus to all who, like him, are devoting all their energies to the salvation of souls:

Suppose he had set his heart on assisting the starving, hungry crowds, and, in order to accomplish it, had gone to work to reduce taxation; to increase the opportunities of the wage-earning class to help themselves; to invent new forms of employment, or by various plans to increase their ability to earn money. Supposing he had given himself up to this, and thus expended his life in the struggle; does anyone, acquainted with the main causes of poverty, think that through any alterations in the laws, or by any other success that might have attended his efforts, anything like the number of poor people would have been benefited, or to anything like the extent which has been the case, as the result of what he has been enabled to do in the direct work of saving them from sin?

(a) Supposing he had set to work to make money in order to bestow it on the poor, and had succeeded, what would the scattering of a few thousand dollars have been compared with the sum that reformed people have earned for themselves, or saved from public places and gambling hells as the result of their regenerated characters, and of those habits of sobriety, industry and economy which flow from salvation?

(b) Or suppose he had started upon the track of social reform and had achieved remarkable success in that direction, which would not have been certain, the beneficial results to the poor people must necessarily have been immensely behind what has been accomplished through his revivals, by the influence of which many, saved from the poverty which serfdom to sin entailed, have transported themselves to comfortable cottages and dwellings, and in many instances have advanced to respectable social positions.

(c) Or suppose that, in order to alleviate the lot of the poor, he had given all his time and taxed all his energies to shorten their hours of toil, and to cheer and alleviate their existance, and had succeeded as well as such reformers usually do. Who would claim that the result would begin to compare with what he has accomplished?

In thousands of homes where once nothing was known but cursing, quarrelling and misery, there is now the spirit of contentment and song of praise and gladness, while hundreds of individuals literally sing their way through all the hardship, persecution and difficulty they are called to endure in seeking to rescue their fellows from the abyss out of which they themselves have been lifted by the glorious salvation of the cross.

(d) Suppose that, out of pity for the poor who suffer from disease, he had embarked in the study and profession of a physician, and suppose that he had prospered in this profession far beyond an average practitioner, what success could he possibly have accomplished in the removal and prevention of disease compared with what has been wrought through these wonderful revivals? If cleanliness and clothing and warmth and abstinence from intoxicants and narcotics, together with the practice of morality and the use of nourishing food, with kindness, tender nursing, happiness and love, not only prevent disease, but go far in the majority of cases in effecting its cure, then what multitudes of precious children and fathers and mothers are hale and hearty to-day, and likely to continue so, who, but for his loyalty to the evangelistic call, would have been suffering on sick beds or lying cold and stark in the dark and cheerless grave!

(e) Suppose that, lured by the fascinating claims of the poor drunkard, he had thrown himself in his behalf into any or all of the various temperance reformation enterprises. Could he have hoped to have delivered as many hundreds from the chains of the dark fiend as through the instrumentality of his revivals have been rescued?

Or could he have ever dreamed, in his most sanguine moments, of being able to make any infinitesimal proportion of the number of abstainers that this movement has produced? Could he have hoped to have created any such portion of enlightened public opinion on the subject, or to have created such an amount of execration of the drink traffic and abhorrence of it as a fortune-making business as he has been enabled to thus bring about? We think not; we are sure not.

Supposing he could have produced by merely human efforts the material, earthly well-being aimed at; if he could have removed the heavy burdens of the poor; if he could have increased their wages threefold; if he could have transferred them to comfortable dwellings; if the sick could have been healed, or their diseases prevented; if the drunken could on any large scale have been made sober — would these things necessarily have brought happiness to the people? Does misery only dwell with the poor, the sick, the harlot and the drunkard?

Moreover, may not all these outside evils be taken away and still leave the heart a prey to cankering cares, jealousies, envyings, strifes, lusts, bitterness, hatreds, revengeful tempers and the like, which, together or apart, are the authors of nearly all the miseries of men, making life an intolerable burden, though passed in gilded chambers on the couches of ease, or in the possession of health and wealth and all else that earth can give or human power create?

Therefore, it follows that this plan for removing misery in this world — the plan to which the Spirit of God led seven years ago and in the working out of which He has sustained him — has gone much deeper than any human methods could possibly have done, not only dealing with results, but healing the festering disease itself and opening in the soul an ever-flowing fountain of gladness, which, while it sustains the spirit in the endurance of the afflictions and hardships that remain, transmutes them into sources of blessing, both for this life and the life to come.

His life is also a forcible illustration of the following revealed truths which challenge the faith of every child of God.

1. "Trust in the Lord with all thine heart, and lean not unto thine own understanding. In all thy ways acknowledge Him and He shall direct thy paths."

2. "Give and it shall be given unto you." He has been an ever springing fountain of liberality, and has bountifully proved that "he that watereth others shall himself be watered." He is an exemplification of Wesley's advice to "make all you can, save all you can and give all you can." Though himself poor, yet he has been enabled to make many spiritually rich, and also to distribute thousands of dollars to help assuage temporal misery, and drive wolfish want from the door of the poor. Himself too full of trust and busy in his Master's business to worry about his own necessities of this life, he has sought first the kingdom of God and His righteousness and all "these things have been added unto him."

3. "The kingdom of heaven suffereth violence, and the violent take it by force." In what may be termed the *audacity* of faith and persistent prayer, his equal is seldom met. God honors it and grants great blessings.

4. "There is no man that hath left house, or brethren, or sisters, or father, or mother, or wife, or children, for my sake and the gospel's, but he shall receive an hundred-fold, brethren, and sisters, and mothers, and children and lands, with persecutions; and in the world to come eternal life." He has given up all the comforts that come from home and association there with loved ones, and has verified the blessedness of this promise, for hundreds of homes all over the land greet him with welcomes as tender as if he were a father, a brother or a son. Nor, as we have seen, does he lack the spice of persecution, with which the Master flavors the dishes of all those whom He delights on earth to use and honor.

5. "If any man serve me, him will my Father honor."

Had Bro. Weber heeded the doleful prophecies of mistaken advisers when he forsook all and entered the evangelistic field, or had he have served self and sought his own promotion, he never would have exemplified the truth of this blessed promise, which challenges the best thought of all who would seek and secure abiding honors. Honors that the river of death cannot drown or the fires of judgment consume. Honors compared with which, D. D., L. L. D., and like degrees, with all those highest in the gift of kingdoms, empires and republics, combined with all others which worldlings love and the world can give, magnified a million-fold, are but like bursting bubbles which amuse for a moment only and then vanish forever.

These all are but flickering tallow candles, which glimmer for an instant and then go out.

Such are among the most tempting honors that this world can offer. Is it any wonder, then, that Jesus said, "I receive not honor from men," and that thousands of His humble followers have counted it a privilege to follow in His footsteps?

And that He also questioned, "How can ye believe which receive honor, one of another, and seek not the honor that cometh from God only?" The cup of man's capacity of receiving honor can contain but a limited amount. When filled with earthly honors, there is no room for those which are enduring, and which come from God. A part of the honor which Jesus promises to them that serve Him, He often gives while they are still on earth, as with Paul, Wesley and a host of others; but this is only as a grain of sand to the seashore, compared with what awaits beyond. the honor, which, beginning with the King's "Well done" before an assembled universe, His grand reception into the society of the redeemed and high angelic hosts, continues to increase with man's capacities to receive, as he reigns a king and priest unto God and the Father forever more.

Like many others, Bro. Weber has been given, for his encouragement, a part of this infinite reward while here on earth. God already has given him a name, among men and angels, as an illustrious soul-saver. A name more highly valued in heaven's kingdom, and more to be coveted, than all honorary degrees and titles high of church or state. A name which bids fair to shine with increasing lustre as the "firmament" and "as the stars forever and ever."

As this book goes to press, he is in the midst of another mighty soul-saving "Tornado," at Alpena, Mich., in which the pastor reports the power of God being displayed in a wonderful way, over three hundred having professed conversion.

He still is a comparatively young man. He hopes yet, by God's grace, to win thousands more for his Master. The story of his life will never end. We have been permitted to write and read this fragmentary, yet thrilling, section of it. It may never all be put in print, but it all is being written by an unseen hand. In more attractive form than this, in the burning characters of some new language, yet to be unfolded among the revelations that await us in the Celestial City, we may be permitted to peruse it.

May we each be among the number, who, having "washed our robes and made them white in the blood of the Lamb," and having "turned many to righteousness," shall, with "everlasting joy upon our heads, enter through the gates into the city, to go out no more forever!"

For the triumphs of our King herein recorded, for the mighty efficiency of the cleansing blood and the indwelling Spirit, and for the soul-entrancing prospects of God's children here and hereafter, let us each, while we live, when we die and throughout Eternity,—

>"Praise the Father,
>Praise the Son
>And praise the Holy Ghost."— AMEN.

The End.

THE REVIVALIST.

A monthly paper devoted to the maintenance of a Revival Spirit and the advancement of Revival Work. Edited and published by

REV. MARTIN WELLS KNAPP.

Its Motto: Salvation, Present and Full, Free and for All.

FACTS IN ITS FAVOR.

1. It makes a specialty of the most important and grandest theme in the universe Revivals.
2. It is a foe to sham revivals, and advocates only that kind of revival work which will stand the test of the Word, Life, Death, Judgment, and Eternity.
3. It holds persistently that the baptism of the Holy Spirit is an indispensable qualification to successful revival work.
4. It is the child of the Holy Spirit and an intense desire to glorify God.
5. Any profit that may come from its publication will be devoted to God's work.
6. One page is prepared especially for the unconverted, which makes the paper of great value to scatter among them.
7. It has a wide field before it, as there are only very few papers devoted solely to this theme.
8. It is condensed, "much in a little." It aims to eliminate from its columns all dross that would simply add to its size without increasing its value, and to present only the unalloyed gold of pure Revival Truth.
9. It commends itself especially to busy workers. Every moment to such is more precious than diamonds, and they feel that they can not take time to hunt up revival arrows that are buried in columns of miscellaneous matter. The Revivalist presents them in a quiver, where they can be caught at a glance.
10. It is cheap. Only 30 cents per year. So cheap that it can be taken without conflicting with the claims of any other paper, and can be sown broadcast among the poor and the unconverted.
11. It is dedicated to God, and for all the good it has done or ever may do, He shall have all the glory.

INDORSEMENT.

The following from THE WORD AND THE WAY, Saratoga Springs, N. Y., one of the brightest and best monthlies in the land, is a sample of the kindly way the REVIVALIST is being mentioned by many. Especial attention is called to the words that we have emphasized,—

"The first number of 'THE REVIVALIST' has been received at this office. We are very much pleased with the paper, and **we think it should be read by Christians everywhere.** The publisher of this paper is the Rev. M. W. Knapp, Albion, Mich., which is a sufficient guarantee that its pages will be filled with such matter as true Christians are always glad to read. Other papers are published through the land that take up special lines of work; but this is the first ever known to us whose **special line of work will be to promote revivals of religion.** We most heartily commend this evangelist and his publication, 'THE REVIVALIST,' to the Christian public."

It is believed that this paper is to be used of God in winning many souls to Christ. Would you like a share in the work and the reward? You can have it,—

1. *By praying for its success.*
2. *By sending at once your subscription.*
3. *By getting a list of subscribers for it.*
4. *By lending it after you have read it, and by giving subscriptions to the poor and the unconverted.*

SAMPLES WITH SPECIAL OFFERS FREE.

Your co-operation in this work is invited. "The King's business requires haste." Address

THE REVIVALIST PUBLISHING CO., Albion, Mich.

OUT OF EGYPT INTO CANAAN;

Or, LESSONS IN SPIRITUAL GEOGRAPHY.

By REV. MARTIN WELLS KNAPP,

Author of "Christ Crowned Within."

PRICE, 80 CENTS. :•: :•: **TO MINISTERS, 60 CENTS.**

CONTENTS.

Illustrative Map: In Egypt, or Spiritual Bondage—The Red Sea, or Spiritual Deliverance—The Sinai Wilderness, or Spiritual Twilight—Kadesh Barnea, or the Believers' Waterloo—Desert Wilderness, or "Wretched Religion"—Entering Canaan—Canaan, or Spiritual Sunshine—Out of Canaan into Babylon—Back from Babylon—Out of Canaan into Heaven—Canaan: Contrasts and Inquiries—The Author's Experience.

EXTRACTS FROM NOTICES.

—The book begins with a map, representing, by a beautiful object lesson, the whole subject. Egypt and Babylon are black, the Red Sea is red, the wilderness is slate color, Canaan is white, etc., etc. The way is traced in white for the direct march, in black for the wanderings. It is a strikingly suggestive map. The book contains fourteen chapters, and traces minutely the correspondencies between the movements and experiences of the Israelites and the believer. Egypt represents the kingdom of darkness; the Red Sea is conversion. Between the Red Sea and Kadesh Barnea, the period from conversion to the point of receiving entire sanctification, Kadesh Barnea is defeat. The wilderness represents backsliding. Jordan is entering the land of Canaan. Canaan is union with Christ; Babylon is the fallen state; *i. e.* fallen from spiritual Canaan. We do not hesitate to pronounce this book well adapted to the instruction of the people in Divine things. It can not help being useful.—*Christian Witness and Advocate of Bible Holiness.*

—Its method of presentation is original. It is well written, and worthy of extensive circulation.—*Christian Standard and Home Journal.*

—The plan strikes me as original, the ideas Scriptural, the language pungent and yet sweet, the comparisons apt and numerous, while the whole is pervaded by an earnest evangelism. Blessings on the book and its devoted writer!—REV. J. W. RAWLINSON.

—If any one has made careful study of the great spiritual truths so aptly illustrated by the history of Israel in Egypt and delivery therefrom, that man is our Brother Knapp. The *Advocate* contained several articles from his pen upon this subject, and we are pleased to see these and others elaborated and otherwise adapted to the permanent page. The spiritual tone of the volume is high, the literary work creditable, the illustrative matter appropriate to its purpose, and the mechanical execution in accordance with the well-known reputation of the Cincinnati house.—*Michigan Christian Advocate.*

—The author's style abounds in illustrations of the thought he wishes to stress, which are apt, and, at times, striking.—*Wesleyan Christian Advocate.*

—You have furnished, by God's help, two valuable books. . . . They can't help doing good. REV. THOMAS C. MOOTS.

—The great truths of Christian experience are interestingly presented in this book.—*Guide to Holiness.*

OUT OF EGYPT INTO CANAAN.—Continued.

—His unique "Map" will be examined with interest. . . . That he has apprehended truly and made a book which will be a blessing to many, there can be no doubt. Glowing, as it does, with holy fire, it manifests his eminent fitness for evangelistic work to which he has consecrated himself. The printer and book-binder have made the book attractive to the eye.—*The Baltimore Methodist.*

—In the wonderful light of this work, one will take deepest pleasure in reading the story of the *exode* again, and, we are sure, will see a beauty and significance in it never before discovered. He will be astonished, also, to see how easily every outward step and act admits of inward and spiritual application, and while he will pity the Israelites that they wandered so long before reaching Canaan, he will surely regret that with the bright companionship of Mr. Knapp, the author, the journey for himself had not been longer.—*Herald of Gospel Liberty.*

—It is an able, clear, and forcible statement of the higher-life doctrine under the plan of a journey, the roads of which are clearly and distinctly marked. . . . We most heartily commend it to our readers.—*Central Methodist.*

—Crowded full of choice instruction and counsel. . . . We can not too highly commend the design of the work, or the manner in which the design is executed.—*Wesleyan Methodist.*

—It hits a real want in the holiness literature not otherwise filled.—REV. ISAIH REID.

—Volume contains much of instruction and encouragement to all who will live godly.—*Western Christian Advocate.*

—It is written in a pleasing style.—*The Free Methodist.*

—A GRAND NEW BOOK.—It more fully deals with the subject indicated by the title than any book yet published. It is direct, pointed, going right at the matter in hand, so briefly and clearly, that it is like a new inspiration to read it.—*The Highway.*

—If I ever write an article on "Books that have helped me," I am sure that next to the Bible I must place your "Out of Egypt."—REV. T. H. MURLIN.

—A book well worth reading. The author is . . . a successful evangelist who has a warm heart, a vivid imagination, and who withal possesses a goodly share of common sense.—*The Methodist Young People.*

—It bristles with practical points that can not fail to be wholesome to Christians. It is written in a very simple style, easily understood, free from unnecessary verbiage, and eminently suited for the use of the laity. We trust many of our readers will procure the book and read it.—*Evangelical Messenger.*

TRACTS BY THE SAME AUTHOR.

	EACH.	DOZ.
FIRE FROM ABOVE	5c.	50c.
HOW I CAME TO BE AN EVANGELIST	3c.	30c.
THE MODEL CLASS-LEADER	1c.	8c.
"HOLINESS A HOBBY"	1c.	8c.
FIVE DOLLARS GIVEN AWAY. For the unconverted	1c.	8c.
AN ECHO FROM THE BORDER LAND. For the unconverted	1c.	5c.
THIS LIFE AND THE LIFE TO COME. Diagram. For the unconverted	2c.	10c.
THE RIVER OF DEATH. A Chart showing how men are lost. For the unconverted	3c.	15c.
THE TWO RAILROADS (Chart)	5c.	

THE REVIVALIST PUBLISHING CO., ALBION, MICH.

"OUT OF EGYPT INTO CANAAN."

BY REV. B. S. TAYLOR.

This beautiful book, by Rev. M. W. Knapp, has been recently issued by the author, who is an evangelist residing in Michigan. It gives me great pleasure to bring it before your readers, as one of the best of holiness books—clear, Scriptural, delightful. It outlines forcibly the spiritual interpretation of the "Exodus," the way out, and the way in. "He brought us out from thence, that he might bring us into the land which he sware unto our fathers." The English style is peculiarly simple, idiomatic, and will be intensely attractive to young people. It ought to go into every Sunday-school library in the world, to the exclusion of tons of romantic trash, skeptical philosophy, and infidel "science," falsely so called. It will be a great rival to the "Christian's Secret of a Happy Life," which has had an enormous sale. This book has some likeness to "The Pilgrim's Progress," simple in language, and yet remarkably adapted to lead young believers into the life and power of holiness, and to make its readers more than ever fond of the Old Testament riches of glory and beauties of holiness therein portrayed. It is intensely practical. Theories and speculations are all left out. Nothing but the clearest and plainest teachings of the Scripture are admitted. It breathes a beautiful spirit; is kind, charitable, patient in teaching truth, and exposes error so tenderly that it would please a hypocrite himself to be thus unmasked. . . . In particular, let me call attention to Chapter II, and the twenty-six "Excuses" there exposed. That ought to be put into a gospel arrow tract form, and scattered all over the land. The tone of the book is that of a practical and successful soul-winner, who demonstrates his skill as a "workman that needeth not to be ashamed."—*From Christian Witness, Boston.*

CONVERTED BY A BOOK.

The rich spiritual rewards which are sometimes reaped in circulating books for Jesus' sake, when the Holy Spirit deigns to use them, is forcibly illustrated by the following extract from a worker's letter. She writes of "OUT OF EGYPT INTO CANAAN," as follows: "I sold one to a young lady. She was a Church member, but unconverted, and when I saw her again she said: 'I would not take *ten dollars* for that book. *It was the means of my conversion.*'"

BY

REV. MARTIN WELLS KNAPP,

EDITOR OF "THE REVIVALIST," AND AUTHOR OF "CHRIST CROWNED WITHIN," "OUT OF EGYPT INTO CANAAN," AND "REVIVAL TORNADOES."

"I am come to send fire on the earth; and what will I, if it be already kindled?" — JESUS.

THE REVIVALIST PUBLISHING CO.,
ALBION, MICH.

PRICE, $1.10.

CHRIST CROWNED WITHIN.

12mo. 199 pp. Price, 75 Cents.

By Rev. Martin Wells Knapp.

CONTENTS.

Christ Crowned Within.—The Soul's Desire.—The Object of Man's Creation.—Promised.—The Object of his Enthronement.—The Great Need of the Church.—Results of his Enthronement.—Purity.—A Divine Fullness.—Perfect Love.—Holiness.—Growth and Fruit.—Power and Prosperity.—A Stable Experience and Spiritual Enlightenment.—Assurance and Humility.—Peace, Joy, and Divine Guidance.—False Fear Banished.—Religion Made Easy.—Heaven on Earth.—Heaven Above.—When and How Attained.—How Retained.

COMMENDATIONS.

It will doubtless be useful in stimulating the reader to a higher life.—*Northwestern Advocate.*

A very attractive book.—*Michigan Advocate.*

The method is original, the style is attractive, and the spirit most delightful.—*Christian Witness.*

I shall prize it among my treasures.—REV. C. A. JACOKES.

It is clear, Scriptural, and warm with the pulsations of Divine life.—REV. N. TAYLOR.

The evangelistic fire of the author glows on every page.—REV. F. L. McCOY.

It is one of the best books ever printed. It is worth its weight in gold.—*The Word and Way.*

I like your book much. It avoids all machinery and dogma, and is a clear, simple, beautiful, Scriptural handling of your theme, "Christ Crowned Within."—REV. T. H. JACOKES.

I think in the whole realm of literature on the higher life which I have had the pleasure of reading, this is the cream.—REV. C. H. SWEATT.

COMMENDATIONS—Continued.

My soul feasted while reading "Christ Crowned Within." Doubtless the Holy Spirit will use the book to lead many into the blissful realm where Jesus reigns without a rival; where all the heart forces are united in the willing service of the King of kings.—ABBIE MILLS, *author of "Quiet Hallelujahs," Rockford, Ill.*

The book is not written in any controversial spirit, but sets forth in a simple and yet most effective manner our high calling of God in Christ Jesus. Happy are all they who live in the sunshine of the divine presence.—*Free Baptist, Minneapolis, Minn.*

The book is full of good things.—REV. G. D. WATSON.

"Christ Crowned Within" is the title of a most interesting and useful book now on our table. The type is clear, the chapters short and Scriptural, exegesis clear, striking, and in perfect harmony with inspired truth. The book deserves a wide circulation, and will be a benediction to all who read it. We heartily commend it to the public.—*Methodist Standard.*

We must add our testimony. This is no ordinary book these excellent people are praising so. We have the delightful book kindly sent us by the publishers, and it is a mine of soul-wealth to us, a garden of spices, a breeze from heaven. We are not extravagant in our description. Read the book yourself.—*Hubbard Times Hubbard, Iowa.*

I have read 'Christ Crowned Within" with pleasure and profit. I am in full sympathy with it, teachings It will be helpful to any Christian seeking the way of holiness and inspiring to the life consecrated to God."—REV. JOHN MCELDOWNEY.

I can heartily commend it for its originality, simplicity, and sweetness. "Christ Crowned Within!" I am conscious that he is so crowned to-day.—REV. EDGAR LEVY.

"Christ Crowned Within" is a useful book to the devout heart. It is a treasury of the burning thoughts of those who have lived nearest the Master in this world.—CHAPLAIN MCCABE.

BOOKS AND TRACTS BY THE SAME AUTHOR.

	Each.	Dozen.
REVIVAL TORNADOES,.................................	$1 00	$7 20
CHRIST CROWNED WITHIN,.............................	75 cts.	5 40
FIRE FROM ABOVE,.....................................	5 cts.	50 cts.
HOW I CAME TO BE AN EVANGELIST,.................	3 cts.	30 cts.
THE MODEL CLASS LEADER,............................	1 ct.	8 cts.
"HOLINESS A HOBBY,".................................	1 ct.	8 cts.
FIVE DOLLARS GIVEN AWAY. For the unconverted,......	1 ct.	8 cts.
AN ECHO FROM THE BORDER LAND. For the unconverted,	1 ct.	5 cts.
THIS LIFE AND THE LIFE TO COME. Diagram. For the unconverted....................................	2 cts.	5 cts.
THE RIVER OF DEATH. A Chart showing how men are lost. For the unconverted.............................	2 cts.	5 cts.
THE TWO RAILROADS. Chart,...........................	2 cts.	5 cts.
LETTER ENVELOPES WITH SIGNET AND TEXTS, per 25	15 cts.	
THE REVIVALIST, a monthly, devoted solely to the promotion of Scriptural Revivals........................	30 cts.	

Address all orders to

THE REVIVALIST PUBLISHING CO.,
ALBION, MICHIGAN.

A MINE OF GOLD.

Each one of the Books in the following list is a Spiritual Nugget, worth more than its weight in Gold:

Forty Witnesses. By OLIVER GARRISON,	$1 00
Life of Charles G. Finney,	50
Lectures to Professed Christians. By FINNEY,	1 50
Revival Lectures. By FINNEY,	1 75
Biography of Bishop Hamline. 471 pages,	1 50
White Robes. By G. D. WATSON, D. D.,	50
Coals of Fire. By G. D. WATSON, D. D.,	50
The Christian's Secret of a Happy Life. By MRS. H. W. SMITH,	75
Aggressive Christianity. By MRS. BOOTH,	50
Godliness. By MRS. BOOTH,	50
Popular Christianity,	75
Love Enthroned. By REV. D. STEELE, D. D.,	1 25
Full Salvation. By REV. B. S. TAYLOR,	50
A Dollar Cruden's Concordance. (Postage, 16c.)	1 00
Perfect Love. By J. A. WOOD,	1 00
"The Boy Preacher"—Thomas Harrison,	1 00
Life of Frances Ridley Havergal,	1 25
Poems of Frances Ridley Havergal. Complete in two volumes,	3 00
Total,	$18 75

A FULL SET will be sent to any address, post-paid, for $17.00.

☞ Remittance with order. Twenty per cent off from retail price to ministers. Postage paid on each book, except "Cruden," when the full retail price is paid.

Address **THE REVIVALIST PUBLISHING CO., ALBION, MICH.**

www.ingramcontent.com/pod-product-compliance
Lightning Source LLC
Chambersburg PA
CBHW021157230426
43667CB00006B/438